This study reconstructs the historical Pontius Pilate and looks at the way in which he is used as a literary character in the works of six first-century authors: Philo, Josephus and the four evangelists. The first chapter provides an introduction to the history and formation of the imperial Roman province of Judaea. The following two chapters examine the references to Pilate in Philo and Josephus, looking at each author's biases before going on to assess the historicity of their accounts. The next four chapters consider the portrayal of Pilate in each gospel, asking how a first-century reader would have interpreted his actions. Each chapter asks what this portrayal shows about the author's attitude towards the Roman state, and what kind of community found this useful. The conclusion distinguishes between the 'historical Pilate' and the different 'Pilates of interpretation' preserved in our first-century literary sources.

Helen K. Bond is Lecturer in New Testament at the University of Aberdeen. Her other publications include *The Allegro Qumran Collection* (in collaboration with George G. Brooke, 1996).

SOCIETY FOR NEW TESTAMENT STUDIES

MONOGRAPH SERIES

General Editor: Richard Bauckham

100

PONTIUS PILATE IN HISTORY AND INTERPRETATION

Pontius Pilate in history and interpretation

HELEN K. BOND

CAMBRIDGE
UNIVERSITY PRESS

PUBLISHED BY THE PRESS SYNDICATE OF THE UNIVERSITY OF CAMBRIDGE
The Pitt Building, Trumpington Street, Cambridge CB2 1RP, United Kingdom

CAMBRIDGE UNIVERSITY PRESS
The Edinburgh Building, Cambridge, CB2 2RU, United Kingdom
40 West 20th Street, New York, NY 10011–4211, USA
10 Stamford Road, Oakleigh, Melbourne 3166, Australia

© Helen K. Bond 1998

First published 1998

Printed in the United Kingdom at the University Press, Cambridge

Typeset in Times 10/12 pt [CE]

A catalogue record for this book is available from the British Library

Library of Congress Cataloguing in Publication Data

Bond, Helen K. (Helen Katharine)
Pontius Pilate in history and interpretation / Helen K. Bond.
    p.   cm. – (Monograph series / Society for New Testament Studies: 100)
Based on the author's thesis (doctoral) – Durham University.
Includes bibliographical references and index.
ISBN 0 521 63114 9 (hardback)
1. Pilate, Pontius, 1st cent.
2. Governors – Palestine – Biography.
3. Jews – History – 168 BC–135 AD.
4. Philo, of Alexandria – Contributions in the biography of Pontius Pilate.
5. Josephus, Flavius – Contributions in the biography of Pontius Pilate.
6. Bible. N.T. Gospels – Criticism, interpretation, etc.
7. Jesus Christ – Trial.
I. Title.
II. Series: Monograph series (Society for New Testament Studies): 100.
DS122.B66 1998
933'05'092–dc21   97–45970 CIP

ISBN 0 521 63114 9 hardback

To Evelyn, John and David Bond
With love and thanks

CONTENTS

PREFACE

That Jesus of Nazareth was crucified under Pontius Pilate, the fifth prefect of the imperial Roman province of Judaea, is one of the surest facts of Christianity; it is attested not only by the earliest Christian traditions but also by the Roman historian Tacitus (*Annals* 15.44). As the judge of Jesus, Pilate has earned an important place both in the New Testament and Christian creeds and also in popular imagination. The picture of an official washing his hands in an attempt to avoid responsibility and the eternally unanswerable question 'What is truth?' (John 18.38) are inextricably linked with Pilate, even by those who profess little or no Christian commitment.

In view of Pilate's significance it is not surprising to find many varied treatments of the historical governor over the last century, both on an academic and on a popular literary level.[1] Two factors generally have influenced these presentations. First of all, the sources at the historian's disposal are relatively thin and those which are available appear to give contradictory views of Pilate. The Jewish writers Philo and Josephus describe Pilate in negative terms; a harsh, cruel man who was the enemy of the Jewish nation. The Christian gospels, however, are generally interpreted as presenting a governor who, although weak and indecisive, recognized the innocence of Jesus and attempted to save him from execution. To a large extent any reconstruction of the 'real Pilate' has depended upon the relative value set upon each source by the historian.[2] In the second place, several influential interpretations of Pilate over the last century appear to have been coloured, whether consciously or not, by the social and political environments of

[1] For material prior to 1888 see Müller, *Pontius*, pp. v–viii. Full details of works referred to by author in this introduction can be found in the bibliography.
[2] There are, of course, many references to Pilate in apocryphal writings but, due to limitations of space, this study will look at first-century sources only.

their authors. Thus these 'Pilates' may reflect as much the writer's contemporary society as first-century Judaea under Pilate's administration.

At the turn of the century the standard work on Pilate was by G. A. Müller, *Pontius Pilatus, der fünfte Prokurator von Judäa und Richter Jesu von Nazareth* published in Stuttgart in 1888. Müller's favourable view of the governor was largely based on Pilate's portrayal in the gospels and tended to dismiss the testimony of the Jewish writers as tendentious. Despite E. Schürer's picture of a contemptuous, intolerant and reckless Pilate in his *Geschichte des jüdischen Volkes im Zeitalter Jesu Christi* (1886–1890), it was Müller's interpretation which was taken up and developed in Germany by E. von Dobschütz (1904) and H. Peter (1907). Pilate was seen as a reasonably able governor finding himself faced with a series of difficult situations involving a turbulent race of people in a difficult province. In Britain, A. Souter, writing an article on Pilate in 1908, similarly concluded that whilst Pilate could show a lack of tact and was not the stuff from which heroes were made, he was 'doubtlessly in many respects a competent governor'. F. Morison, writing a popular account in 1939, presented a sympathetic portrayal of Pilate whose rule over Judaea rather resembled that of a British colonial governor. C. H. Kraeling, writing in the *Harvard Theological Review* in 1942, argued that Pilate's actions in at least one incident were determined by thoroughly practical considerations rather than an arbitrary act of provocation as the Jewish sources would have us believe.[3] With few exceptions, this relatively favourable interpretation of Pilate, based largely on the characterization of the governor in the gospel accounts, dominated the first half of the twentieth century.[4]

In the former Soviet Union Pilate and acts associated with him, such as the washing of hands, were particularly prominent in works

[3] Kraeling, 'Episode', referring to Pilate's erection of iconic standards in Jerusalem (Josephus, *JW* 2.169–74; *Ant.* 18.55–9). See chapter 3 for fuller details.

[4] One notable exception, however, was I. Broydé whose article in the *Jewish Encyclopaedia* (1905) emphasized Pilate's cruelty. Though less negative than Broydé, G. T. Purves in 1900 had also thought that Pilate made little effort to understand the Jews, that he was a man without high moral qualities and of a feeble character.
In response to R. Eisler's *Messiah* (ET 1931), this period also saw several works dealing with strictly historical questions, particularly the precise dating of Pilate's administration; these offered no assessment of Pilate's competence as a governor or of his character. See, for example, Holzmeister, 'Wann'; Hedley, 'Pilate's'; de Laet, 'Successeur'. Dibelius, 'Herodes', though a theological analysis of the Lukan trial narrative, offers no characterization of Pilate.

written during the Stalinist era. The weak Pilate of the gospels was regarded as a particularly appropriate figure to reflect the results of an abnegation of ethical responsibility, moral compromise and a devotion to selfish concerns such as several authors felt was fostered by Stalinist ideology. Paramount amongst these works was M. Bulgakov's *The Master and Margarita* written in 1938. In Bulgakov's original interpretation of the trial scenes Pilate becomes a credible and moving figure whose downfall is his own moral cowardice. By betraying his own personal feelings, Pilate is to suffer for all eternity.[5]

This favourable, or at worst weak, view of Pilate was shattered after the Second World War by E. Stauffer in *Christus und die Caesaren* (1948) and a number of works which followed.[6] He suggested that Pilate was the personal appointee of Sejanus, the allegedly anti-Jewish prefect of the Praetorian Guard. The conflicts recounted by Philo and Josephus and numismatic evidence illustrate a deliberately aggressive attempt to provoke the Jewish people, the enactment of a policy masterminded by Sejanus. The intention was to rouse the whole nation to open rebellion which was then to be brutally crushed, resulting in the annihilation of the entire race. Sejanus' fall in 31 CE, however, prevented the realisation of his plans and left Pilate in a precarious position, a precariousness adequately illustrated by the governor's vacillating behaviour in the trial of Jesus (which Stauffer concludes occurred in 33 CE). In Stauffer's reconstruction of the extreme anti-Jewishness of Sejanus and Pilate and their worldwide attempt to annihilate the Jewish race, it is difficult not to hear echoes of similar Nazi objectives only a few years previously.

In this interpretation the value of the Jewish sources has come into prominence; no longer are they seen as hopelessly biased and untrustworthy. In contrast to previous attempts to harmonize the conflicting portrayals of Pilate in the various sources (which, as we have seen, generally tended to put more emphasis on the evidence of the gospels), Stauffer's interpretation stressed the historical value

---

[5] M. Bulgakov *The Master and Margarita* (1938, first published 1966–7). See later Chingiz Aitmatov, *Plakha* (*The Place of the Skull*), 1986, which also involves Pilate in a commentary on Stalinist Russia. In general see Ziolkowski, 'Pilate and Pilatism'.

[6] *Christ* (ET 1955), especially pp. 118–20, 103; 'Münzprägung' and *Jerusalem*, pp. 16–18. The link with Sejanus and an anti-Jewish conspiracy had already been tentatively expressed by A. D. Doyle in 1941: cf. 'Pilate's', especially p. 192. Stauffer, however, expressed these opinions much more forcibly, drawing on historical evidence to back them up.

of both Christian and Jewish tradition. This neatly created two Pilates, the Pilate of Philo and Josephus and the Pilate of the gospels, with a specific historical event – the fall of Sejanus – to account for the change.

This picture of Pilate's harsh unyielding character, riding rough-shod over the religious sensitivities of the people he was sent to govern, has exerted a tremendous influence over Pilate research and still finds several adherents today. Stauffer's views were quickly endorsed by E. Bammel[7] and taken up in particular by several Jewish writers. In 1961 P. Winter published his influential book *On the Trial of Jesus,* taking a similar line to Stauffer. Winter maintained that Philo's description of Pilate's brutal and vicious character was the most historically trustworthy we possess. H. Cohn, writing in 1967 agreed with this estimate, characterizing Pilate as a governor full of 'wild wrath and insensate onslaughts'.[8] M. Stern in 1974 strongly criticized Pilate, agreeing with Stauffer in seeing a considerable deterioration between the Jewish people and Rome throughout his term of office due to a series of clashes in line with Sejanan policy.

The reconstruction of Stauffer and his followers has also had a profound effect upon non-Jewish scholarship. The revisers of Schürer, though not nearly so negative in their appraisal of Pilate's character and governorship as Stauffer, continued to uphold Schürer's original rather negative view of Pilate.[9] J. Blinzler, though aware of the bias behind the accounts of Philo and Josephus, regarded Pilate as contemptuous of the Jewish people in his province and eager to avail himself of every opportunity of letting them see it.[10] P. L. Maier took up Stauffer's hypothesis of a Sejanan and a post-Sejanan phase in Pilate's governorship and on the basis of this similarly set the crucifixion in 33 CE.[11] E. M. Smallwood, too, in her book *The Jews under Roman Rule* (1976) agreed that Pilate exhibited a blatant disregard for his subjects' religious sensibilities; though she showed more caution with regard to Sejanus' alleged conspiracy, noting only that Pilate was 'possibly implementing Sejanus' policy'.[12] Recently Stauffer's hypothesis was

---

[7] See the following works: 'Syrian'; 'Philos'; 'Pilatus'.
[8] H. Cohn, *Trial*, p. 16.
[9] Schürer, *History*, vol. 2, pp. 383–7.
[10] See both *Trial* and 'Pilatus'.
[11] Maier, 'Sejanus'; 'Episode'; see also his historical novel *Pontius Pilate*.
[12] Smallwood, *Jews*, pp. 160–70.

endorsed by H. Hoehner in his article on Pilate in the *Dictionary of Jesus and the Gospels* (1992).[13]

Yet right from the beginning Stauffer's views met with some opposition, an opposition which has increased over recent years. As early as 1950 E. Fascher argued that Tiberius would not have allowed Pilate to remain in office for ten years if his rule were really so blatantly provocative and unpopular. In 1965 H. E. W. Turner challenged Stauffer's theory on several grounds. In particular he cast doubt over Sejanus' anti-Judaism, a fact attested only by Philo in an extremely rhetorical work, and highlighted the deficiencies of our knowledge of numismatics for this period. Turner saw in Pilate a carelessness with respect to Jewish sensitivities but no deliberate policy of provocation pursued on instructions from Rome. A similar line was taken by H. Wansbrough in 1966 who saw in Pilate a governor zealous in his attempts to honour the Emperor, acting with the greatest possible leniency compatible with maintaining public order. S. G. F. Brandon too refused to regard Pilate's actions as deliberately provocative whilst A. Strobel in 1980 stressed the difficulty of Pilate's commission and put his clashes with the people down to a mixture of obstinacy and weakness within his character.[14] An important step against the deliberately provocative Pilate was taken in 1981 with the publication of J. P. Lémonon's book *Pilate et le gouvernement de la Judée*. According to Lémonon, what led to trouble with his Jewish subjects was not Sejanan influence but Pilate's character and conception of the role of a provincial prefect. He expected to be master in his own province, attempting to honour the Emperor by bringing Judaea in line with other provinces and ignoring the sensitivities of the people in the process. He attempted to gain respect by use of force, a strategy that showed little political sense and earned him a poor reputation. Similar views were taken up by R. E. Brown in *The Death of the Messiah* (1994).[15] The Jewish scholar D. R. Schwartz, however, went even further and argued that we need not assume that the grounds for the friction between Pilate and the people

---

[13] Similar views were expressed in Hoehner's earlier work *Herod*, pp. 172–83. For other unfavourable treatments of Pilate see Buckley, 'Pilate'; Roth, 'Pontius'; Horsley and Hanson, *Bandits*, pp. 38–9. Sandmel ('Pilate') and Hilliard and Clavier ('Pilate') presented more neutral pictures of the governor.

[14] Brandon, 'Pontius'; Strobel, *Stunde*, especially pp. 99–137.

[15] See particularly pp. 695–705.

'were to be found in the particular characteristics of Pilate's personality, policies or administration. Rather the friction was inherent in the very phenomenon of Roman rule in the land many Jews considered to be God's'.[16]

B. C. McGing in 'Pontius Pilate and the Sources' (1991) largely based his thesis upon Lémonon's reconstruction, though regarding Pilate slightly more favourably, and argued in a similar manner to Strobel that the Pilate of the Jewish sources – a governor prepared to confront the Jews and to resist them stubbornly, yet at the same time indecisive, able to give way and not inclined to bloodshed – could fairly easily be reconciled with the Pilate of the gospels. McGing's work highlights a growing tendency amongst modern scholars: no longer is it necessary to see a Pilate of Jewish writers and a diametrically opposed Pilate of Christian sources, with a historical event, such as Sejanus' fall, to account for the change. For these writers a careful analysis of Philo and Josephus, read in their historical context and taking their individual biases into account, shows no real discrepancy with the Pilate encountered in Christian sources.

Pilate research today therefore broadly encompasses two different interpretations of the historical prefect. On the one hand he is seen as deliberately provocative, of a callous disposition, merely a minion of Sejanus and his anti-Jewish plot. The events of the Jewish literature belong to the time before Sejanus' fall whilst the crucifixion of Jesus of Nazareth takes its place afterwards. The other approach rejects the theory of an anti-Jewish plot of Sejanus, reading all the sources in context and suggesting that there is no fundamental difference between the Pilates encountered in each one. With the recent publications referred to above, it is this second view which is gradually becoming the dominant one.

Aims of the present work

Despite this interest in Pilate, there has never been a full-length academic treatment of the historical governor in English. One aim of the present work is to provide such a compilation and an assessment of the various literary, archaeological and numismatic sources relevant to the Judaean governor. Although my own interpretation will be generally similar to that taken by Lémonon

[16] Schwartz, 'Pontius', p. 399.

and McGing, my historical reconstruction of each event will not always concur with theirs.

A historical assessment of Pilate is important – he was a historical man involved in a historical and historic trial – yet the major aim of this work lies in a slightly different direction. It is an attempt to see how this real historical figure was used by various Jewish and Christian authors of the first century CE as a literary character in their writings. How do Philo, Josephus and the four gospels portray Pilate and what rhetorical concerns have shaped these interpretations of the governor? In particular, have these differing literary presentations of the Roman prefect been influenced by their authors' attitudes towards the Romans with whom they have come in contact? This is a particularly relevant question in the case of the gospels where, with the exception of Luke-Acts, Pilate is the only Roman to be described in any detail. As the above survey of research illustrates, even modern writers can consciously or unconsciously allow their own contemporary situation to affect their description of Pilate. It is all the more likely that first-century writers allowed their own situation to colour their portrayals: they were not engaged in constructing purely 'historical' accounts but were consciously interpreting historical events to speak to the needs of their readers or to produce a certain response. This is the case with Josephus and Philo just as much as with the evangelists. It would be a mistake to regard the Jewish accounts of Pilate as 'historical' in contrast to the 'theological' portrayals of the gospels: all these presentations of Pilate to a greater or lesser extent reflect the rhetorical aims and contemporary understandings of their authors. It is the political situations leading to such presentations which I aim to investigate.

The political background and rhetoric of Josephus and Philo have been the subject of many articles and books and so this study will concentrate on that of the gospels. It is necessary to ask how Pilate is being presented in each gospel and, in the case of Matthew and Luke (and perhaps John), how significant are the changes from Mark's account?[17] What kind of readers would have found such presentations of the representative of Rome useful? In general, what does this say about the attitudes of different first-century Christian communities towards their Roman overlords?

It is often assumed, and expressed quite clearly by Winter, that

---

[17] I shall follow the majority of scholars regarding the priority of Mark.

the various presentations of Pilate in the gospels take their place in a linear development in which Pilate becomes progressively friendlier towards Jesus and anxious to acquit him, whilst more and more blame is heaped upon the Jewish leaders. This process, beginning with Mark's gospel and ending with the apocryphal fourth-century gospel of Nicodemus, is claimed to be directly proportional to Roman persecution of Christianity. Winter writes: 'There is a definite connection between two facts: the more Christians are persecuted by the Roman State, the more generous becomes the depiction of Pontius Pilate as a witness to Jesus' innocence'.[18] Yet is this picture a little too simplistic? There is no evidence to suggest the existence of a gradual increase in Roman persecution of Christianity stretching from its earliest days until Constantine's victory at Milvian Bridge altered imperial policy; rather persecution, especially in the earliest century of Christianity, tended to be sporadic and confined to certain areas.[19] Suggested persecutions under Nero, Domitian or Trajan do not appear to have affected all Christians in every part of the Empire. It would appear rather odd, then, if four gospels emanating from different geographical parts of the first-century Empire were really to fit so neatly into such a development as is generally presumed. It would be much more reasonable to expect a complex variety of different interpretations of Pilate, addressing different political situations, without necessarily exhibiting any common line of development; quite possibly the author of a later gospel might portray Pilate in harsher terms than an earlier one if such a picture were more appropriate to the social or political needs of his readers. Furthermore, is it necessarily the case that a persecuted community would portray Pilate as favourable towards Jesus? This could undoubtedly be put to good apologetic effect if the gospel was generally aimed at a Roman readership; but if a gospel was written exclusively or principally in order to strengthen a Christian community in their faith or to encourage them at a time of persecution, would a weak, ineffectual Pilate be of much use? Surely in such circumstances a picture of Jesus quietly and courageously enduring a trial at the hands of a harsh Roman judge would be more relevant? The whole of the

---

[18] See Winter, *Trial*, p. 59.

[19] See, for example, Sherwin-White, 'Persecutions', pp. 199–213, and Garnsey and Saller, *Roman*, p. 202. Ste Croix ('Why?', p. 15), notes that persecution at this period was from *below* – the result of popular agitation coming to the governors' ears rather than as a result of an imperial edict.

'progressively friendlier Pilate' theory thus needs careful re-examination in the light of the differing interpretations of Pilate found in the four canonical gospels.

Methodology

The first chapter gives a general introduction to the history and formation of the imperial Roman province of Judaea and the powers and duties of its equestrian governors, with particular reference to Pilate. This draws upon Roman and Jewish sources, both literary and epigraphic. The next two chapters examine the references to Pilate in the Jewish writers Philo and Josephus. There are three reasons for taking these authors at this point. First, their date. Philo, writing around 41 CE, is our earliest literary reference to Pilate whilst Josephus, writing around the mid-seventies and mid-90s of the first century CE, is probably later than Mark's gospel but roughly contemporary with the other three. Second, the two Jewish writers form a natural pair since a certain similarity in background and rhetorical aims leads at times to a similarity in their portrayals of Pilate. Third, the bulk of what we can reconstruct of the historical Pilate is derived from the accounts of Philo and Josephus. By treating their accounts first we will already have formed some picture of the historical man before going on to analyse the way in which he is interpreted by the four evangelists. The remaining four chapters will deal with the portrayal of Pilate in each gospel in turn.

The material will be arranged slightly differently in the analysis of the Jewish writers than with the Christian ones. This is because the rhetorical interests and attitudes towards Rome shown by Philo and Josephus have already been investigated in great detail by other writers.[20] Each chapter will therefore begin with a description of these interests and attitudes, and the subsequent discussion of Pilate as a literary character within the works will go on to show how the portrayal of the prefect fits into, and has been influenced by, the general rhetorical aims of each work. Each chapter will end with an examination and reconstruction of the historical events behind the rhetoric.

With the gospels, however, the first two steps are reversed. This is

---

[20] For example, Goodenough, *Politics* and Bilde, *Flavius*. See chapters 2 and 3 for fuller details.

largely because there has been less research and less consensus reached regarding the relation of each gospel writer to his Roman overlords. After a consideration of the general themes in each evangelist's passion narrative, each chapter will give a more detailed description of how the writer concerned presents the prefect as a literary character, asking how a first-century reader would have understood and interpreted Pilate's actions. When this has been established we will ask whether the portrayal of Pilate in each case gives any indication as to the author's attitude towards the Roman state, and what kind of readers might have found this useful. After all four Roman trial narratives in the gospels have been analysed, the possible historical events behind them will be discussed.

The conclusion will be in two parts. It should by then be possible to distinguish between the 'historical Pilate', the Roman knight sent by Tiberius to take charge of the province of Judaea, and the many different Pilates of interpretation preserved in the writings of six first-century Jewish and Christian authors.

ACKNOWLEDGEMENTS

Many people have contributed to the writing of this book over the past few years with both advice and friendship. Unfortunately, I can mention only a few of them here.

Professor Jimmy Dunn of Durham University deserves special thanks for his kindness, encouragement and inspiring supervision of my doctoral dissertation which formed the basis of this book. I am also indebted to Professor Dr Martin Hengel for all his helpful comments and generosity throughout a year spent at Eberhardt-Karls University, Tübingen. Other people who have made helpful suggestions to the manuscript include Professor Martin Goodman and Dr Loren Stuckenbruck (both of whom examined my dissertation), Professor Dr Sandy Wedderburn, Professor Jackson Hershbell, Dr Margaret Thrall (the former editor of this series) and, in particular, Professor Dr Klaus Haacker who sent me several detailed and useful suggestions. These people will not agree with all that I have written in the following pages – I would like to thank them for their help and apologize for the remaining errors which are entirely my own.

It is impossible to embark on a doctoral dissertation or a book without the support and encouragement of close friends and colleagues. My former colleagues at Northern College, Manchester, kept me smiling throughout the revisions – especially Revd Dr Martin Scott and Revd Frankie Ward – and my new colleagues at Aberdeen University have allowed me research time to finish off the manuscript. Thanks too go to my friends Lisa Bage, Mike Fraser and, especially, Keith Raffan. Most of all, I would like to take this opportunity to thank my mother for proofreading the entire manuscript and my father for drawing the map of Judaea. To them, and to my brother David, this book is dedicated.

ABBREVIATIONS

ABD	*Anchor Bible Dictionary*, ed. D. N. Freedman, vols. 1–6, New York/London: Doubleday, 1992
AJT	*American Journal of Theology*
ANRW	*Aufsteig und Niedergang der römischen Welt*, ed. H. Temporini and W. Haase, Berlin: de Gruyter, 1972–
ATR	*Anglican Theological Review*
BETL	Bibliotheca ephemeridum theologicarum lovaniensium
Bib.	*Biblica*
BN	*Biblische Notizen*
BSac.	*Bibliotheca Sacra*
BTB	*Biblical Theology Bulletin*
BZ	*Biblische Zeitschrift*
CAH	*Cambridge Ancient History*. 2nd edn, vol. 10
CBM	ed. G. F. Hill, *Catalogue of the Greek Coins of Palestine in the British Museum*, (London: 1914)
CBQ	*Catholic Biblical Quarterly*
Chrysostom	
Hom. in Matt.	*Homilies on Matthew*
Cicero	
Ad Fam.	*Ad Familiares*
CRINT	*Compendium rerum iudaicarum ad Novum Testamentum*, ed. S. Safrai and M. Stern, 2 vols. Van Gorcum & Co, Assen, 1974
Dig.	*Digesta Justiniani*
DNTT	*Dictionary of New Testament Theology*, ed. C. Brown, vols. 1–3, Exeter: Paternoster, 1975–8
ETL	*Ephemerides theologicae lovanienses*
Epiphanius	
Adv. Haer.	*Against Heresies*

Eusebius
 EH   *Church History*
 Chron.   *Chronicle*
 DE   *Proof of the Gospel*
EvT   *Evangelische Theologie*
ExpTim   *Expository Times*
FB   *Forschung zur Bibel*
HTR   *Harvard Theological Review*
IDB   *Interpreter's Dictionary of the Bible*, Nashville: Abingdon, 1962
IEJ   *Israel Exploration Journal*
Ignatius
 Sm.   *Letter to the Smyrnaeans*
 Ph.   *Letter to the Philadelphians*
 Pol.   *Letter to Polycarp*
 Eph.   *Letter to the Ephesians*
ILS   *Inscriptiones Latinae Selectae*, ed. H. Dessau, Berlin, 1892–1916
Irenaeus
 Adv. Haer.   *Against Heresies*
JBL   *Journal of Biblical Literature*
Jerome
 In Matt.   *Commentary on the Gospel of Matthew*
JJS   *Journal of Jewish Studies*
Josephus
 Ant   *Antiquities of the Jews*
 JW   *Jewish War*
JQR   *Jewish Quarterly Review*
JRS   *Journal of Roman Studies*
JSJ   *Journal for the Study of Judaism*
JSNT   *Journal for the Study of the New Testament*
JSNTSup   JSNT Supplement Series
JSOT   *Journal for the Study of the Old Testament*
JSPSup   Journal for the Study of the Pseudepigrapha Supplement Series
JTS   *Journal of Theological Studies*
LTK   *Lexicon für Theologie und Kirche*
LXX   The Septuagint
m.   Mishna
MTZ   *Münchener theologische Zeitschrift*
NS   New Series

NovT	*Novum Testamentum*
NovTSup	Novum Testamentum Supplement Series
NTS	*New Testament Studies*
NTT	*Norsk Teologisk Tidsskrift*
OCD	*Oxford Classical Dictionary*, 2nd edn, Oxford: Oxford University Press, 1970

Origen
   In Matt.   *Commentary on the Gospel of Matthew*

p.	Palestinian Talmud
PBSR	Papers of the British School at Rome

Pliny (the Elder)
   NH   *Natural History*

Pliny (the Younger)
   Ep.   *Letters*

PW	*Real-Encyclopädie der classischen Altertumswissenschaft*, ed. A. G. Pauly-Wissowa, Stuttgart/ Munich, 1894–1972
RA	*Revue d'assyriologie et d'archéologie orientale*
RB	*Review Biblique*
RGG	*Religion in Geschichte und Gegenwart*

Seneca
   Epist. Mor.   *Epistulae Morales*

Severus
   Chron.   *Chronicle*

SNTSMS   Society for New Testament Studies Monograph Series

Strabo
   Geog.   *Geography*

Suetonius
   Aug.   *The Lives of the Caesars*, ii, Augustus
   Tib.   *The Lives of the Caesars*, iii, Tiberius
   Gaius   *The Lives of the Caesars*, iv, Gaius
   Claud.   *The Lives of the Caesars*, v, Claudius

Tacitus
   Ann.   *Annals*
   Hist.   *Histories*

TBei	*Theologische Beiträge*
TDNT	*Theological Dictionary of the New Testament*, vols. 1–5, ed. G. Kittel; vols. 6–10, ed. G. Friedrich, Grand Rapids: Eerdmans, 1964–76

Tertullian
  Apol.   *Apology*
TLZ   *Theologische Litteraturzeitung*
TS   *Theological Studies*
UBS4   United Bible Societies Greek New Testament, 4th (revised) edn, Stuttgart: Deutsche Bibelgesellschaft,1993
Virgil
  Georg.   *Georgics*
VT   *Vetus Testamentum*
ZDPV   *Zeitschrift des deutschen Palästina-Vereins*
ZNW   *Zeitschrift für die neutestamentliche Wissenschaft*

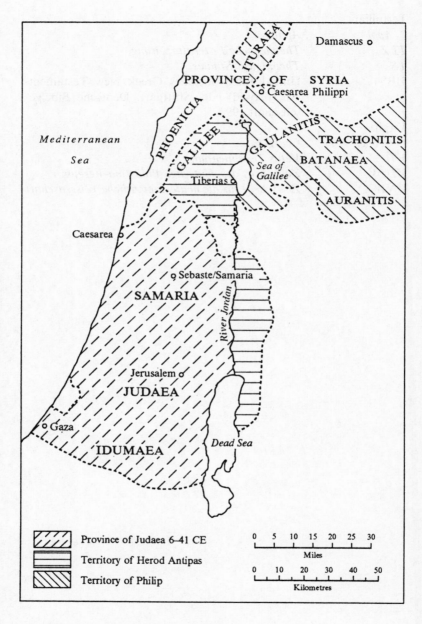

The Roman province of Judaea, 6–41 CE

1

PONTIUS PILATE AND THE ROMAN
PROVINCE OF JUDAEA

Pontius Pilate was the fifth governor of the Roman province of Judaea, holding office from 26–37 CE.[1] The small province had been brought under Roman rule only two decades earlier. The events which led to this, however, go back another decade still to the death of Herod I in 4 BCE.[2]

In the final codicil of his will, the king divided his kingdom between three of his sons: Philip and Antipas received a quarter each; the remaining half, including Judaea, was to go to Archelaus. Since Herod I was a vassal king, or *rex socius*, it lay with Augustus either to ratify the will as it stood or to appoint another successor. Both Archelaus and Antipas journeyed to Rome:[3] Archelaus anxious to have his succession ratified; Antipas to plead for the greater legitimation of an earlier will in which he had been named

---

[1] Gratus was sent to Judaea some time after Tiberius' accession in 14 CE (*Ant.* 18.32–3) and spent eleven years in the province (18.35), taking us to c. 25/6 CE. Pilate was dismissed shortly before Tiberius' death in March 37 after governing for ten years (18.89), indicating that he took up his duties c. 26 CE. The suggestion of D. R. Schwartz (following Eisler, *Messiah*, pp. 13–20) that Pilate actually took up his post in 19 CE is unconvincing. He maintains that all the references in Josephus' *Antiquities* given above which point to a date of 26 are Christian forgeries designed to refute the *Acta Pilati* circulated during the principate of Maximin Daia in 311. In this work Jesus' execution occurred in 21 CE; if Josephus' records could be tampered with to show that Pilate had only appeared in the province in 26 CE then the work could be proved to be a hoax. There are two major problems here. First, it is difficult to see how every copy of *Ant.* could have been altered at such a late date (there are no textual variants here). Second, this reconstruction assumes that these Christian forgers were quite happy to accept that Jesus' crucifixion occurred at the incredibly early date of 21 CE. Would it not have been more effective to add an identifiable date to Josephus' reference to Jesus' execution rather than alter Pilate's dates? See Schwartz, 'Pilate's Appointment', pp. 182–201.

[2] For more detailed historical surveys of this important period see Schürer, *History*, vol. 1, §§ 16–7, pp. 330–427; Smallwood, *Jews*, pp. 105–19; Lémonon, *Pilate*, pp. 33–41; Hoehner, *Herod*, pp. 18–39.

[3] Josephus, *JW* 2.14, *Ant.* 17.219.

as sole heir.[4] The two Herodians were joined by a group of relatives who, according to Josephus, openly supported Antipas but whose real purpose in appearing before the Emperor was to secure direct Roman rule over the former kingdom.[5] This sentiment was shared by yet another delegation composed of fifty delegates from Judaea, supposedly joined by eight thousand Jews living in the capital, who pleaded with Augustus to unite their country to Syria and to entrust the administration to the Syrian legate.[6] Clearly Josephus would have us believe that both the people and the nobility of Judaea would prefer to be governed by Romans rather than a successor of Herod.

Yet Josephus' record can only be accepted with some caution. A central apologetic purpose in both the *Jewish War* and the *Antiquities of the Jews* was to show that the troubles leading up to the revolt of 66 CE were initiated by a small rebellious faction and that the people generally acquiesced to Roman rule.[7] This purpose could be served all the better if an initial request for Roman rule actually came from the people themselves. In all probability, there were some who feared that Archelaus might turn out even more tyrannical than his father and to whom direct Roman rule seemed the better prospect, but their numbers and influence were not as great as Josephus would have us believe. Many would have remembered Rome's heavy-handed and often brutal interference in Judaean affairs over the last sixty years, such as Pompey's desecration of the Holy of Holies in the Temple, Crassus' use of gold from the Temple treasury to raise money for his Parthian campaign, or his selling the inhabitants of four small towns into slavery after Julius Caesar's death to help pay for the civil war.[8] Furthermore, in view of Rome's eagerness to extend direct rule over the whole Near East at this period and the extra revenues the imperial fiscus stood to receive by the annexation of Judaea, Augustus' decision not to turn Herod's territory into a Roman province would have been extremely curious if the population had generally requested it.[9]

---

[4] *JW* 2.14, *Ant.* 17.146; for the earlier will see *JW* 1.646, *Ant.* 17.146–7. On Herod's six wills see Hoehner, *Herod*, Appendix I, pp. 269–76.

[5] *JW* 2.22, *Ant.* 17.227.   [6] *JW* 2.91, *Ant.* 17.314.

[7] For further details and secondary literature see chapter 3 on Josephus.

[8] See Goodman, *Ruling*, p. 10.

[9] On Rome's expansionist policies in the Near East see Millar, *Roman*. Goodman also thinks it unlikely that the Jews sent to Rome were genuine representatives of the Judaeans: cf. *Ruling*, p. 16.

At this stage, Augustus decided to uphold Herod's final will.[10] Antipas was allotted Galilee and Peraea; Philip was given Batanaea, Trachonitis, Auranitis and certain parts of Zeno[11] around Panias.[12] Both were given the title 'tetrach', literally the ruler of a fourth part of a kingdom. Salome was proclaimed mistress of Jamnia, Azotus and Phasaelis and given the palace of Ascalon.[13] The remainder, amounting to half of the kingdom and comprising Idumaea, Judaea and Samaria (along with jurisdiction over Salome's estates), was given to Archelaus with the title 'ethnarch' and the promise that he would be given the title 'king' if he proved himself worthy. The cities of Caesarea, Samaria, Joppa and Jerusalem were to remain in his control whilst the Greek towns of Gaza, Gadara and Hippos were annexed to Syria.[14]

In 6 CE, however, Augustus was once again forced to consider the government of Archelaus' half of the kingdom.[15] Our primary evidence again comes from Josephus who alleges that both the Jews and the Samaritans under the ethnarch's authority appeared before Caesar to denounce his 'cruelty and tyranny'. Augustus summoned Archelaus to him in Rome, subsequently banishing him to Vienne in Gaul and formally annexing his territory into a Roman province. Yet although Josephus stresses Archelaus' brutality, he records no specific charges, nor does his short description of his reign furnish us with many examples. In the virtual anarchy which reigned in the kingdom after Herod's death, Archelaus is said to have put down a protest at Passover with excessive force.[16] As ethnarch, he deposed two high priests (a practice established by his father) and married unlawfully.[17] Perhaps this scarcity of evidence indicates that Josephus' source here, Nicolas of Damascus, ended at this point.[18] Or perhaps, as M. Goodman suggests, the fall of Archelaus was due

---

[10] *JW* 2.93–100, *Ant.* 17.317–20.   [11] *JW* 2.95; Zenodonis in *Ant.* 17.319.

[12] Or Ituraea; cf. Luke 13.1.

[13] This was bequeathed by her on her death in 10 CE to the Empress Livia, and, on her death in 29 CE, to Tiberius. The estate was administered from 10 CE onwards by imperial financial agents known as 'procurators' resident in Jamnia, rather than by the prefect of Judaea (as in *Ant.* 18.158; see Smallwood, *Jews*, p. 158).

[14] Lémonon puts the value of Archelaus' territory at 400 talents. For his discussion of the evidence see *Pilate*, p. 106.

[15] *JW* 2.111 dates the events to the ninth year of Archelaus' reign. That it was actually the tenth year, as *Ant.* 17.342 records, seems more likely as this is supported by Dio Cassius (55.27) and an allusion to the tenth year of Archelaus' reign in Josephus (*Life* 5).

[16] *JW* 2.11–13, *Ant.* 17.213–18.   [17] Ibid. 17.339–41.

[18] Suggested by Thackeray, *Jewish*, vol. 2, p. 364, note a.

not to charges of brutality but rather to dynastic intrigue.[19] This is the reason given by Dio Cassius and possibly also by Strabo.[20] If the problem was Archelaus' brutality, Augustus could easily have given his land to Antipas, Philip or another Herodian; there was no compelling reason why Judaea should be turned into a province. Josephus does not even say that the people asked for a Roman governor this time. But if the problem was fighting amongst the Herodians, that would give Augustus the perfect opportunity to remove the Jewish princes and subject the ethnarchy to direct Roman rule. Both the confiscation of Archelaus' property into the imperial treasury and the imposition of direct taxation were financially valuable to Rome.[21]

If it is correct to see dynastic intrigue as the root of the problem confronting Augustus, then any delegations from Jews and Samaritans could have played only a minor role in the affair, if any at all. The views of the people in Archelaus' territory were therefore not a determining factor in the Emperor's decision. How, then, did they respond to direct Roman rule? The violence after Herod's death, which was primarily directed at Roman targets, and the troubles which accompanied the imposition of the census taken for taxation purposes at the inauguration of the province, all suggest that pagan rule was not so universally welcomed in Judaea as Josephus would have us believe.[22]

Judaea was now transformed into a third-class imperial province.[23] These provinces, which were few in number, tended to be

---

[19] Goodman, *Ruling*, p. 39.

[20] Dio Cassius 55.27.6; Strabo, *Geog.* 16.2.46. Strabo's evidence is not entirely clear. Speaking of Herod I he writes, 'However, his sons were not successful, but became involved in accusations; and one of them [i.e. Archelaus] spent the rest of his life in exile . . . whereas the others [i.e. Antipas and Philip], by much obsequiousness, but with difficulty, found leave to return home, with a tetrachy assigned to each'. The 'accusations' could be from either the inhabitants of Archelaus' ethnarchy (so Josephus) or from the Herodians (so Dio). But the final part of the citation suggests that all three brothers were in Rome at the decisive time when Archelaus was exiled (i.e. 6 CE, not 4 BCE). This may suggest dynastic in-fighting.

[21] *JW* 2.111, *Ant.* 17.344; Goodman, *Ruling*, p. 39.

[22] The principal goal of the unrest after Herod's death seems to have been national independence – cf. *JW* 2.49–50, 51, 54, 62, 68, 71 and 75. See Hengel, *Zealots*, pp. 325–30. On the census see ibid. pp. 127–38 and Schürer, *History*, vol. 1, pp. 399–427. Josephus characteristically transforms what was probably general unrest in 6 CE by attributing all the troubles to the activities of two men, Judas the Galilean and a Pharisee named Saddok, the founders of the 'fourth philosophy' – cf. *JW* 2.118; *Ant.* 18.3–10, 23–5; Hengel, ibid. pp. 76–145.

[23] Strabo, *Geog.* 17.3.25, describes imperial and senatorial provinces and at 17.840 lists the three types of imperial province. In contrast to quieter senatorial provinces,

those which were least important in terms of expanse and revenue. Often they were territories in which the indigenous population presented particular problems, where 'owing to a tenacious and individual culture, or lack of it, the strict implementation of ordinary regulations seemed impossible'.[24] The governors of these provinces were drawn from the equestrian order and commanded only auxiliary troops.[25] Although technically independent, the new province was to a large extent under the guidance of the powerful and strategically important neighbouring province of Syria. The Syrian legate, a man of consular standing, had three Roman legions at his disposal to which a fourth was added after 18 CE.[26] He could be relied upon to intervene with military support in times of crisis and could be called upon as an arbitrator by either the Judaean governor or the people if the need arose.[27]

Throughout most of the first century, Rome's control of the Judaean region was comparatively tenuous and uncertain.[28] The borders of the province underwent several alterations whilst certain areas fluctuated between Roman and Herodian rule. Initially, Judaea consisted of Archelaus' territory minus several Greek cities. After the brief reign of the Herodian Agrippa I (41–4 CE), the whole of the king's territory reverted to Roman rule. The province was now at its maximum extent, covering not only Archelaus' former territory but also Galilee and Philip's share of the

imperial provinces tended to be the more turbulent ones in which troops were needed, an arrangement which (as Dio Cassius observed) skilfully allowed the Emperor to control the army since most of the legions were to be found in his own provinces: cf. Dio Cassius 53.12.1–4.

[24] Schürer, *History*, vol. 1, pp. 357–8.

[25] Other such imperial provinces with an equestrian governor at the head were Mauretania Tingitana, Caesariensis and Thrace. For more details see Levick, *Government*, p. 15 and Stevenson, *CAH* vol. 10, p. 211. Although governed by a man of equestrian rank, Egypt was an exception to this since its size and importance made it unwise to entrust it to a senator.

[26] These were the VIth Ferrata, Xth Fretensis and IIIrd Gallica and, after 18 CE, the XIIth Fulminata. These four legions were still stationed in Syria during Pilate's governorship (Tacitus, *Ann.* 4.5), Lémonon, *Pilate*, p. 62.

[27] For example, Longinus came to Jerusalem 'with a large force' when he feared that Fadus' demand that the high priestly vestments be kept in Roman custody might cause a revolt (*Ant.* 20.7); Petronius intervened when entrusted by Gaius with a special mandate to erect his statue in the Jerusalem Temple. Presumably his legions would have proved useful in a riot (*JW* 2.185, *Ant.* 18.261; Philo, *Embassy* 207); and delegations from the people appealed successfully to the Syrian legates against Pilate, Cumanus and Florus (*Ant.* 18.88; *JW* 2.236–44/*Ant.* 20.118–136; *JW* 2.280–3). See further Lémonon, *Pilate*, pp. 60–71.

[28] See Millar, *Roman*, pp. 55–6.

kingdom.[29] In 53 CE the province was reduced in size by the donation of Philip's former territory to Agrippa II.[30] Further territory was lost the following year when parts of Galilee, including Tiberias and Tarichaea, and the city of Julias in Panaea along with fourteen neighbouring villages were added to Agrippa II's kingdom.[31] This was the extent of Judaea until the outbreak of revolt in 66 CE.

The new province was small. Pilate's governorship belonged to its first phase when it measured only approximately 160 kilometres north to south and 70 km west to east (see the map on p. xxvi). Yet, despite its size, its borders encompassed several different groups of people. Predominant were the Judaean Jewish population situated at the centre of the province and, to the south, the Idumaean Jews.[32] Both these Jewish groups looked to Jerusalem as their cultural and religious centre. This city continued as a place of pilgrimage for Jews from all over the Roman world, particularly during the three great festivals. It was cosmopolitan and trilingual: archaeological excavations have revealed a high proportion of inscriptions written in Greek as well as Hebrew and Aramaic.[33] The many gifts lavished upon the Temple by Jewish pilgrims and gentile visitors alike, besides the increase in trade due to the numbers of visitors, assured the city's place at the centre of the Judaean economy.[34] The Herodians had poured wealth into their capital city whilst the Temple itself provided employment for a large number of craftsmen until 64 CE.[35] To the north were the Samaritans with Mount Gerizim as their religious centre; feuds between

[29] This was given to Agrippa on Philip's death. *JW* 2.247.

[30] *Ant.* 20.138, *JW* 2.247.

[31] *Ant.* 20.158–9. Several scholars date this last alteration to 61 CE because the last issue of coins by Agrippa II mentions an era which began in 61. This, however, would contradict Josephus who links the reduction of territory to Felix's governorship which ended c. 60 CE. For a fuller survey of territorial changes throughout the province's history see Lémonon, *Pilate*, pp. 35–6, maps pp. 38–41.

[32] Despite having been forcibly converted to Judaism by John Hyrcanus at the end of the second century BCE, the Idumaeans seem to have regarded themselves as completely Jewish (*JW* 4.270–84). There is also no evidence that the Judaean Jews regarded them as anything other than Jewish; Josephus has Herod I referred to as a 'half-Jew' because of his Idumaean background only once and this is in an extremely polemical speech (*Ant.* 14.403).

[33] See Hengel (*Hellenization*, pp. 7–18) who stresses the extent of Greek culture and language in other parts of Judaea, Samaria and Galilee in the first century.

[34] On the Judaean economy, especially the period shortly before the revolt, see Goodman, *Ruling*, pp. 51–75.

[35] *Ant.* 20.219–22.

the Samaritans and the Jews are frequently referred to by Josephus. The province also contained two predominately pagan cities – Caesarea and Sebaste – which had been completely rebuilt on the lines of Graeco-Roman cities by Herod I. They contained temples dedicated to Caesar and held four-yearly festivals with gladiatorial combats and games.[36] The frequent riots and troubles between these different peoples, each with their own religious and cultural sensibilities, attest to the difficulties involved in governing such a variety of peoples in a confined area.

Under the Roman governors Judaea had, to a certain degree, two capital cities. The traditional capital, Jerusalem, continued as the focus of Jewish religious life whilst the Roman governor resided in Caesarea together with his troops, family and entourage, transforming the city into the Roman administrative headquarters.[37] The governor occupied the palace built by Herod which then became known as the praetorium.[38] The choice of Caesarea was judicious for three reasons. First, and undoubtedly most importantly as far as the military governors were concerned, the city's location by the sea made it a good strategic choice.[39] There was less chance of being surrounded and trapped in a revolt; the harbour built by Herod I made communication with Rome easier; and, in cases of emergency, the Syrian legate could reach Caesarea with greater speed and ease than Jerusalem. Second, it respected the religious character of Jerusalem. Although many Jews lived in Caesarea, its largely Greek character made it more agreeable to the pagan governor and his troops who could live there without fear of offending Jewish religious sensitivities. Third, although the choice of Caesarea may have appeared to favour the pagan inhabitants of the province, it was neutral ground as far as the largest ethnic groups – Jews and Samaritans – were concerned. Neither could feel that the other group commanded more of the governor's attention.

On occasion, however, the governor did move to Jerusalem. This was especially important during festivals when the crowds and

[36] *JW* 1.403, *Ant.* 15.296–8 on Sebaste; *JW* 1.408–16, *Ant.* 15.292–8, 331–41, 16.136–41, Pliny, *NH*, 5.14–69 on Caesarea. See also Millar, *Roman*, p. 355.
[37] The first evidence for this comes from Pilate's era (*JW* 2.169–74, *Ant.* 18.55–9); Florus also lived here (*JW* 2.332), as did Felix (Acts 23.23–4) and Festus (Acts 25.1–13). It seems reasonable to suppose that all the governors made Caesarea their capital.
[38] Acts 23.35. It was a Roman custom for governors to occupy the palace of the former sovereign: see Lémonon, *Pilate*, p. 118.
[39] Smallwood, *Jews*, p. 146.

religious fervour generated could potentially lead to rioting. The presence of the governor with his troops helped to check such outbreaks. Although there is some dispute over whether the governor's Jerusalem residence was the Antonia fortress or Herod's palace, the latter is probably the likeliest. The commanding position of the beautiful palace meant that it was convenient for maintaining law and order.[40] Members of the Herodian family visiting Jerusalem had to stay in the Hasmonaean palace.[41]

In all, fourteen governors were sent to the province.[42] Most ruled between two and four years, though Felix remained approximately eight years (52–60). By far the longest periods of office belong to Gratus, who ruled eleven years (15–26) and Pilate, who ruled a similar length of time (26–January 37). It is no coincidence that both these governorships occurred under the principate of Tiberius (14–37). One of the features of Tiberius' provincial administration was that he retained men in office for a long time. This may have been due partly to his dislike of taking decisions.[43] Josephus, however, suggests that a further motive was to protect provinces from the rapacity of the governors:

> For it was a law of nature that governors are prone to engage in extortion. When appointments were not perma-

[40] See *Ant.* 17.222, *JW* 2.301 and *Embassy* 299, 306. For a description of the palace see *JW* 5.177–83, 1.402 and *Ant.* 15.318. Lémonon gives an account of the archaeological excavations (*Pilate*, pp.121–2). Herod's palace is also favoured by Schürer, *History*, vol 1, pp. 361–2 and Smallwood, *Jews*, p. 146.

[41] Agrippa II stayed here during the governorship of Festus (*Ant.* 20.189–90). This is presumably also where Antipas stayed when he was in Jerusalem for the Passover: cf. Luke 23.7.

[42] Seven were before Agrippa I: Coponius (6–c. 9 CE); Ambibulus (or Ambibuchus) (c. 9–12); Annius Rufus (c. 12–15); Valerius Gratus (c. 15–26); Pontius Pilate (26–37); Marcellus (37); Marullus (37–41). Seven ruled after Agrippa: Cuspius Fadus (44–c. 46); Tiberius Iulius Alexander (c. 46–8); Ventidius Cumanus (48–c. 52); Antonius Felix (c. 52–c. 60); Porcius Festus (c. 60–2); Albinus (62–4); Gessius Florus (64–6). For details see Schürer, *History*, vol. 1, pp. 382–98, 455–70.

It is possible that Marcellus and Marullus were actually the same man – Μάρκελλος in *Ant.* 18.89 being a corruption of Μάρυλλος in *Ant.* 18.237 (or the other way around). Marcellus was appointed provisionally by the Syrian legate Vitellius and may have been confirmed in this post by Gaius. Thus when Josephus speaks of the Emperor *sending* Marullus, he is using the verb ἐκπέμπω to signify an official appointment. See Schürer, *History*, vol. 1, p. 383 and note. D. R. Schwartz holds a different view regarding these two men. He suggests that they were not actually independent governors of Judaea at all since after Pilate's suspension the province was annexed to Syria until 41 CE: cf. *Agrippa*, pp. 62–6.

[43] Tacitus, *Ann.* 1.80, Dio Cassius 58.23.5–6. For Tiberius' provincial policy see Levick, *Tiberius*, pp. 125–47.

nent, but were for short terms, or liable to be cancelled without notice, the spur to peculation was even greater. If, on the contrary, those appointed kept their posts longer, they would be gorged with their robberies and would by the very bulk of them be more sluggish in pursuit of further gain.[44]

The long tenures of Gratus and Pilate are therefore perfectly in keeping with this provincial policy.

Pilate and his fellow governors of Judaea, as was customary in a relatively unimportant imperial province, were drawn from the equestrian order. The only exception seems to have been the freedman Felix; the comments of both Tacitus and Suetonius on his low birth suggest that the appointment of a freedman was unprecedented, thereby indirectly confirming that the others were equestrians.[45] This was the middle rank of the Roman nobility, coming after senators but before curials. To possess the *nomen* or *dignitas equestris* a man needed free birth, certain moral standards and, most importantly, wealth. Under the Empire the census evaluation for admission to equestrian rank was 400,000 sesterces.[46] It was possible for men of lower rank to be promoted to the order following exceptional military service. Augustus, himself originally of equestrian background, introduced a series of measures to raise the standing of this order in the eyes of the public and to restore it to its ancient prestige.[47] Roughly every five years the order was reviewed, paying particular attention to the origins, respectability and fortune of those belonging to its ranks. The long-disused ceremonial parade, or *transvectio*, of 15 July was reintroduced and accompanied by an inspection; again this was an attempt to make the civic hierarchy clearly visible.[48] Augustus' aim was to establish an order of men possessing *dignitatio*, or fitness for public office. In essence the order was to be 'a huge reservoir which would enable

---

[44] *Ant.* 18.170–3: see also Tacitus, *Ann.* 4.6.

[45] Suetonius, *Claud.* 28; Tacitus, *Hist.* 5.9. Although Tacitus speaks of the province being entrusted to 'knights or freed*men*', there is no evidence to suggest that any other governor belonged to this class. See Lémonon, *Pilate*, p. 37. Felix, though a manumitted slave, had probably already joined the equestrian order. Scholars are divided on this question; see Lémonon, ibid. p. 55, n. 69.

[46] Pliny, *NH*, 33.32.

[47] On Augustus' rank see Suetonius, *Aug.* 2.5. On the equestrian order in the early Empire generally see especially Nicolet, 'Augustus', pp. 89–128; Garnsey and Saller, *Roman*, pp. 23–6, 112–18.

[48] Suetonius, *Aug.* 38.3; Dio Cassius 55.31.2.

the *res publica* to recruit, in sufficient numbers, suitable candidates for various essential offices'.[49]

Equestrians could serve the *res publica* in a variety of ways: serving on jury panels; as publicans supervising the collection of taxes; from the reign of Claudius onwards they might be found in certain magistracies in the senate if no senators came forward. But the most common public service for an equestrian was in military office; this corresponds closely to the original meaning of *equites*, or cavalry. Equestrians might be prefects of a cohort or *ala*, or military tribunes. Certain duties in Rome were also undertaken by men of equestrian rank such as the prefect of the imperial body-guard, the 'Praetorian Guard'.[50] Under Augustus it became pos-sible for equestrians who had progressed through the military ranks to serve the *res publica* in a specific capacity as provincial prefects such as we find in Judaea; the highest of these was the governorship of Egypt.

This office-holding minority came to resemble senators in that they derived honour from the rank of their office.[51] Roman politics was essentially a quest for fame, power and wealth; a man in public office was continually striving and competing against his contem-poraries. The old republican aspirations of *virtus* and *gloria* were still very much alive in the early Empire. Men still pursued a reputation for great deeds in the service of the state, the approval of the 'best men' and fame which would live on after their death. Along with this went the pursuit of wealth; riches honourably gained were a natural part of the achievement of glory.[52] With the emergence of the principate, however, pride in personal achieve-ment in public life could only be celebrated 'in an uneasy combina-tion of personal glory and loyalty to the Emperor'.[53] Officials could only take as much *gloria* from their public deeds as was consistent with their position; they had to be careful to stress their obedience to the Emperor at all times. In military campaigns, *gloria* would go to the Emperor, not to the general.[54]

A man's chances of promotion to public office depended not so much on individual competence as his connections and influences

---

[49] Nicolet, 'Augustus', p. 99.

[50] Dio Cassius 52.24.2–6. See Ferguson, 'Roman Administration', pp. 649–65.

[51] On Roman political ideology see especially Wiseman, *Roman*, pp. 1–44 and Earl, *Moral*.

[52] Wiseman, *Roman*, pp. 12–13. Cicero amassed over 2 million sesterces during his year as proconsul of Cilicia without breaking any laws (*Ad Fam.* 5.20.9).

[53] Wiseman, ibid., p. 8.   [54] Earl, *Moral*, pp. 90–1.

in the imperial court.[55] Equestrians often needed the support of senatorial patrons to secure a post from the Emperor. Powerful and prestigious posts such as the prefecture of an imperial province were in the Emperor's direct gift; sanction by the senate was only a formality. In view of the competitive spirit amongst the nobility, however, emperors had to be extremely careful in selecting men for these public offices. Tiberius is said not to have chosen men with outstanding *virtutes* (great deeds coupled with moral qualities) because of the dangers to his own position. But at the same time he feared public scandal and so was careful not to select men who might bring Rome into disrepute on account of their vices.[56] In general, men of mediocre qualities could be counted on to steer a middle path. In deciding who should hold office, Tacitus tells us, Tiberius 'took into consideration birth, military distinction, and civilian eminence, and the choice manifestly fell on the worthiest men'.[57] Yet despite these good intentions, governors often turned out to be less competent than had been hoped and charges of maladministration were frequent.[58] By 4 BCE provincials could bring some capital charges against officials.[59] The old republican laws of *lex Julia* and *repetundae* originally did not cover the misconduct of equestrian governors, but by the time of Claudius and Nero, and possibly earlier, these governors could be indicted according to *repetundae*.[60] A governor could not be tried whilst holding office;[61] he would be relieved of his command and subsequently tried in Rome.

Once in office, the responsibilities of the governor of Judaea were primarily military. This aspect is emphasized by the title of the governor which, before the reign of Agrippa I (41–4 CE), was 'prefect' (*praefectus*/ἔπαρχος). A mutilated limestone inscription found in Caesarea in 1961 confirms this title, at least in Pilate's case. The following words are still legible:

---

[55] Saller, *Personal* and Lintott, *Imperium*, pp. 168–74. On equestrian careers generally see Pflaum, *Carrières*, vols. 1–3. Nothing is known of Pilate's career prior to Judaea, though in all probability he secured his office by attracting imperial attention in military campaigns.

[56] Tacitus, *Ann.* 1.80.

[57] Ibid. 4.6 (Grant, *Tiberius*, p. 156); see also *Ann.* 3.69.

[58] Brunt, 'Charges', pp. 189–223 and Levick, *Tiberius*, p. 135. Lucilius Capito, the procurator of Asia, was tried in 23 CE; C. Silanus, the proconsul of Asia, was convicted of extortion aggravated by violence in 22 CE. Tacitus, *Ann.* 3.66–7, 4.15.3–4; Dio Cassius 57.23.4–5.

[59] Brunt, 'Charges', pp. 190–227.   [60] Ibid., p. 198.   [61] Ibid., p. 206.

.........S TIBERIÉVM
.........NTIVS PILATVS
.........ECTVS IVDA E
....

Although complete reconstructions of the inscription are tentative and extremely hypothetical in nature, and we are not certain as to what kind of a building was referred to by TIBERIÉVM,[62] two things are clear. One is that the second line refers to Pontius Pilate, presumably giving his first name in the mutilated left section; second, the third line gives his official title which, in all probability, is to be reconstructed as *'Praefectus Iudaeae'*. The appointment of men to a military prefecture shows the determination of the early Emperors to hold on to a newly subjugated territory and to bring the native inhabitants under Roman control. Under Claudius, however, 'prefect' was changed to a civilian title, 'procurator' (*procurator*/ἐπίτροπος), which may have been 'designed to reflect the success of the pacification process in the areas concerned'.[63] After Claudius' reforms, the title 'procurator' denoted not simply a fiscal agent (as it had done previously) but a public official taking on the same governmental duties as the former prefect.[64] Only in Egypt was the title 'prefect' retained, possibly indicating the continued military character of the governor.

Rome had few officials in its provinces; an imperial province would be administered only by the prefect and a small number of personal staff including perhaps companions, scribes and messen-

[62] Several scholars have assumed that the Tiberiéum was a temple dedicated to the Emperor. Although Tiberius appears not to have encouraged his own cult, epigraphic evidence affirms its existence (e.g. ILS 162, 3.474, 933, 4.454, cited by Lémonon, *Pilate*, p. 31, note 37). However, the mutilated state of the inscription means that we cannot be sure to what kind of building it referred. Lémonon suggests that the small size of the block would indicate that it is not a dedication but simply a brief inscription recording the name of a secular building. He therefore suggests (pp. 26–32) a simple *fécit* for the final line rather than the *dédit* or *dédicavit* proposed by other scholars.

[63] Garnsey and Saller, *Roman*, p. 23.

[64] This change in title under Claudius goes a long way in explaining the apparent confusion of the principal literary texts here. Philo, Josephus, the NT and Tacitus refer to various governors as ἔπαρχος (*praefectus*), ἐπίτροπος (procurator) and ἡγεμών (governor), apparently indiscriminately. For tables and a detailed analysis see Lémonon, *Pilate*, pp. 45–8. On the role of procurators and Claudius' reforms in his provincial government see Jones, 'Procurators', pp. 115–25; Sherwin-White, 'Procurator', pp. 11–15; Lémonon, *Pilate*, pp. 50–8; Brunt, 'Procuratorial', pp. 461–89.

gers.[65] Due to this small Roman presence, the governor's concerns had to be limited to essentials, principally the maintenance of law and order and the collection of taxes. To undertake this the governor possessed *imperium*, or the supreme administrative power in the province including both military and judicial authority.[66]

In order to uphold law and order, an equestrian governor had only auxiliary troops at his disposal. In Judaea these amounted to five infantry cohorts and one cavalry regiment.[67] These were usually drawn from non-citizen inhabitants of a province, or occasionally from neighbouring countries. Since Jews were exempt from military service on religious grounds, the Judaean auxiliaries were drawn from pagan provincials only.[68] The Roman governors seem to have inherited the troops of the Herodians drawn predominately from Caesarea and Sebaste.[69] The auxiliaries were organized into cavalry divided into *alae* (generally five hundred men, but sometimes a thousand) and infantry divided into centuries from which cohorts of five hundred or a thousand men were formed.

These auxiliary troops were stationed throughout the province. The majority would remain at the governor's military and administrative headquarters in Caesarea; smaller garrisons were scattered throughout the Judaean fortresses.[70] Although not a strategically important site, Jerusalem's position as the centre of the Jewish cult meant that it too needed to be guarded by a permanent garrison. One cohort was permanently posted in the Antonia fortress; it was commanded by a tribune and may have been partially mounted.[71] These troops carried out police duties in both the Temple Mount and the town itself.[72] Another camp was located in the western part of the town at Herod's palace; numbers here would be increased during festivals by the presence of the governor and a number of Caesarean troops.[73]

On the rare occasions when these auxiliary forces were not able

---

[65] Lintott, *Imperium*, pp. 50–2.

[66] Tacitus, *Ann.* 12.60. This is probably what Josephus refers to by ἐξουσία in *Ant.* 18.2.

[67] On the following paragraph see Webster, *Imperial Army*, pp. 142–55; Maxfield, *Military*, pp. 32–6; Spiedel, 'Roman Army', pp. 224–32; Schürer, *History*, vol. 1, pp. 362–7, vol. 2, pp. 95–6. One of these infantry cohorts may well have been the *cohors II Italica civium romanorum voluntariorum* referred to in Acts 10; see Hengel, *Between*, p. 203, n. 111.

[68] This was a ruling of Julius Caesar, *Ant.* 14.204, 13.251–2.

[69] *Ant.* 19.365, 20.122, 126; *JW* 2.41, 51–2, 236.

[70] *Ant.* 18.55: *JW* 2.408, 484–5.   [71] *JW* 5.223–4, Acts 21.31, 23.23.

[72] *JW* 2.224.   [73] See Isaac, *Limits*, pp. 279–80.

to check riots and disturbances amongst the people, the prefect would call upon the Syrian legate to intervene with his legions. In this respect one feature of Pilate's governorship is noteworthy. Throughout Pilate's term of office, Syria had three successive legates. The first was L. Aelius Lamia: he held the position until 32 CE and, although we do not know the exact year of his appointment, was probably already the legate when Pilate came to Judaea in 26. He was followed by L. Pomponius Flaccus from 32 to c. 35. Third was L. Vitellius from 35 to c. 39, the legate responsible for Pilate's eventual deposition.[74] Of these three legates, the tenure of the first, Lamia, deserves special attention. Both Suetonius and Tacitus testify that Tiberius gave provinces to men whom he never allowed to leave Rome.[75] Both writers suggest that Tiberius' motivation was fear that eminent men should be out of his sight, but it may be that Tiberius was in fact trying out a form of centralized government whereby provinces were governed from the capital.[76] Lamia appears to have been one of these men.[77] The two subsequent legates, however, both governed their province from Antioch.[78]

The implication of all this is that for the first six years of Pilate's governorship there was no Syrian legate in residence acting as a general overseer and mediator in Judaean affairs. Although Lamia conducted his official duties from Rome, the problems of long-distance communication would inevitably mean that he lost a certain degree of contact with his province. The distance would also mean that it was much more difficult for embassies from Judaea to contact the legate. Exactly what powers Lamia's Syrian deputies and assistants would have had in dealing with Judaean affairs is uncertain.[79] From Pilate's point of view, the absence of the legate was not entirely advantageous. It could be argued that he might recklessly misgovern the province, misusing the fact that the people had no strong advocate in Syria. Possibly some of this was true, yet if his behaviour had been completely provocative towards the people we would expect them to have complained immediately to

---

[74] See Schürer, *History*, vol. 1, pp. 261–3.
[75] Tacitus, *Ann.* 1.80: Suetonius *Tib.* 63 (probably also § 41).
[76] See Levick, *Tiberius*, p. 125 and Stevenson, *CAH*, p. 649.
[77] Tacitus, *Ann.* 6.27.   [78] For Vitellius see Tacitus, *Ann.* 6.32.
[79] Possibly the commanding officer Pacurius (*Ann.* 2.79; Seneca, *Epist. Mor.* 12.8–9) acted as one of Lamia's deputies (Stevenson, *CAH*, pp. 649); though what powers he would have had over the Judaean governor or to intervene in Judaea are unknown.

Flaccus on his arrival in 32 CE. As far as we know, this was not the case.[80] It is more likely that the absence of the governor presented difficulties for Pilate. Unlike his predecessors, he could not rely upon the immediate support of the legions in case of unrest. This would mean that any potential uprising had to be put down quickly before it could escalate. Until 32 CE, therefore, Pilate would have been more dependent on his auxiliaries than any previous governor.

The pagan character of these auxiliary troops, however, could on occasion be threatening for the Jewish inhabitants of the province. When trouble broke out between pagans and Jews, it was all too easy for the pagan auxiliaries to show partiality towards their own people.[81] This animosity could also manifest itself in over-brutal treatment of the Jewish population.[82] Although Josephus is doubtlessly exaggerating when he blames these pagan troops for sowing the seeds of the revolt of 66 (*Ant.* 19.366), their one-sidedness and anti-Jewishness could not have led to stability in the province or Jewish confidence in the imperial forces.

A further aspect of the maintenance of law and order was the prefect's supreme judicial power within the province. In Judaea, the prefect had the authority to try and execute provincials and probably also citizens within his area of jurisdiction.[83] He would presumably have a system of assizes to which cases could be brought and receive a hearing.[84] The precise division of judicial competence between the governor and native courts varied in different provinces.[85] There is not enough evidence to determine whether or not Jewish courts could inflict the death penalty at this period; scholarly opinion is sharply divided on this issue. The Roman governor would doubtless wish to maintain his jurisdiction in political offences but it is not impossible that Jewish courts were able to

---

[80] Given Josephus' apologetic interest in showing that one of the factors leading to the Jewish revolt was continued misgovernment by the Roman governors, he would surely have recorded such an event had he known of it.

[81] *JW* 2.268, *Ant.* 20.173–8.   [82] *Ant.* 18.62.

[83] Jones ('I Appeal', pp. 51–65) and Sherwin-White (*Roman*, p. 10) both assert that governors could not execute Roman citizens under their provincial jurisdiction at this period. Garnsey, however, suggests that even by late republican times provincial governors were empowered to execute civilian citizens by the *ius gladii*. If the accused felt that his case would not obtain a fair hearing in the governor's court he had the right to appeal to Caesar: cf. 'Criminal', pp. 51–9. In favour of Garnsey's case are the trial of Paul (who within Luke's narrative is a Roman citizen, Acts 25.6–12) and Florus' execution of men of equestrian rank (*JW* 2.308).

[84] Lintott, *Imperium*, pp. 55–6.   [85] Ibid., p. 57.

execute when their own Law had been contravened.[86] The Jewish Law was tolerated by Rome not primarily out of respect for its antiquity or morality but as a reward for military assistance given by the Jewish people to Julius Caesar during the civil war.[87]

Besides the military and judicial activities crucial for maintaining law and order, the second essential duty of a Roman prefect was to oversee the collection of taxes. The heaviest of these was the *tributum*; by the first century CE this was primarily a tax on provincial *land*.[88] The amount of tribute required from each person was worked out by means of a census. The frequency with which the census was held depended on the province and was often irregular.[89] Only one census appears to have been conducted in Judaea, that organized by Quirinius at the formation of the new province in 6 CE.[90]

When it came to the collection of taxes, Rome relied a great deal on previously established local systems. In the case of Judaea, this meant relying on the τελῶναι, Hellenistic tax-farmers introduced into Palestine under the Ptolemies.[91] This system continued with very little change until the third or fourth century CE. Roman tax-collectors, or *publicani*, were introduced for a short time after

---

[86] Evidence generally brought in favour of the Jewish courts having capital powers under the Romans are: the rule concerning gentile trespassers in the Temple (*JW* 6.124–6, *Ant.* 15.417; also confirmed by an inscription, *RA* 23 (1882) p. 220) which may be an extraordinary concession; the execution of any Jew trespassing in the Holy of Holies (Philo, *Embassy* 307) which may be hypothetical; the execution of a priest's daughter (m.sanh 7.2b); the death of Stephen (Acts 6.12–15, 7.57–9) which could have been an illegal lynching; and the death of James (62 CE, *Ant.* 20.200–3) which occurred at a time when Judaea had no governor and may have been illegal. Winter suggests that the penalty of strangulation was introduced after the abolition of Jewish capital jurisdiction in 70 CE (*Trial*, pp. 67–74); however, there is little evidence for this.

Arguments in favour of the curtailment of Jewish powers of capital punishment are: the statement of John 18.31 (though this could be theologically motivated); the gospel accounts generally; and several rabbinic sources, though it must be admitted that these can only be used with care – see Lémonon, *Pilate*, pp. 81–90. More generally see Juster, *Juifs*; Lietzmann, 'Prozeß'; Catchpole, *Trial*, pp. 234–6; and Strobel, *Stunde*, pp. 18–45.

[87] Garnsey and Saller, *Roman*, pp. 169–70.

[88] Shaw, 'Roman Taxation', p. 813.

[89] For example, Sicily had a census every five years, whilst in Egypt it was every fourteen. See Shaw, ibid., p. 814.

[90] *Ant.* 18.3–4, 20.102, *JW* 7.253, Acts 5.37, Tacitus *Ann.* 2.6. Luke 2.2 probably also refers to this – see Schürer, *History*, vol. 1, pp. 399–427. Millar (*Roman*, p. 48) suggests that it was simply a coincidence that Judaea was formed into a province at the same time as Quirinius was taking a census of Syria.

[91] For the tax system in Judaea see Herrenbrück, 'Wer Waren' and 'Vorwurf'; he describes the τελῶναι as 'Hellenistischer Kleinpächter'.

Pompey's conquest in 63 BCE, but they proved unsuitable due to their lack of local knowledge and experience, and were not used after 44 or 47 BCE. The τελῶναι were responsible for a wide range of both direct and indirect taxation – taxes on produce, traffic, border taxes and excise duties. These men were generally rich, respected Jews with influence within the Jewish community. They would bid at auction for the right to raise a specific tax for one year. Supervising these was the governor, acting as the Emperor's personal financial agent, assisted by slaves and freedmen. Less scrupulous governors could misuse this task to enrich themselves.[92] The revenues from Judaea went to the public treasury (*aerarium*) rather than the imperial treasury (*fiscus*), even though it was an imperial province.[93] When essential amenities such as roads or water supplies were required separate charges were levied.[94]

In accordance with general Roman practice, not only the collection of taxes but the entire day-to-day administration of the nation was left largely in the hands of the Jewish high priest and aristocracy in Jerusalem. The scarcity of Roman officials meant that efficient government had to rely to a great extent upon the co-operation of local authorities.[95] The Romans expected them to act as mediators, representing the feelings of the people to the governor and the expectations of the governor to the people. In return, local aristocracies could expect their own privileged position to be safe-guarded by Rome. In Judaea, however, the Roman governors met with a problem. Fearing potential rivals, Herod I had executed most of the prominent Judaean notables when he came to power and replaced them with his own favourites.[96] These men had no influence over the people and were deeply despised and resented.[97] Worse still, recognising the political prestige of the high priesthood, Herod had deliberately set about diminishing its role in the eyes of the people. He took it upon himself to appoint and depose high priests at will, generally favouring men from less well-known Zadokite backgrounds as they posed the least threat. When Judaea became a Roman province in 6 CE, therefore, there was no natural Judaean elite to whom Rome could entrust the running of the nation. The prefects had to rely instead on men whom Herod had

---

[92] Josephus, *Ant.* 18.172, 176, *JW* 2.273, 292; Philo, *Embassy* 199; Tacitus, *Ann.* 4.6.
[93] Schürer, *History*, vol. 1, p. 372.   [94] Shaw, 'Roman Taxation', p. 824.
[95] Schürer, *History*, vol. 1, p. 376.   [96] *JW* 1.358, *Ant.* 14.175, 15.6.
[97] *JW* 2.7. See Goodman, *Ruling*, pp. 37–41.

advanced, men who generally did not command a great deal of prestige amongst the people. As a result of occasional concessions won from Rome this newly promoted aristocracy might sometimes rise in the estimation of the people but in general the people preferred to deal directly with the governor rather than call on these men as intermediaries.[98]

Perhaps in an attempt to heighten the prestige of the high priesthood amongst the people, the Romans promoted an unknown priestly family to the office, that of Ananus b. Sethi.[99] Whatever the origins of this family, in accordance with Roman status criteria Ananus was presumably a wealthy man. In the period 6–41 CE, the high priesthood was almost entirely in the hands of this family.[100] Ananus, his son-in-law Caiaphas, and three of his sons were appointed to the office; the tenures of the two men from other families were brief.[101] But the Romans, like Herod, recognized the political importance of the position and exercised their control by appointing and deposing high priests at will. Only men who could be relied on to pursue an actively pro-Roman policy would be chosen.[102] Before the reign of Agrippa, the choice of the high priest usually fell within the competence of the Judaean prefect.[103] On his accession in 41, Agrippa restored the high priesthood to the pro-Herodian family of Boethus. From this time on, the appointment of the high priesthood passed completely into Herodian hands: first to Agrippa I, then Herod of Chalcis and later Agrippa II.[104]

As a puppet of the Roman and later Herodian rulers, the high priesthood could never hope to regain its former position in Judaean society. A blatant example of Roman control was that the high priestly vestments worn at the festivals remained in Roman

---

[98] Examples are the people's actions when confronted by Pilate's standards and the threat of Gaius' statue in the Temple. See Goodman, ibid., p. 45. For a more positive assessment of the prestige of the aristocracy see McLaren, *Power* and E. P. Sanders, *Judaism*, pp. 322–38.

[99] Goodman, *Ruling*, p. 44. On the possible origins of Ananus b. Sethi and his family see Stern, *CRINT*, vol. 2, p. 606.

[100] *Ant.* 20.198.   [101] Smallwood, 'High Priests', pp. 14–16.

[102] Ibid., p. 22.

[103] Only in two exceptional cases did the legate of Syria intervene: *Ant.* 18.26 when Quirinius replaced Joazar by Ananus, and *Ant.* 18.90–95 when Vitellius dismissed Caiaphas and replaced him with Jonathan.

[104] *Ant.* 19.297, 316, 20.15, 103 (Herod of Chalcis); 20.104, 213 (Agrippa II). Josephus records that this was the result of a Jewish petition (*Ant.* 15.403–5, 18.90–5, 20.6–16).

custody until 37.[105] Following Herodian practice, the Romans took charge of these vestments, allowing them to be restored to the high priest seven days before each festival for purification.[106] That such holy vestments, essential to the religious life of the community, should be in pagan hands would have been offensive to Jewish piety and served as a permanent reminder of their subjugation to Rome.[107]

Unlike his predecessor, Gratus, who had no less than four changes of high priest in his eleven-year governorship, Pilate made no change to the incumbent of the high priesthood.[108] This was presumably not out of any wish to respect Jewish sensitivities but rather because he found in Gratus' last appointee, Caiaphas, a man who could be relied on to support Roman interests and who could command some respect amongst the people.[109] Caiaphas was deposed by Vitellius in the wake of Pilate's own removal from the province.[110]

One final task of the Roman prefect of Judaea needs consideration – the striking of coins. The minting of gold and silver coinage was the sole prerogative of the Emperor, though on exceptional occasions important cities might mint silver coins. Following the Hasmonaeans, Herod I and Archelaus, the prefects of Judaea struck only bronze coin. All these rulers followed the Seleucid monetary system, striking coins with a value of 1 Perutah (Jewish) = 1 dilepton (Seleucid).[111] The Roman governors may have continued to use the established monetary system in an attempt to avoid arousing hostility amongst the Jews by the introduction of a new one.[112] It was not until the rule of Agrippa I that the *Roman* monetary system was introduced into

[105] They were restored to Jewish control after an appeal to Vitellius, the legate of Syria, who wrote to Tiberius on behalf of the people (*Ant.* 15.405, 18.90–5).

[106] *Ant.* 18.90–5. On the high priest and his vestments see E. P. Sanders, *Judaism*, pp. 99–102, 319–27.

[107] The dispute flared up again in the governorship of Fadus who wanted to take the vestments back into Roman custody (*Ant.* 20.6); the matter was referred to Claudius who decided in favour of Jewish custody in 45 (*Ant.* 20.6–16).

[108] *Ant.* 18.33–5. Joseph, called Caiaphas, was appointed in 18/19 CE. According to John 18.33 he was the son-in-law of Ananus (or Annas).

[109] Caiaphas may have offered the governors some monetary reward for the office (so Catchpole, *Trial*, p. 249). Possibly Ananus offered Pilate financial inducements to keep his son-in-law in the office until his own son was old enough to take over.

[110] *Ant.* 18.90–5. On Vitellius' journeys to Jerusalem see Smallwood, *Jews*, pp. 172–3 and, less likely, Hoehner, *Herod*, pp. 313–16.

[111] Maltiel-Gerstenfeld, *New Catalogue*, pp. 31–2, table on p. 34.

[112] Maltiel-Gerstenfeld, *260 Years*, p. 32.

Judaea.[113] Coins were struck only when necessary; accordingly only five prefects/procurators issued coinage (Coponius, Aristobulus, Gratus, Pilate and Felix).[114]

Pilate's coins are important since, along with the inscription referred to earlier, they constitute our only specific archaeological link with the prefect. The following three coins were struck:[115]

(a) *Obverse*
Three ears of barley; the central upright, the others drooping, tied together by the stalks with two horizontal bands.
ΙΥΛΙΑ ΚΑΙCΑΡΟC

Reverse
What looks like a *simpulum* with upright handle.
TIBEPIOY ΚΑΙCΑΡΟC
Date LIZ (year 16) 29/30 CE.

(b) *Lituus* with crook facing right.
TIBERIOU ΚΑΙCΑΡΟC

Wreath with berries, tied below with 'X'.
Date LIZ (year 17) 30/1 CE.

(c) As above.

As above but
Date LIH (year 18) 31/2 CE.[116]

Pilate seems to have struck coins in only three successive years: 29/30, 30/1 and 31/2 CE, corresponding to the fourth, fifth and sixth years of his rule. The coins follow the usual practice for coins struck in Judaea in that they contain no portrait of the Emperor but only a Greek inscription recording his name. One side of each of the coins contains a purely Jewish representation: the three ears

---

[113] The location of the procuratorial mint is uncertain. Caesarea or Jerusalem is the likeliest possibility. In the absence of literary or historical proof that these coins were struck in Jerusalem, Hill (*CBM* (Palestine), p. ci) and Meyshan ('Jewish Coinage', p. 46) favour Caesarea since the prefect/procurator and his entourage were stationed there. Meshorer (*Ancient*, p. 186), however, favours Jerusalem for two reasons: (1) this was the former capital and location of Archelaus' mint, and (2) an uncirculated 'mint-piece' was found in Jerusalem; it was one of the coins issued by Pontius Pilate with the strips from the mould still attached (now in the collection of the Institute of Archaeology, Hebrew University of Jerusalem). Kadman, too, favours Jerusalem: cf. 'Development', p. 100, n. 2.

[114] For designs see Hill, *CBM* (Palestine).

[115] Dating Pilate's coins is made particularly difficult by the fact that several specimens are crudely struck and other dates have occasionally been proposed. See Kindler, 'More'.

[116] Descriptions are based on Hill, *CBM* (Palestine), pp. 257–60, nos. 54–82. See also Madden, *Coins*, pp. 182–3, nos. 12, 14–15; Reifenberg, *Ancient*, p. 56, nos. 131–3.

of barley and the wreath. The other sides each contain a distinc-
tively pagan symbol connected with the Roman cult: the *simpulum*
(a sacrificial vessel or wine bowl) and the *lituus* (an augur's crooked
staff, wand). Whilst both these symbols were used in Roman
coinage generally, Pilate was the first to use them on Judaean coins.
Yet Pilate was not the first to deviate from purely Jewish designs on
Judaean coinage.[117] Of the Hasmonaeans, Alexander Jannaeus
appears to have gone furthest in borrowing from Seleucid designs.
Under Herod I and his son Archelaus the coins show more
numerous symbols of a pagan origin, in particular the tripod with
lebes (copper/bronze basin or cauldron), the *caduceus* (a herald's
staff, often associated with Mercury), *aphlaston* (an ornamental
ship's bow, often decorated with protective deities) and the eagle.
Although the early prefects used only Jewish designs, Gratus seems
to have experimented in his first few years with pagan representa-
tions such as the *caduceus* and *kantharos* (a drinking vessel with
handles which was often used in cultic rituals). The use of these
symbols may have stemmed from a desire to emphasize important
features from both Judaism and the Roman cult, such as wine
offerings.

Given the history of pagan designs throughout Judaean coinage,
particularly from Herod and Gratus, Pilate's coins do not seem to
be deliberately offensive. Had he wished to antagonize his Jewish
subjects or introduce the imperial cult, he would surely have struck
coins bearing images of the Emperor or other pagan gods/goddesses
rather than simply cultic vessels. The fact that neither Marcellus
nor Marullus appear to have seen any necessity to issue coins with
a new design and Agrippa I was presumably content to use Pilate's
coins until issuing his own in 42/3 suggests that these coins were not
unduly offensive. Furthermore, the fact that one side of each coin
always bears a purely Jewish design may suggest that Pilate
deliberately depicted both Jewish and Roman symbols in an
attempt to continue the attempt of Herod I and his successors to
integrate Judaea further into the Empire.[118] The use of pagan
vessels may show a certain lack of sensitivity but hardly reflects
deliberate offensiveness.

Pilate's coins have often been used to substantiate a link between
the prefect and Sejanus, the allegedly anti-Jewish commander of the
Praetorian Guard and a man with considerable influence over

---

[117] See Bond, 'Coins', for fuller details.   [118] Hengel, *Hellenization*, p. 41.

Tiberius.[119] E. Stauffer suggested that as part of a worldwide action against the Jews Sejanus ordered Pilate in 29 CE to put provocative pagan symbols on his coins. The intention was to rouse the Jews to open rebellion which was then to be brutally crushed; Sejanus' fall in 31 CE, however, prevented the final realization of these intentions.[120] E. M. Smallwood, too, notes that Pilate's last issue of coinage corresponds to the year of Sejanus' death, suggesting that with the removal of Sejanus Pilate did not dare to issue any more offensive coins.[121]

Several points from the preceding discussion, however, go against such a direct link between Pilate and Sejanus. First, pagan symbols, although relatively rare, had already been used on Jewish coins. Intervention by Sejanus is not necessary to explain Pilate's use of such designs. Second, the *simpulum*, as a symbol of the Pontifex, appears to have been more offensive than the *lituus*. If Pilate were acting according to an anti-Jewish plan of Sejanus, we would expect the symbols to become more and more provocative; as it is, the more provocative symbol gave way within a year to the *lituus* which was then used without change the following year. Third, the simplest way to provoke the Jews, and to bring Judaea in line with other Roman provinces would have been to put an image of the Emperor on the coins; this Pilate did not do. Fourth, the argument that Pilate issued no more coins after Sejanus' death ignores the fact that the coins would have been used for several years *after* the date on which they were issued. Coins struck in 31/2 would be still in use well after Sejanus' downfall. There is no evidence that any of Pilate's coins were restruck with another design, and if they had been recalled then a need would have quickly arisen for a new coin before Agrippa's issue in 42/3. If there is any truth in Philo's statement that Tiberius issued instructions after Sejanus' death to all provincial governors ordering them, amongst other things, to respect the Jews and their laws (*Embassy* 161), then the prolonged use of offensive coins in Judaea would be inexplicable.

From these arguments, therefore, a direct link between Pilate's

---

[119] Only Philo, *Embassy* 159–60 and the beginning of *In Flaccum* (followed by Eusebius, *EH* 2.5.5), records Sejanus' anti-Jewish policy. Whilst Suetonius (*Tib.* 36.1), Tacitus (*Ann.* 2.85.5) and Dio Cassius (157.18.5a) write of an expulsion of Jews from Rome in 19 CE, they do not associate it with Sejanus. Unfortunately, Tacitus' account of 30/1 CE in the *Annals* has not survived.
[120] Stauffer, *Jerusalem*, pp. 16–8.   [121] Smallwood, *Jews*, p. 167.

coins and an anti-Semitic plot of Sejanus seems unlikely (if, in fact, such a 'plot' ever existed).[122] But what is possible is that the coins more generally reflect a less compromising attitude felt within the Empire towards the Jews. Pilate may have felt less inhibited by Jewish sensitivities than his predecessors, especially those under Augustus who seems to have particularly favoured the Jews.[123] Perhaps the memory of Jewish favours towards Julius Caesar had begun to give way to irritation at their lack of co-operation with Roman rule, an irritation which may have expressed itself at other times throughout Pilate's governorship.

With this brief overview of Pilate and conditions in Judaea during its earliest phase as a Roman province, we are in a better position to turn to our six literary descriptions of the prefect. We will start with Philo of Alexandria, first examining his characterization of Pilate and then attempting to piece together the historical events behind the narrative.

[122] It is possible that Philo has deliberately portrayed Sejanus as anti-Semitic in order to highlight Tiberius' leniency towards the Jews; see Hennig (*Seianus*, pp. 160–79) who doubts Sejanus' anti-Jewishness and Schwartz, 'Josephus and Philo', pp. 35–6.

[123] Philo, *Embassy* 157–9. Philo is, of course, going out of his way to acknowledge the favourable attitude shown towards the Jews by the Emperors prior to Gaius, but some truth probably lies behind his description of Augustus' favour.

2

PILATE IN PHILO

Our earliest surviving literary reference to Pontius Pilate is found within the writings of the diaspora Jew, Philo of Alexandria. His *Embassy to Gaius* (or *Legatio ad Gaium*) describes how Pilate offended against the Jewish Law by setting up aniconic shields in Jerusalem. The Jewish leaders appealed to Tiberius who ordered Pilate to remove them (§§ 299–305).[1] The incident is found within a letter supposedly from Agrippa I to Gaius Caligula, attempting to dissuade the Emperor from setting up his statue in the Jerusalem Temple (§§ 276–329). However, modern scholars are agreed that the letter as we now have it is clearly the work of Philo himself.[2] It is perfectly feasible that Agrippa wrote a letter to Gaius and also that Philo, who was in Rome at the time, knew something of its contents.[3] Yet, in accordance with historiography of his day, Philo has presented the letter in his own stylistic terms.

Philo's account of Pilate is historically important in that, although belonging to Egypt, he was a contemporary of the events which he relates in Palestine.[4] He would also have had access to reasonably reliable information through his family connections

[1] For the view that substantial sections of the *Embassy* and In *Flaccum* recording Pilate's anti-Jewish attitude have been lost see J. Morris in Schürer, *History*, vol. 3.2, pp. 359–66. Against this see Colson (*Embassy*, pp. xxiv–v) and Smallwood (*Legatio*, p. 43).

[2] Lémonon (*Pilate*, p. 208) notes the similar treatment of speeches by the author of Acts and Tacitus in *Ann.* 11.24.

[3] Josephus gives two different versions of events. In *JW* 2.203 it is Gaius' death which prevents the erection of the statue; but in *Ant.* 18.289–304 Agrippa prepared a magnificent banquet for Gaius and, being offered any favour he chose to name, asked for the plans regarding the statue to be abandoned. This account is suspect: the banquet has all the marks of Jewish legend such as Esther's banquet to save her people (Esther 5.1–8); or Salome's request for John the Baptist's head (Mark 6.21–9). Zeitlin argues that Philo's letter was composed in accordance with his theology: cf. 'Did Agrippa?', pp. 22–31.

[4] He lived from roughly 30 BCE to 45 CE (*OCD*, p. 684).

with Agrippa.[5] However, Philo's 'historical' writings, comprising the *Embassy to Gaius* and the *In Flaccum*, are marked by strong rhetorical and theological concerns.[6] This is particularly prominent in his assessment of the character and actions of Roman Emperors and officials. Therefore, whilst Philo's account of Pilate doubtlessly contains a core of historical fact, his description of Pilate's character and intentions has very likely been influenced by his rhetorical objectives. For this reason, I shall outline Philo's general theological and rhetorical aims before attempting to reconstruct the historical event behind the story. The text runs as follows:

> (299) Pilate was an official who had been appointed procurator of Judaea. With the intention of annoying the Jews rather than of honouring Tiberius, he set up gilded shields in Herod's palace in the Holy City. They bore no figure and nothing else that was forbidden, but only the briefest possible inscription, which stated two things – the name of the dedicator and that of the person in whose honour the dedication was made. (300) But when the Jews at large learnt of this action, which was indeed already widely known, they chose as their spokesmen the king's four sons, who enjoyed prestige and rank equal to that of kings, his other descendants, and their own officials, and besought Pilate to undo his innovation in the shape of the shields, and not to violate their native customs, which had hitherto been invariably preserved inviolate by kings and Emperors alike. (301) When Pilate, who was a man of inflexible, stubborn and cruel disposition, obstinately refused, they shouted, 'Do not cause a revolt! Do not cause a war! Do not break the peace! Disrespect done to our ancient laws brings no honour to the Emperor. Do not make Tiberius an excuse for insulting our nation. He does not want any of our traditions done away with. If you say that he does, show us some decree or letter or something of the sort, so that we may cease troubling you and appeal to

[5] Philo's brother Alexander was the Alabarch of Alexandria (*Ant.* 18.259); Agrippa borrowed money from this man (18.159–60). In 41 CE the same brother married Agrippa's daughter Berenice (19.276). Although Agrippa himself was not directly involved in the event concerning Pilate which Philo relates, he would have learnt the details from his four relatives who were involved (*Embassy* 300).

[6] See, for example, Thatcher's discussion of *Embassy* 299–305 in 'Philo'. He categorizes Philo's writing here as a 'hortatory discourse'; see pp. 216–17 and notes.

our master by means of an embassy'. (302) This last remark exasperated Pilate most of all, for he was afraid that if they really sent an embassy, they would bring accusations against the rest of his administration as well, specifying in detail his venality, his violence, his thefts, his assaults, his abusive behaviour, his frequent executions of untried prisoners, and his endless savage ferocity. (303) So, as he was a spiteful and angry person, he was in a serious dilemma; for he had neither the courage to remove what he had once set up, nor the desire to do anything which would please his subjects, but at the same time he was well aware of Tiberius' firmness on these matters. When the Jewish officials saw this, and realized that Pilate was regretting what he had done, although he did not wish to show it, they wrote a letter to Tiberius, pleading their case as forcibly as they could. (304) What words, what threats Tiberius uttered against Pilate when he read it! It would be super-fluous to describe his anger, although he was not easily moved to anger, since his reaction speaks for itself. (305) For immediately, without even waiting until the next day, he wrote to Pilate, reproaching and rebuking him a thousand times for his new-fangled audacity and telling him to remove the shields at once and have them taken from the capital to the coastal city of Caesarea (the city named Sebaste after your great-grandfather), to be dedicated in the Temple of Augustus. This was duly done. In this way both the honour of the Emperor and the traditional policy regarding Jerusalem were alike preserved.[7]

Philo's *Embassy* and *In Flaccum* are a complex interweaving of theology and political rhetoric. Philo uses theology to make political points and, at the same time, the political rhetoric en-hances his theology. Both have influenced the way in which Philo has portrayed Pilate. Although any rigid separation between the two is artificial to Philo's thought, for the sake of clarity it is easier first to examine Philo's theological outlook, one which he shares with other Jewish writers of his day, and how this has influenced even the words used to describe Pilate, and then to go on to consider the more concrete political situation behind the works and the way in which this too has shaped the characterization of Pilate.

[7] Smallwood's translation, *Legatio*, pp. 128–30.

The theology behind Philo's historical works

Throughout Philo's 'historical' writings runs the common Jewish conviction that God is the divine protector of his people. The enemies of Israel are synonymously the enemies of God; he will not hesitate to intervene in history to vindicate his people and to judge their oppressors.[8] The measure by which Roman Emperors, officials and non-Jews generally are judged is by their attitude towards the Jewish nation and its Law. In accordance with this overriding theological framework the characters within the story tend to become stereotyped; at one extreme are those who respect the Jewish nation and thus become paragons of every virtue; at the other are those who want to abolish the Law and inflict sufferings on the Jewish people; often these characters end up suffering themselves.

Paramount amongst those who respected the Jewish Law is the Emperor Augustus. He approved of the Jews, allowing those in Rome to meet on the Sabbath and to send their 'first fruits' to Jerusalem. He and his family gave dedications to the Temple, ordered regular daily sacrifices to be made to the 'Most High God' at their own expense, and protected Jewish interests in the monthly distribution at Rome.[9] Because of these benefactions Philo regards Augustus as 'the Emperor whose every virtue outshone human nature'. He goes so far as to claim that 'almost the whole human race would have been destroyed in internecine conflicts and disappeared completely, had it not been for one man, one princeps, Augustus, who deserves the title of "Averter of Evil"'. He is a 'wonderful benefactor'.[10]

A similar picture emerges of Tiberius. Philo mentions nothing of his alleged life of vice on Capri,[11] nor of his expulsion of Jews from

---

[8] This idea can be found in other places throughout Philo's writings: see Williamson, *Philo*, p. 32.

[9] *Embassy* 154–8; also 309–18.   [10] *Embassy* 143–8.

[11] Smallwood (*Legatio*, p. 164) argues that Philo's description of Gaius' life with Tiberius on Capri as 'moderate' and 'healthy' (§ 14) casts doubt on the reliability of Tacitus, Suetonius and Dio Cassius when they write of Tiberius' debauchery and Suetonius' reference to Gaius' depravity there (*Gaius* 2): 'If Philo had been able to represent his enemy Gaius as leading a thoroughly disreputable life before as well as after his accession, he would hardly have failed to do so'. Yet Philo's description at this point is conditioned by two motives. First, he is concerned to paint a favourable portrait of Tiberius from whom Gaius should have learnt to respect the Jewish Law. Second, he goes on to show that Gaius' anti-Judaism and other crimes were a result of his illness; that is, that anti-Judaism is 'unhealthy', or the result of madness.

Rome in 19 CE.[12] Instead, an 'upheaval in Italy' is briefly alluded to and associated with Sejanus who was 'contriving his attack'. Immediately after Sejanus' death Tiberius realized that 'the charges brought against the Jews living in Rome were unfounded slanders' and issued instructions to his provincial governors 'to change nothing already sanctioned by custom, but to regard as a sacred trust both the Jews themselves, since they were of a peaceful disposition, and their laws, since they were conducive to public order'.[13] Tiberius is therefore credited with giving 'peace and the blessings of peace to the end of his life with ungrudging bounty of hand and heart', and possessing a 'fine character'.[14] Augustus' wife Julia (Livia) donated costly items to the Jerusalem Temple and receives praise for her natural ability, pure education and intellect.[15] The Syrian legate Petronius, because of his favourable disposition towards the Jews, is similarly described in glowing terms.[16]

Those characters within the story who do *not* respect the Jewish Law, however, are characterized in an even more exaggerated manner. Central amongst these is the character of Gaius Caligula. Philo alleges that he 'felt an indescribable hatred for the Jews', that he 'swelled with pride, not merely saying but actually thinking that he was a god', that he was 'devoid of human feeling', a megalomaniac and a fool, an 'iron-hearted, pitiless creature', a 'universal destroyer and murderer' and countless other such descriptions.[17] The Roman prefect Flaccus also attacked the Jews; his 'naturally tyrannical' nature achieved his designs through cunning. The final year of his prefecture of Egypt was characterized by the lack of fair and impartial hearings in disputes in which Jews were denied free speech. The 'boundless excesses of his unjust and lawless actions' are described in detail.[18]

Not only Gaius and the prefect of Egypt but also lesser Roman officials are described in similar language. Capito, the collector of revenues in the imperial estate of Jamnia, is accused of 'robbery and embezzlement', 'evading accusations by slandering those whom he had wronged'.[19] Gaius' councillors Helicon and Apelles also receive brief but damning character sketches for both helped to

---

[12] Josephus, *Ant.* 18.79–83; Suetonius, *Tib.* 36; Dio Cassius 57.18.5a; Tacitus, *Ann.* 2.85.
[13] *Embassy* 159–61; also 298.   [14] Ibid. 141–2.   [15] Ibid. 319–20.
[16] Ibid. 245–6.   [17] Ibid. 77, 87–9, 133, 162, 190–4, 346.
[18] *In Flaccum* 1, 24, 32, 107, 135.   [19] *Embassy* 199.

poison the Emperor's mind with their intense hatred of the Jews.[20] Philo's description of the Alexandrian mob is also extremely vehement; they are accused of attacking the Jews with 'insane and bestial fury', 'madness and frenzied insanity'. These 'ruthless men' subjected the Jews to all kinds of cruelty, so pleasing Gaius.[21]

Of these aggressors, three are specifically said to have met with an unpleasant fate. The arrest, exile and murder of Flaccus are described in minute detail, taking up almost half of the treatise (*In Flaccum* 104–91). F. H. Colson has highlighted the vindictive way in which Philo gloats over this.[22] Gaius' advisers, Apelles and Helicon, 'received the wages of their sacrilege' later, and Philo describes their gruesome deaths.[23] It is quite possible that the missing ending to the *Embassy*, had it ever been written, described both a change in the fortunes of the Jews under Claudius and a graphic description of Gaius' assassination.[24] The underlying theme is that no one can challenge God's people and their laws with impunity. Philo remarks that Flaccus' fate 'was caused, I am convinced, by his treatment of the Jews, whom in his craving for aggrandizement he had resolved to exterminate utterly', a fact which Flaccus himself is said to have realized before his death.[25]

This interest in characterization and strongly emotional language marks Philo's writings as 'pathetic history'. A similar theologically inspired history and characterization is found throughout many Jewish works of the last two centuries BCE.[26] One example is the book of Esther in which the King's official Haman, furious that Mordecai the Jew will not bow down and worship him, sets out to destroy the Jewish nation utterly.[27] The characterizations of the actors within the story are extremely sparse but Haman is described as boastful and conceited.[28] Similarly, Nebuchadnezzar and Holo-

---

[20] Ibid. 166–72, 203–5.   [21] Ibid. 120–1, 132–3, 201; *In Flaccum* 59, 68.
[22] *In Flaccum*, p. 301.   [23] *Embassy* 206.
[24] Ibid. 373. Williamson, *Philo*, p. 32. The statement in *In Flaccum* 191 that Flaccus 'also' suffered may imply that the fate of another, quite possibly Sejanus, was included in a lost opening section.
[25] *In Flaccum* 116, 170–5.
[26] The *Embassy* and *In Flaccum* also have similarities with the theologically based history-writing in the OT (though there is not so much stress on characterization in the OT) and especially with Greek historical essay writing and moral tales (though here, of course, there is not the same theological outlook); see Borgen, *Philo*, p. 50.
[27] Esther 3.13, 9.24–5.
[28] Ibid. 5.9–12, 6.6. Talmon argues that the book of Esther is a 'historicized wisdom tale', or an enactment of standard wisdom motifs, which explains why the

phernes in the apocryphal book of Judith want to demolish all the sanctuaries in Judaea, so that Nebuchadnezzar alone would be worshipped by all peoples (3.8, 6.4). Holophernes is boastful and arrogant (6.18–19), trusting in the might of arms (9.7) and treating Israel with contempt (14.5). Both he and Haman pay for their attitudes towards the Jews with their lives (Esther 7.10, Judg. 13.8).

Even closer are the parallels between Philo's works and Maccabean literature; here there are even verbal similarities in the descriptions of the oppressors.[29] In particular, 2 Maccabees, with its dramatic interest in the characters involved, is especially close to Philo's historical works. Here again, characters are judged according to their attitude towards the Jewish Law. Thus Onias, Judas, Eleazar and the seven brothers and their mother receive high commendation[30] whilst Simon, the feuding high priests Jason and Menelaus, Seleucid officials and Antiochus himself are described in terms reminiscent of Philo's vocabulary for impious men.[31] Antiochus has several parallels with Gaius: he wanted to dedicate the Jerusalem Temple to Zeus (6.2), he is savage (5.11), merciless (5.12), audacious (5.15–16), proud (5.17), a murderer and blasphemer (9.28) and has pretensions of being more than human (5.21, 9.8). Quite possibly the Seleucid king served as a model for Philo's

characters exhibit few 'real' qualities: cf. 'Wisdom', pp. 419–55. Philo never directly cites Esther, possibly because its stark storyline and the absence of all the key religious concepts of Judaism did not lend themselves to his philosophical speculations.

[29] To take only the description of Pilate: the word ἁρπαγή is used of Tryphon's spoiling the land (1 Macc. 13.34–5) and Apollonius' attempt to seize the Temple treasury (4 Macc. 4.10); αἰκία is used of the tortures of the seven sons and their mother (2 Macc. 7.42), αἰκίζομαι in 2 Macc. 7.1, 13, 15 and Philopater's torture of the Jews (3 Macc. 4.14); ἄκριτος of the Hasidim who were wrongfully put to death rather than profane the Sabbath (1 Macc. 2.37); φόνος (2 Macc. 4.35, 3 Macc. 3.25); ὠμότης is used of men from Joppa (2 Macc. 12.5), Philopater (3 Macc. 5.20, 7.5) and his friends (6.24). The verbal similarities are not strong enough to suggest a literary dependence but both Philo's historical works and the Maccabean literature appear to have grown out of the same cultural and theological outlook in Alexandria. See Brownlee, 'Maccabees', pp. 201–15.

[30] Onias 3.1, 4.2, 15.12; Judas 8.7, 12.38, 42, 45, 13.14, 15.7–17; Eleazar 6.18, 23, 31; seven brothers 7.1–41.

[31] The author of 2 Maccabees does not use the same vocabulary as Philo but the sense is extremely similar. For Simon see 3.5, 11, 4.1, 4, 6. Jason accepts bribery (4.7) and shows boundless wickedness (4.8–10, 13, 19, 5.6, 7, 8). Menelaus has the 'temper of a cruel tyrant and the fury of a savage beast' (4.25, 32, 47, 50, 13.4–8). Nicanor is sent to exterminate the entire Jewish race (8.9), is impious (8.14) and a villain (8.34, 15.3, 5, 6, 32, 35). On Lysimachus see 4.39, 40, 42. Antiochus Epiphanes is described in 1 Macc. 1.10, 24, 3.29, 35, 6.11–13 and 4 Macc. 4.15, 5.2, 14, 8.1, 9.15, 30 (a description taken from 2 Macc.).

description of Gaius. All those who oppose the Jewish nation receive their just retribution from God who protects his people.[32]

Turning back to the *Embassy*, Philo's description of Pilate perfectly conforms to this common picture of the Roman official bent on undermining the Law of his Jewish subjects. He is described as wanting to annoy the Jews rather than honouring Caesar. His disposition is inflexible, stubborn and cruel, spiteful and angry, lacking in courage and unwilling to do anything to please his subjects. His administration showed his venality and violence and was a series of thefts, assaults, abusive behaviour, frequent executions of untried prisoners and endless savage ferocity.

An important point here is that none of the adjectives used to describe Pilate, particularly those in §§ 301–2, is used exclusively of him throughout Philo's historical writings; every single one is also used to describe another character.[33] The general charge of annoying the Jews rather than honouring Caesar was also levelled against the Alexandrian mob.[34] Pilate's 'inflexible, stubborn and cruel disposition' in § 301 similarly has parallels: ἄκαμπτος (inflexible) was used of cruel captors who allow their captives to go for money, not mercy;[35] αὐθάδης (stubborn) described the evil speech of the Alexandrian crowd;[36] ἀμείλικτος (cruel) twice summarized the character of Gaius.[37] The long list of Pilate's misdeeds in 302 is likewise paralleled elsewhere. Δωροδοκία (taking of bribes), for example, is used of the bribes given to Flaccus' accusers by Isodorus.[38] Of the eleven remaining words used to describe Pilate here, four are used of Flaccus – ὕβρις (violence or pride), ἐπήρεια (abusive behaviour), ἄκριτος (the condemnation of untried prisoners), φόνος (murder, execution).[39] Seven are also used of the Alexandrian mob and their leaders – ὕβρις, ἁρπαγή (thefts), αἰκία (insulting treatment, assaults; this is even linked with ὕβρις in one instance), ἐπήρεια, ἀργαλέος (vexatious, troublesome), ὁμότης (savagery, cruelty), and ἔγκοτος (spiteful).[40] All of these words are

---

[32] In 3 Maccabees many Alexandrian Jews were abused and underwent a 'cruel and ignominious death' (3.25–6) at the hands of the proud and wicked king (2.2–3). However, God's providence intervened, thwarting the king's plans to level Judaea and destroy the Temple. In this story, the king is not killed but instead has a miraculous conversion in the final chapter (7.9).

[33] This is also noticed by McGing, 'Pontius', pp. 432–3.   [34] *In Flaccum* 51.

[35] Ibid. 60.   [36] Ibid. 35.   [37] Ibid. 182; *Embassy* 350.

[38] *In Flaccum* 140.

[39] Ibid. 177 (ὕβρις); 103 (ἐπήρεια); 54 (ἄκριτος); 189 (φόνος).

[40] Ibid. 40, 95, 136 (ὕβρις); 56–7, 62, 69, *Embassy* 122, 129 (ἁρπαγή); *In Flaccum* 71–2, 96, *Embassy* 128 (αἰκία, linked with ὕβρις in *In Flaccum* 59); *Embassy* 134

used frequently to refer to Gaius except ὕβρις, αἰκία and
ἐπήρεια.[41] Tiberius describes Pilate's action as 'new fangled'
(καινουργός, § 305), the same word is used to describe the cruelty
of the Alexandrian mob, Gaius' statue and the Emperor's 'new
fangled acts of megalomania'.[42]

It is clear that Philo's description of Pilate is not a personalized
attack but a patchwork of set words and expressions regularly used
by this writer to describe the enemies of the Jews, most notably
Gaius and the Alexandrian mob. This is supported by *In Flaccum*
105 which gives a general description of a corrupt governor:

> Some, indeed, of those who held governorships in the time
> of Tiberius and his father Caesar, had perverted their office
> of guardian and protector into domination and tyranny
> and had spread hopeless misery through their territories
> with their venality [δωροδοκία], robbery [ἁρπαγή], unjust
> sentences, expulsion and banishment of quite innocent
> people, and execution of magnates without trial [ἄκριτος].
> But these people on their return to Rome, after the
> termination of their time of office, had been required by
> the Emperor to render an account and submit to scrutiny
> of their doings, particularly when the aggrieved cities sent
> ambassadors.

There are clear parallels here with the description of Pilate in
Embassy 299–305. The sense of corrupt rule is the same: three
words in the short description are identical; there is even a reference
to an embassy at which the misdeeds of the governor will come to
light, a clear parallel to Pilate's fear in § 302.[43] In fact, the only
concrete allegations made against Pilate in *The Embassy to Gaius*
are precisely those also found here – venality, robbery and executions of prisoners without trial. When these are removed, little
remains but character slurs – inflexible, stubborn, cruel, violent,

(ἐπήρεια); *In Flaccum* 21, 95 (ἀργαλέος); 59, 66 (ὀμότης); and *In Flaccum* 19
(ἔγκοτος).
[41] *Embassy* 105 (ἁρπαγη); 126, 124 (ἄκριτος); 66 (φόνος); 334, *In Flaccum* 182
(ἀργαλέος); *Embassy* 341 (ὀμότης); 199, 260 (ἔγκοτος); 260 (βαρυμήνιος).
[42] *In Flaccum* 59; *Embassy* 217, 348.
[43] It is unlikely that Philo was thinking specifically of *Pilate's* administration here;
if he were, the reference to governors under Augustus would be out of place. It is
more likely that the passage gives, as it claims, an account of corrupt governors in
general. Philo would doubtlessly have had enough personal experience of governors
of Egypt and other provinces without needing to think of Pilate at this point.

insulting treatment, abuse, ferocity and anger – that is, nothing which could be positively verified or denied. Historically, Pilate may have been of a harsh, unyielding disposition, or at least may well have appeared so in Jewish eyes,[44] yet Philo's description of him is doubtless exaggerated in accordance with his own theological rhetoric.[45] Pilate acted against the Jewish Law and so is described in precisely the same terms as other 'enemies' of the Jews: Gaius, Flaccus, Capito and the Alexandrians.[46]

Political rhetoric

The *Embassy* is not simply a timeless theological tract. It is related to a concrete historical and political situation which has also to some degree shaped the narrative involving Pilate.

Agrippa's letter, in which the reference to Pilate occurs, is a passionate appeal to the Emperor Gaius not to desecrate the Jerusalem Temple by the erection of his statue but to respect Jewish tradition like former emperors. On a larger scale the whole *Embassy* contains a similar plea. E. R. Goodenough suggested that the book was composed early in the reign of Claudius and that it is an attempt to persuade the new Emperor not to follow the Jewish policies of Gaius but those of his predecessors, Augustus and Tiberius.[47] Philo pursues this aim in several ways, three of which are of importance for the passage involving Pilate.

First, a recurring theme of the *Embassy* (and the *In Flaccum*) is the assertion that the Jewish nation are loyal subjects of Rome. As long as their native customs are not interfered with, they want to be

---

[44] The clashes later narrated by Josephus would have contributed to such a reputation, *JW* 2.169–77; *Ant.* 18.55–62, 85–7.

[45] Of course, a description composed of stereotyped language does not *necessarily* have to be historically inaccurate. Yet Philo's characters are extreme 'types'; there is no middle ground. In all probability a proportion of his charges against Pilate and other 'negative' characters has some basis in truth whilst other cases have been exaggerated.

[46] Unlike his description of Gaius' advisors and Flaccus, Philo narrates no miserable fate in the case of Pilate; he is only an incidental character in the story. There may, however, be a slight hint in Tiberius' angry rebuke and order that the shields be removed immediately (§ 305) that the proud and cruel Pilate, like Flaccus (*In Flaccum* 116), was humiliated before the people he was sent to govern.

[47] *Embassy* 206 mentions events after Claudius' accession. See Goodenough, *Politics*, pp. 19–20 and Lémonon, *Pilate*, pp. 207–8; this view is assumed by Schwartz, 'Josephus', p. 32. Eusebius (*EH* 2.18.8) states that Philo read what he had written concerning Gaius' hatred of God before the Roman senate, possibly indicating an attempt to influence Claudius' policy.

peaceful members of the Empire. During the conflict over Gaius' statue, the Jewish leaders tell Petronius that they are striving for two ends: 'respect for the Emperor and obedience to our hallowed laws'.[48] The exchange between Pilate and the Jews centres upon the same theme: as loyal members of the Roman Empire, the Jews do not want to be disrespectful towards their Emperor (they refer to him as δεσπότης, master); yet as loyal Jews they cannot tolerate any dishonour shown to their God and his Law. The story illustrates that there is no fundamental conflict between these two positions. By removing the shields 'both the honour of the Emperor and the traditional policy regarding Jerusalem were alike preserved' (§ 305). For Philo it is clear that 'disrespect done to our ancient laws brings no honour to the Emperor' (§ 301); Pilate's action therefore can only have been 'with the intention of annoying the Jews rather than of honouring Tiberius' (§ 299). Respect for the Jewish Law and for the Emperor goes hand in hand: a model Emperor like Tiberius recognized this immediately (§§ 304–5).

Second, Philo tries to persuade Claudius to adopt the policies of Augustus and Tiberius rather than those of Gaius by his use of characterization. As noted previously, this stems to a large extent from Philo's theological conviction that God protects Israel and that the enemies of the Jews are the enemies of God; but this theological conviction can be turned to good political effect. Both Augustus and Tiberius are depicted as men of the highest moral standing, whose long reigns were peaceful and prosperous; their respect for the Jewish Law and refusal to tamper with ancestral customs are repeatedly emphasized. Gaius, in contrast, set himself up as the enemy of the Jews, making an attempt on the Temple and blatantly disregarding Jewish Law in his absolute hatred for the people; he is described as a fool, a murderer and a madman. The *Embassy* and *In Flaccum* clearly show that anti-Judaism is a characteristic of the low born, base or disloyal. Sejanus' anti-Jewish policy stemmed from his own disloyalty; Flaccus' actions were due to fear for his own position and because he had become 'utterly enfeebled' and 'incapable of solid judgement'; Capito's slanderous allegations were prompted by fear of exposure; Gaius' own delusions and hatred for the Jews were the result of madness caused by illness.[49] In contrast, Augustus' gifts to the Temple were 'proof of

[48] *Embassy* 236; also 160, 230–2; *In Flaccum* 48.
[49] *Embassy* 160 (Sejanus); *In Flaccum* 10, 16 (Flaccus), 199 (Capito).

his truly imperial character'.[50] Clearly Claudius is to recognize not only that devotion to Judaism is perfectly in harmony with loyalty to the Emperor, but also that respect for Judaism is the mark of a great man.

This leads to two tendencies within the scene with Pilate. First, Philo stresses Tiberius' concern in such a comparatively small issue, where no images were concerned and the offending shields were erected not in the Jewish Temple or a synagogue but in the Roman governor's headquarters. The smallness of Pilate's offence is highlighted so that Tiberius' concern to rectify a small infringement of the Jewish Law is in marked contrast to Gaius' planned desecration of the Jerusalem Temple. Second, Philo emphasizes the baseness and depravity of Pilate's character in order to highlight Tiberius' virtuous imperial character.

A third way in which Philo tries to persuade Claudius not to adopt Gaius' policies is by means of a veiled threat. This has a double thrust: both the Emperor himself and the peace of the Empire are at risk if Claudius does not respect the Jewish Law. The fates of Flaccus, Helicon, Apelles (and possibly Gaius in the lost ending of the *Embassy* and Sejanus in the lost opening of *In Flaccum*) show what happens to a ruler or official who sets himself against Judaism. Further, there are references to a great number of Jews all over the Empire who would rise up to defend their religion should the need arise.[51] The warnings of the Jewish spokesmen in § 301, 'Do not cause a revolt! Do not cause a war! Do not break the peace!', are perfectly in keeping with this theme. Philo warns that a deliberate attack on the Jewish Law, such as he claims Pilate initiated, could indeed result in war and revolt throughout all the Jews resident in the Empire. The threats of § 301, therefore, have in all probability been exaggerated in accordance with Philo's political rhetoric.

Finally, one more feature of Philo's political rhetoric deserves attention: his positive portrayal of the Herodian dynasty. Given the historical circumstances this portrayal makes good sense. Agrippa I played an important role in Claudius' succession and was rewarded with 'the whole of his grandfather's kingdom' which he ruled from 41–4 CE.[52] If, as seems likely, the *Embassy* was written shortly after Claudius' accession in 41, Agrippa was still on the Judaean throne.

---

[50] *Embassy* 157.   [51] Ibid. 216–17.
[52] Josephus, *JW* 2.206–17, *Ant.* 19.236–77.

It is possible that Philo wanted to persuade Claudius that Judaea should permanently be ruled by a Herodian. This would account for not only the glowing description of Agrippa himself (who was related to Philo by marriage),[53] but also that of the four Herodian princes in the conflict with Pilate who enjoy 'prestige and rank equal to that of Kings' and are the natural representatives of their people. In this passage, the conflict quickly becomes polarized between the Herodians with their entourage and Pilate. Tiberius, however, as arbitrator, upholds the Jewish position without a moment's hesitation (§§ 304–5). Philo thus shows that both the Herodians and Tiberius share the same basic view that loyalty to God is not incompatible with loyalty to the Empire. The Herodians are therefore the natural leaders of Judaea; they enjoy popular support and share the same views as the Emperor. In contrast, the Roman governor Pilate wants to please neither his people nor the Emperor (§ 303). The poor picture of Pilate, therefore, highlights not only Tiberius' good qualities but also those of the Herodians.

Philo's Pilate

In summary, Philo's characterization of Pilate has been shaped by his theological outlook, in which, in a similar way to other Jewish theological-histories of his period, he depicts the prefect in stereo-typed language reserved for those who act against the Jewish Law: he is inflexible, stubborn, spiteful and cowardly by disposition; his rule is characterized by corruption – bribery, violence, thefts, assaults, the condemnation of untried prisoners and continuous executions. Further references in the narrative can be accounted for by Philo's political rhetoric: the character of Pilate has to be denigrated to contrast unfavourably with Tiberius and the Herodians. The description of Pilate's motivation in setting up the shields (i.e. to annoy the Jews, § 299) is also part of this rhetoric, as is the suggestion that Pilate's actions were serious enough to provoke a war or revolt (§ 301).

The historical event

When the nature of Philo's rhetoric is recognized, it is possible to come to some plausible reconstruction of the historical event

---

[53] *Embassy* 278, 286.

behind *Embassy* 299–305. Philo's own interpretation seems to be confined to his description of Pilate's character and motivation, not to the actual events. This is not surprising for two reasons. First, Philo was probably in possession of reasonably accurate facts through his friendship with Agrippa I, four of whose close relatives were involved in the incident. Second, Philo could not afford blatantly to misrepresent the facts. His argument at this point depends on showing Tiberius' respect for the Law by his reaction to an incident caused by Pilate; if Philo's description of the event could easily be proved false, then his argument would lose all its force. Therefore it was possible to exaggerate, even to distort, Pilate's character but the facts of the incident had to be reasonably accurate.

Pilate's crime

The most obvious starting point is: In what way did Pilate's shields offend against the Jewish Law? According to *Embassy* 133 synagogues in Alexandria also contained 'gilded shields' (ἀσπίδες) set up in honour of the Emperor, and Josephus tells us that even Solomon's Temple contained shields. What was different about those set up by Pilate? Smallwood's translation of the relevant passage (*Embassy* 299) reads:

> He set up gilded shields in Herod's palace in the Holy City. They bore no figure and nothing else that was forbidden, but only the briefest possible inscription, which stated two things – the name of the dedicator and that of the person in whose honour the dedication was made.[54]

Several scholars have assumed either that the shields were inoffensive or that the offence was only slight. Philo's narrative is therefore taken to show the extreme sensitivity of the Jewish people regarding their Law.[55] Certainly, in accordance with his apologetic aims,

---

[54] Smallwood, *Legatio*, p. 128.

[55] The majority of scholars assume that this incident took place after a similar incident recounted by Josephus in which Pilate introduced iconic standards into Jerusalem: cf. *JW* 2.169–74, *Ant.* 18.55–9. Smallwood (*Legatio*, p. 304) suggests that the incident with the standards awakened the Jews to the fact that even aniconic objects could have (presumably religious) significance for the Romans and they were therefore anxious to keep these out of Jerusalem too. In short, although the shields were themselves inoffensive, 'they feared that the introduction of aniconic shields was the thin end of the wedge' and could be the forerunner of a definite contra-

Philo has played down the offensiveness of the shields; he stresses that they 'bore no figure', an obvious contrast to Gaius' statue. Yet the incident would lose all sense and parallelism if the shields were not offensive.[56] The basic aim is to show how a minor infringement of the Law upset the Jews and how severely Tiberius remonstrated with the perpetrator. Some contravention of the Law has to be present, otherwise Philo (in the guise of Agrippa) has at best only succeeded in pointing up the idiosyncrasies and hypersensitivities of his people; at worst he would have described a threatened revolt against a Roman prefect who had not transgressed the Law. Neither would be likely to sway Gaius, within the context of the narrative, or Claudius, the probable recipient of the whole work.[57] In fact, Philo clearly states that there *was* something offensive about the shields. He writes that they bore no figure and nothing else that was forbidden (ἔξω τινὸς ἐπιγραφῆς ἀναγκαίας), i.e. *except* a necessary inscription.[58] Obviously something about the inscription was forbidden. Philo elaborates on this: the inscription revealed two things (ἢ δύο ταῦτα ἐμήνυε),[59] the name of the dedicator (ἀναθέντα) and the one in whose honour the dedication was made (ὑπὲρ ὃ ἡ ἀνάθεσις). The offence caused by Pilate's shields therefore lay in the wording of the inscription which contained the names of Pilate and Tiberius.[60]

In all probability Pilate referred to himself in the same way as on the Caesarea inscription: (unknown first name) Pontius Pilatus; possibly adding his title: Praefectus Iudaeae. Since neither of these contravened the Law, the offence must have been in the name of

vention of the Law. Maier ('Episode', p. 118) asserts that there was 'no theological justification per se for the attitude of the Jerusalemites on this occasion' which may, he suggests, explain why Josephus makes no reference to it. Schürer, *History*, vol. 1, p. 386 and Schwartz, 'Josephus', pp. 29–31 both assume the shields were inoffensive. In this respect, scholars have been too influenced by Philo's rhetorical attempt to play down Pilate's crime, discussed above.

[56] Lémonon also makes this point: cf. *Pilate*, p. 217.

[57] Gaius already felt an indescribable hatred for the Jews (*Embassy* 133, 346) because they refused to accept his divinity (353, 357) and held their dietary sensibilities and monotheism in contempt (361, 367).

[58] P. S. Davies argues persuasively for the translation 'necessary inscription' rather than 'of a minimum size' suggested by Colson and Smallwood ('Meaning', pp. 109–10).

[59] Again, P. S. Davies suggests the reading 'revealed' for ἐμήνυε, which is regularly used for the 'revelation of profoundly important facts', rather than simply 'to state' ('Meaning', pp. 110–11).

[60] It seems reasonable to assume that Pilate was himself the dedicator: cf. Smallwood, *Legatio*, p. 302. If another person had dedicated the shields it would be odd to find no reference to him or her.

Tiberius. How did Pilate refer to him? The only other known inscriptions from Pilate referring to Tiberius are preserved on the prefect's coins. There Pilate followed the convention set by previous prefects who put only the Emperor's name or its abbreviation on their coins, presumably not to cause offence by the use of the princeps' official title. Pilate's coins accordingly read only 'TIB'. However, it is probable that an honorific inscription destined for the governor's residence would refer to the Emperor by his full title. Augustus' will imposed the title *Augustus* on Tiberius and a senatorial decree of 17 September 14 CE made him *divi filius*. The title *pontifex maximus* was bestowed on him on 10 March 15 CE, a position to which he attached great importance.[61]

The most common way to refer to Tiberius in short inscriptions was: 'Ti. Caesari divi Augusti f. (divi Iuli nepoti) Augusto pontifici maximo'.[62] Silver denarii issued by this Emperor read: 'TI(berius) CAESAR DIVI AVG(usti) F(ilius) AVGVSTVS' on one side: 'PONTIF(ex) MAXIM(us)' on the reverse.[63] It seems reasonable to suppose that Pilate's inscription followed official patterns and referred to Tiberius by his full title, including the phrase *divi Augusti* and quite possibly his position as *pontifex maximus*.[64] This reference to the divine Augustus would be offensive. As G. Fuks notes, the removal of the shields to the Temple of *Augustus* in Caesarea (§ 305) lends further support to the suggestion that it was the reference to the divinity of this Emperor which was offensive.[65] What offended the Jews therefore was the reference to a pagan deity – not Tiberius, as S. G. F. Brandon suggested,[66] but Augustus – and possibly too a reference to the supreme pontificate of the Roman cult situated, as Philo emphasizes, in the holy city of Jerusalem.[67]

[61] ILS 154; for Tiberius' attitude to the position of *pontifex maximus* see Grant, *Aspects*, p. 45.

[62] See ILS 113, 152, 153, 155, 156, 159, 160, 164, 5818, 5829, 5829a; 114 and 6080 omit '*pontifici maximo*'.

[63] See, for example, Matthiae and Schönert-Geiß, *Münzen*, pp. 98–9.

[64] That it was the phrase *divi Augusti* which caused offence was pointed out by Fuks, 'Again', p. 307.

[65] The same offensive reference to the Emperor's divinity may lie behind Jesus' answer to the tribute question in Mark 12.17; see Haacker, 'Kaisertribut'.

[66] Brandon, *Jesus*, p. 74.

[67] A small number of scholars suggest that this incident is identical with Pilate's introduction of military standards recorded by Josephus: for example, Colson, *Embassy*, pp. xix–xx; Schwartz, 'Josephus', followed by McLaren, *Power*, pp. 82–3, note 1 and Brown, *Death*, pp. 702–3. This view depends to a large extent upon the prior assumption that the shields described by Philo were inoffensive. Since the

So much we can infer from Philo's description; but is it possible to say anything further about Pilate's motivation in setting up the shields and whether he really intended to cause offence? Here a fuller description of the uses of and designs upon honorific shields in the first century will be of some use.

It was an ancient custom to decorate shields used in warfare, often with the characteristics of the wearer, an abbreviation of his city or a picture.[68] The shields themselves could also be used as decoration, set up in a public place in honour of a person or a god, or as a war trophy. The Greek ἀσπίς, used here by Philo, corresponds to the Latin *clipeus*, a metal or marble disc bearing an image of a god, a hero, or a great man. Our fullest ancient description of such shields comes from Pliny in his *Natural History* 35.[69] In a passage relating to the painting of portraits, Pliny remarks: 'Bronze shields are now set up as monuments with a design in silver, with only a faint difference between the figures' (35.4); such objects, he comments, 'everybody views with pleasure and approval' (35.12). The first to start this custom, he claims, was Appius Claudius in 495 BCE who dedicated shields bearing portraits in the shrine of the goddess of war (35.12). Marcus Aemilius Lepidus set up similar shields in the Basilica Aemilia and his own home in 78 BCE (35.13).[70] A golden shield was set up in honour of Augustus in 27 BCE in recognition of his 'valour, clemency, justice and piety', the four cardinal virtues of the Stoics; a similar one was set up in 19 CE in honour of Germanicus.[71] Coins of Tiberius, variously dated to 22–3 and 34–7 CE, show shields containing a bust of the princeps and the words 'Moderatio' and 'Clementia'.[72] Later, Gaius was awarded the honour of a gold shield which was to be carried to the

---

Jewish reaction in Philo makes little sense, it is claimed, the writer must be simply presenting his own version of the military standards, greatly reducing Pilate's crime to contrast all the more with Gaius' planned desecration of the Temple (see especially Schwartz, 'Josephus'). However, once it is recognized that the shields *did* contravene Jewish Law, there is no need to resort to such harmonizations.

[68] See *PW*, 'Schild', cols. 420–7, especially col. 425; also 'Scutum', cols. 914–20.

[69] Pliny lived c. 23/4–79 CE and was therefore a contemporary of both Pilate and Philo.

[70] These are visible on coins struck in 61 BCE by his son of the same name; see Sandys, *Latin*, p. 95.

[71] Augustus *Res Gestae Divi Augusti* 34; Tacitus, *Ann.* 2.83. The last two examples are cited by Maier, 'Episode', pp. 117–18; see also Levick, *Tiberius*, p. 87.

[72] Levick suggests that Tiberius was offered an honour similar to Augustus' shield: cf. *Tiberius*, p. 87.

capitol every year on a certain day by the Colleges of Priests.[73] Clearly the shields could be used either as religious dedications or as secular marks of honour.[74] The portrait shields also contained an honorific inscription, or *elogium*. This would include the name of the person honoured followed by his offices and triumphs.[75]

Pilate's shields belong to this type. They did not involve a pagan dedication ceremony, as some scholars suppose, but were simply decorative shields set up in honour of the Emperor.[76] They differ in one important aspect, however, in that they did not contain a portrait of the Emperor. This strongly suggests that Pilate deliberately used shields without portraits in an attempt to respect Jewish sensitivities.[77] If this occurred after the commotion caused by the introduction into Jerusalem of military standards containing images of Tiberius narrated by Josephus (which will be described in the next chapter, pp. 79–85), then Pilate's action was both understandable and prudent. He wanted to honour the Emperor without antagonizing the Jewish people. Furthermore, the shields were set

---

[73] Suetonius, *Gaius* 16. A Carthaginian shield, along with a golden statue, was hung above the portals of the Temple in the capitol until the fire of 83 BCE (Pliny, *NH* 35.14). For two further portrait shields see Lémonon, *Pilate*, p. 214. The Arcus Fabianus, restored by Q. Fabius Maximus in 56 BCE, included statues, shields and emblems of victory; see Sandys, *Latin*, pp. 95–7.

[74] Pliny speaks of Appius Claudius dedicating (*dicare*) shields in a goddess' shrine, but uses the secular word *posuit* (*ponere*) when Marcus Aemilius set up shields in the Basilica Aemilia and in his own home.

[75] See Sandys, *Latin*, pp. 93–4. These were generally affixed to statues (*imagines maiorum*) but were also attached to *clipei* to identify the portrait. Formulae giving the name of the person or body responsible for honorific statues were frequent (Sandys, ibid. p. 108); it is less clear whether these were also generally found on *clipei*.

[76] Pelletier suggested that a religious ceremony dedicated the shields to the 'gods in heaven': cf. *Legatio*, p. 375. This was taken up and developed by Lémonon (*Pilate*, pp. 213–17) and also favoured by P. S. Davies ('Meaning', pp. 112–14). Yet dedicatory inscriptions generally contained the name of the god or gods to whom they were dedicated and a dedicatory phrase or abbreviation – for instance *dedit* (Sandys, *Latin*, pp. 83–5); these Pilate's shields did not contain. Besides, the offence concerned the shields themselves, not a dedicatory rite associated with them (*Embassy* 306). Lémonon argues that the Jews thought Pilate had dedicated the shields to the Emperor; but Tiberius disliked divine honours and Pilate is unlikely to have deliberately provoked him on such an issue; besides, Philo clearly says that the shields were set up on *behalf* of the Emperor (ὑπέρ) not 'to' him (Philo is well aware of this distinction, see Gaius' complaint in *Embassy* 357).

[77] Lémonon seems to be over-subtle when he argues that because such shields generally contained images, Pilate's shields, even though aniconic themselves, offended in spirit against the law prohibiting images in that they *suggested* the presence of an image: cf. *Pilate*, pp. 215–16. P. S. Davies, ('Meaning', p. 112) also takes up this suggestion. The presence of the inscription alone would surely emphasize that the portrait was *missing*, not deliberately evoke it.

up inside (ἐν) the governor's residence; they were not on an outer wall where they would be clearly visible to everyone in the city, but inside the Roman administrative headquarters where presumably other objects of a pagan nature might be located. This was certainly the most appropriate place in Jerusalem for such honorific shields. Possibly Pilate realized that the reference to the 'divine Augustus' was technically against the Jewish Law (he did, after all, refrain from using it on his coins). He may have thought that, because of the location of the shields and the fact that the reference to Augustus was part of Tiberius' official imperial title, the Jewish people would not object or, out of reverence for their Emperor, ought not to. If these were his thoughts, of course, he was wrong; the people did object.

But the Jewish reaction itself is interesting and may cast some light on Pilate's later actions. Philo's description is rather oddly constructed. Immediately after the reference to the 'forbidden inscription' he writes: 'But when the Jews at large learnt of his action, *which was indeed already widely known*, they chose as their spokesmen the king's four sons . . . and besought Pilate to undo his innovation in the shape of the shields' (§ 300, my emphasis). This seems to imply a twofold reaction: first of all Pilate's action was 'already widely known', or 'discussed' (περιβόητον ἦν ἤδη τὸ πρᾶγμα); then the 'Jews at large learnt of his action' (ἐπεὶ δὲ ἤσοντο οἱ πολλοί). The sense seems to be that the existence of the shields was generally known before the significance of the reference to Augustus was realized.[78] This would make good historical sense. First-century Judaism, even in Jerusalem, was not monolithic on the question of references to pagan gods. Issues such as Gaius' statue and even Pilate's military standards with their images of Caesar were obvious affronts to the Law and would rouse the Jews to immediate protest. Yet the silver denarii bearing the name and representation of the Emperor were in circulation in the holy city; the Temple tax itself was paid in Tyrian shekels bearing the images of the gods Melkart and Tyche; both apparently were tolerated.[79] It is quite possible that the consequences of Pilate's use of Tiberius' full title were not immediately obvious, or even important, to some Jews. Others, however, recognized that the reference to the 'divine

---

[78] Colson's translation similarly seems to imply that the Jewish outrage was not instantaneous: 'But when the multitude understood the matter which had now become a subject of common talk': cf. *Embassy*, p. 151.

[79] See Bond, 'Coins', pp. 258–60.

Augustus' meant that an allusion to a pagan deity was permanently situated in Yahweh's holy city. Those of a more anti-Roman persuasion may have welcomed a religious reason for ridding Jerusalem of shields honouring the Emperor. Whatever the underlying motivations, the anti-shields lobby became dominant and the four Herodian spokesmen were elected to put the Jewish grievances before Pilate.

The events of *Embassy* 299–305 appear to have occurred at a feast: this is the likeliest explanation as to why four Herodian princes and Pilate should all be in Jerusalem at the same time. If the above reconstruction is correct, it may have taken some time for the Jerusalemites to be generally agreed that the shields were not to be tolerated. The Jewish leaders seem to have specifically waited until the feast to enlist the support of the Herodians whose known pro-Roman sympathies may have presumably carried more weight with the Roman prefect, especially in such a delicate issue. In this case, the shields may already have been in position for some weeks.[80]

The above considerations may help to clarify another puzzling aspect of the affair: Pilate's behaviour after the Herodian delegation. Philo asserts that the Jewish request to send an embassy to Tiberius worried Pilate because he was afraid that they would bring accusations against the rest of his administration (§ 302); a fear which, if there were more than a grain of truth in the description of Pilate's atrocities, would be well founded. The obvious line of action for such a merciless wretch as the perceived Pilate would be to prevent the embassy at all costs and to remove the standards; it would presumably be better to lose face with his people than to lose his position, and possibly his life, at the hands of Tiberius. Philo attributes Pilate's failure to do this to cowardice and the lack of desire to do anything to please his subjects (§ 303). However, as we have seen, Philo's description of Pilate's character and motivation is highly suspect. Yet there is an explanation for Pilate's behaviour which is not entirely out of keeping with Philo's general claims and which fits into the historical situation.

Largely at the instigation of Sejanus, trials of *maiestas*, or treason, were an increasingly frequent feature of Tiberius' reign.[81]

---

[80] Philo's account gives no indication as to how long the shields remained in Herod's palace.

[81] See in particular Bauman, *Impietas*, pp. 71–134, and Levick, *Tiberius*, pp. 180–200.

The old republican law protecting the people and senate of Rome was gradually adapting to the new conditions under the principate, now incorporating any affront to the *divus* of Augustus and any seditious plots – or even verbal slanders – against Tiberius. Although initially indifferent towards affronts to his own person, from 27 CE onwards, and especially in 32 (after Sejanus' execution),[82] Tiberius' growing insecurity led him to take a great personal interest in trials of *maiestas*. Even if Pilate had no connection with Sejanus, it was not a time for a provincial governor to allow his loyalty to the Emperor to be questioned. In fact, as we have seen, Pilate probably set up the shields deliberately to honour the Emperor. Philo is probably correct that the threat of an embassy to Tiberius put Pilate in a dilemma, but not because he was afraid of a poor report being given about his administration. If Pilate did what the people asked and removed the shields he would risk appearing to dishonour not only Tiberius, but more seriously the deified Augustus, especially if they had been up for some weeks without producing a spontaneous outcry and their offence against the Jewish Law was not great. Yet if he did not remove the shields the Herodians would appeal to Tiberius, doubtless giving their side of the affair and showing the insensitivities of the governor.[83] Pilate obviously decided that the latter alternative was the safer; whatever the Herodian delegation claimed, Tiberius could not ignore the fact that the shields had been set up in his honour. It is not impossible that Pilate was in agreement with the Herodians over the writing of this letter: it was safer for him to wait for Tiberius' decision than to act on his own initiative and risk displeasing either the Emperor or the people. The fact that Pilate does not appear to have gone out of his way to stop the Herodians contacting Tiberius supports the view that his exaggerated negative characterization is largely due to Philo's literary and theological art.

Philo's description of Tiberius' reaction is doubtlessly over-exaggerated in accordance with his rhetorical aims, but the general sequence of events seems to support the above hypothesis. The

[82] Tacitus, *Ann.* 6.7.3–5.
[83] Hoehner (*Herod*, p. 183) thinks that the enmity between Antipas and Pilate at the crucifixion of Jesus (Luke 23.12) was caused by the clash here between the Herodians and Pilate over the shields. The execution of some Galileans (Luke 13.1), if it is historical and predates this event, may be another possible explanation for the enmity between the two men. See pp. 194–6.

Emperor acknowledged the Jewish grounds for complaint, ordering Pilate to remove the shields from the holy city. Yet Pilate was not recalled, as he surely would have been if the Herodian letter made any serious allegations against his governorship. Nor is there the slightest hint that Pilate's loyalty to the Emperor was ever in question.[84]

The date of the incident

One remaining question is: When did this incident occur? The majority of scholars assume that it took place in the latter part of Pilate's governorship for one (or all) of the three following reasons.[85]

(1) If Pilate encountered opposition early on in his rule after his introduction of iconic military standards, it is claimed that he would wait some time before bringing in aniconic shields.[86]

(2) The list of Pilate's atrocities in § 302 would have taken some time to commit.[87]

(3) It is claimed that Tiberius' anger at Pilate's high-handed attitude towards the Jewish Law and Pilate's own indecision make best historical sense after Sejanus' assassination in 31.[88]

The first two arguments are far from conclusive. It is not necessary to assume that some years elapsed between the iconic standards and the shields, particularly as Pilate took care that the shields contained no offensive portraits. His principal aim, as we have seen, was not to provoke the people but to honour the Emperor. The list of Pilate's misdeeds in § 302 is part of Philo's stereotyped language applied to those who tampered with the Jewish Law; it

---

[84] Smallwood (*Jews*, p. 167) sees the inscription in Caesarea as a 'sequel to the episode of the shields'. She believes that when Pilate's attempt to show his loyalty to the Emperor failed, 'he conceived and carried out a much more ambitious project in Caesarea'. However, neither the construction of the Tiberiéum nor the incident concerning the shields can be dated exactly and a definite connection between the two cannot be substantiated. Pilate could have erected a secular building in honour of the Emperor at any stage in his governorship.

[85] Often it is simply assumed (e.g. Brandon, *Jesus*, pp. 71–5). The only exceptions to this scholarly consensus are those who think that the incident is identical with that recorded by Josephus concerning standards, see above notes 55 and 67.

[86] For example, Schürer, *History*, vol. 1, p. 386.

[87] For example, Smallwood, *Legatio*, p. 305.

[88] For example, Maier, 'Episode', pp. 113–14; McGing 'Pontius', p. 425; Fuks, 'Again', pp. 501, 504–5.

would certainly be difficult for Philo to give such a list if it were generally well known that this incident occurred in Pilate's first year, yet no certain time length can be established.[89] The strongest argument is that concerning the political situation after Sejanus' death when Pilate would not want to appear to be dishonouring the Emperor by having the shields removed.

Two further arguments can be brought for a later date. One is the fact that the inscription appears to have referred to one person only (ὑπὲρ οὗ is singular). Pilate's coins struck before 29 refer to both Tiberius and his mother Julia, Augustus' wife. Many other communities similarly included Julia in inscriptions and dedications. After her death in 29, the coins refer only to Tiberius. If Julia were still alive we might perhaps have expected her to have been also honoured by the shields. Second, the Jewish spokesmen appeal directly to Tiberius and not to the legate of Syria as was the standard procedure.[90] It may be that the Jewish leaders thought their best course of action was to appeal to the Herodians who, because of their position, could appeal directly to the Emperor. Or, if the incident took place very soon after Sejanus' death, there could be another explanation. Syria was without a legate 'in residence' until Flaccus' appointment sometime in 32. Appeal to the legate would have been difficult before this date as the occupant of the post, L. Aelius Lamia, was in Rome. The Jewish leaders would therefore have been forced to adopt a strategy such as we find in the shields incident in order to bring any pressure on Pilate.[91]

The incident of the shields, therefore, seems to have taken place at a feast shortly after Sejanus' death (17 October 31). This would also provide a historically significant motive for Pilate's erection of the shields: in the politically unstable conditions after Sejanus' fall Pilate wanted to demonstrate his loyalty to Caesar.

---

[89] Smallwood's attempt to match the 'crimes' with known or conjectured events in Pilate's governorship is not convincing: cf. *Legatio*, p. 305.

[90] See p. 5.

[91] For differing reasons Doyle ('Pilate's', pp. 191–3), suggests that this incident occurred at the Passover of 32. Hoehner (*Herod*, pp. 180–1) asserts: 'One objection to this is that it seems unlikely that Pilate would have tried to stir up trouble amongst the Jews so soon after hearing of Sejanus' death, especially since he may not have known about it until the winter of 31/2'. He suggests the Feast of Tabernacles instead. However, by using aniconic shields Pilate seems to have deliberately tried to *avert* trouble.

Conclusion

Philo presents us with a governor bent on annoying his subjects by the unprecedented erection of shields bearing forbidden inscriptions in Jerusalem. His character is described as spiteful, angry, lacking in courage, inflexible, stubborn and cruel; his government shows his venality, violence, thefts, assaults, abusive behaviour, frequent execution of untried prisoners and endless savage ferocity. Yet Philo's description of Pilate conforms to those of other actors within the *Embassy* and *In Flaccum* who disrespect the Jewish nation and their Law, in particular Gaius, the Alexandrian mob and the stereotyped 'corrupt governor' of *In Flaccum* 105. The description of Pilate's character and motivation stems largely from Philo's political rhetoric, in which he tries to persuade Claudius not to adopt Gaius' attitude to the Jews, and from his theology, in which the enemies of Judaism are the enemies of God and are thus portrayed extremely negatively. This 'theologically interpreted history'[92] is found in other Jewish writings of the period, particularly 2 Maccabees, Esther and Judith.

Behind the theological gloss, however, the historical Pilate is just visible; though Philo allowed his imagination to play a part in describing Pilate's character, his description of the facts seems trustworthy. Pilate appears as a governor intent on showing his loyalty to the Emperor. This overriding concern and a fear that the removal of the shields would negate the whole project appear to have been his main priority rather than an attempt to respond to the wishes of his people. But Pilate's erection of the shields was not a deliberate act of aggression as Philo maintains and several modern scholars have supposed. He seems to have gone out of his way to ensure that the shields did not contain portraits of the Emperor and that they were set up inside the headquarters of the Roman administration, surely the most appropriate place in Jerusalem for them. Although he probably realized that Tiberius' full title could be offensive to some Jews, Pilate may have thought that the location of the shields inside the praetorium made them less objectionable. Or, perhaps more likely, he thought that the Jews, like other peoples in the Empire, should not object to honour being shown to their Emperor. The intention behind Pilate's shields in Jerusalem was perhaps the same as that behind

---

[92] Term used by Borgen, *Philo*, p. 50.

his erection of a building known as the Tiberiéum in Caesarea: namely, an attempt to honour Tiberius. The incident is probably to be dated in the troubled times shortly after the death of Sejanus in 31 CE.

3

PILATE IN JOSEPHUS

The Jewish author Josephus refers to Pilate in his two major works: the *Jewish War* and the *Antiquities of the Jews*. The *War*, written c. 75–9 CE, contains two incidents concerning the prefect; the *Antiquities*, published around 93/4 adds two more and describes Pilate's return to Rome.[1] Although both books were written in Rome under Flavian patronage and Josephus himself was born after Pilate's dismissal from Judaea, Josephus was a native of Jerusalem and his description of Pilate probably relies on information passed down to him by his parents and grandparents.[2] Yet, as was the case with Philo, Josephus' dramatic historical narrative has been shaped to some degree by his particular theological and rhetorical aims.

The following discussion will analyse Josephus' works separately, taking into consideration their particular objectives and the role Pilate plays in each one. The historical background behind each incident will then be explored.

The *Jewish War*

In his first literary work Josephus has three important aims: to explain the tragedy which befell the Jewish people, in particular the destruction of the Temple; to attempt to improve the strained relations between Jews and Romans after the war; and, most importantly, to impress upon other nations the futility of revolt against Rome.[3]

---

[1] For detailed discussions of Josephus' life and works see especially Bilde, *Flavius*; Rajak, *Josephus*; Cohen, *Josephus*; Attridge 'Josephus'; Feldman, 'Josephus'.

[2] Josephus was born in the first year of Gaius' reign, 37/8 CE, i.e. a year or two after Pilate's departure (*Life* 5). He probably died around 100 (Attridge, 'Josephus', p. 195). He also claims to be a native of Jerusalem and of priestly descent (*JW* 1.3).

[3] Other aims which are less relevant to this study include praising his Flavian benefactors, especially Titus, and to portray himself in a more favourable light: cf. Bilde, *Flavius*, pp. 75–8.

Josephus understands and interprets the catastrophic political events leading to the war in theological terms.[4] The blame, he maintains, lay with no foreign nation but with the Jews themselves.[5] Internal strife between Jewish factions led to disunity amongst God's people and the transgression of the Law by those in favour of revolt.[6] Throughout the narrative lies the conviction that God has abandoned his people to their sin and now favours the Roman side.[7] God used the Romans to chastise his people: the fall of Jerusalem and the destruction of the Temple were therefore the just punishment for the sins of the nation.[8] This theological interpretation of events has close parallels with the OT, particularly the prophetic understanding of God using foreign nations to chastise his people.[9]

However, Josephus carefully emphasizes that not all the Jewish nation was involved. This ties in with his second apologetic aim, that of attempting to restore the friendlier, pre-war relations between Jews and Romans. He does this primarily by analysing the *causes* of the war, repeatedly stressing that the Jewish people as a whole were not responsible for the revolt; the blame should rather be placed on a small group of rebels who stirred up the nation with their militant aims. These fanatics are variously described as 'tyrants' and 'bandits'.[10] Although admitting their Jewish origin, Josephus wants to show that these men generally did not represent the feelings of the Jewish populace, the majority of whom remained pro-Roman as did the Jewish authorities, Agrippa and the chief priests, and the major Jewish philosophies.[11] By this device,

---

[4] Although the beneficiary of Flavian patronage, Josephus retained his Judaism. His keen sense of the tragedy which befell his people lends a touch of personal anguish to his narrative, for example, 1.9–12, 5.20.

[5] 1.12, 5.257, 6.251.

[6] For example, 2.454–6, 4.314–18, 383–8, 6.99–102.

[7] For example, 3.293, 404, 494, 4.297, 323, 370, 5.2, 39, 343, 6.39, 110, 250, 399, 401, 7.32, 319.

[8] 2.455, 4.323, 5.19.   [9] Bilde, *Flavius*, p. 75.

[10] τύραννοι, λησταί. See, for example, 1.4, 10, 24, 27. The disturbances after Herod's death are similarly ascribed to an extreme nationalistic element (2.53–65). The atrocities of their deeds are described in 4.382–3.

[11] Agrippa makes a speech against the war in 2.345–404; the chief priests, notable citizens and Temple ministers similarly try to prevent it (2.320, 417–18); the people of Tiberias and Tarichaeae wanted peace (3.448, 492); the people in besieged Jerusalem anxiously awaited the arrival of the Romans (5.28, 53, 335); many of the upper classes want to desert (6.113). Josephus claims that the nationalistic Fourth Philosophy founded by Judas the Galilean, which advocated the non-payment of tribute and refusal to tolerate mortal masters, had *nothing in common* with the other philosophies (2.118 – contrast *Ant.* 18.23). By this exaggeration he implies that the

Josephus hoped to exonerate the Jewish people and to show that contemporary Roman ill-treatment was out of place as the people had suffered enough at the hands of their compatriots.

Along with the Jewish nationalists, Josephus also puts blame for the revolt upon the last two Roman procurators of Judaea: Albinus and Florus. Under the governorship of Albinus were sown in the city the seeds of its impending fall (*JW* 2.276) and his successor, Florus, is charged with deliberately wanting war to hide his own excesses.[12] The revolt therefore, according to the *War*, was caused by the agitation of nationalist brigands and the ill-treatment of the nation by its last two governors rather than any innate tendency of the people to rebel. Indeed, they generally tended to be peaceably inclined and should not be held responsible for the atrocities that occurred.

That the resistance of the nationalistic brigands was misguided and futile is stressed throughout the work. The might of Rome and the futility of revolt amongst subject peoples is one of the most dominant themes and, at least as far as Josephus' Flavian patrons would have been concerned, was the most important motive for the work's composition. Josephus uses the Jewish revolt as an example to deter others, especially by his gruesome description of conditions in Jerusalem during the Roman siege.[13] Although he acknowledges Jewish successes against the Romans,[14] the superior might of the Roman army is repeatedly emphasized – its missiles, artillery and its victorious siege engine.[15] Section 3.70–109 contains a long digression on the Roman army – its composition, weaponry, tactics and so on – explicitly to 'deter others who may be tempted to revolt' (§ 108).

But what seals the invincibility of Rome for Josephus is not simply the prowess of its armies but the fact that the Empire has

---

other philosophies were content to accept the Romans, stating this explicitly in the case of the Essenes who obeyed mortal rulers 'since no ruler attains his office save by the will of God' (2.140). Rajak, however, warns against an oversimplified view of Josephus' description, noting that in the earlier stages of the revolt he does admit that there was a middle element who were sometimes behind the war party: cf. *Josephus*, p. 83.

[12] For example, 2.293, 299, 318, 333. A fuller discussion of Josephus' appraisal of Roman governors will be given in the next section, pp. 60–2.

[13] For example, 5.424–38, 512–8, 567–72, 6.1–8, 193–219 (the mother who ate her own baby), 6.201–13 and 7.112.

[14] This is part of his historical concern not to underestimate the Jewish achievements (1.7–8). In fact it enhances the prestige of the victorious Roman armies if their opponents put up a strong fight.

[15] 3.244, 5.269. See also 2.362–79 and Titus' speech in 3.472–84.

God as an ally. God was behind Augustus' success at Actium, he is behind the Empire, shaping its destiny, directing Vespasian to the principate and committing the Empire to him and his son Titus.[16] Revolt against Rome is therefore revolt against God. This is made particularly clear in Josephus' speech to his besieged countrymen in 5.362–419.[17] The message of the *War* is clear: the Jews should have quietly put their trust in God rather than attempted to alter his guidance of history by taking up arms; the passive protest against Gaius' statue illustrates the effectiveness of non-violence and trust in God (2.184–203). The story of the Jewish revolt, however, is a graphic illustration of what happens when a subject nation rises up and takes on the power of Rome and is a dire warning to others of the tragic consequences to which such action leads.

Pilate in the *Jewish War*

In this work Josephus relates two incidents involving Pilate – one describing his introduction of iconic standards into Jerusalem, the other his appropriation of Temple funds to build an aqueduct in the city. Pilate is introduced abruptly and there is no reference to his departure. The texts are as follows:

> (2.169) Pilate, being sent by Tiberius as procurator to Judaea, introduced into Jerusalem by night and under cover the effigies of Caesar which are called standards. (170) This proceeding, when day broke, aroused immense excitement among the Jews; those on the spot were in consternation, considering their laws to have been trampled under foot, as those laws permit no image to be erected in the city; while the indignation of the towns-people stirred the countryfolk, who flocked together in crowds. (171) Hastening after Pilate to Caesarea, the Jews implored him to remove the standards from Jerusalem and to uphold the laws of their ancestors. When Pilate refused, they fell prostrate around his house and for five whole days and nights remained motionless in that position.

---

[16] 1.390, 2.390, 3.6, 404, 5.2.

[17] See also Agrippa's speech shortly before the outbreak of revolt (2.345–404) and its counterpart, that of Eleazar to his fellow Zealots on Masada (7.323–36). For a detailed discussion of these three speeches and the way in which Josephus casts himself in the role of Jeremiah within his speech see Lindner, *Geschichtsauffassung*, pp. 21–48.

(2.172) On the ensuing day Pilate took his seat on his tribunal in the great stadium and summoning the multitude, with the apparent intention of answering them, gave the arranged signal to his armed soldiers to surround the Jews. (173) Finding themselves in a ring of troops, three deep, the Jews were struck dumb at this unexpected sight. Pilate, after threatening to cut them down, if they refused to admit Caesar's images, signalled to the soldiers to draw their swords. (174) Thereupon the Jews, as by concerted action, flung themselves in a body on the ground, extended their necks, and exclaimed that they were ready rather to die than to transgress the Law. Overcome with astonishment at such intense religious zeal, Pilate gave orders for the immediate removal of the standards from Jerusalem.

(2.175) On a later occasion he provoked a fresh uproar by expending upon the construction of an aqueduct the sacred treasure known as *Corbonas*; the water was brought from a distance of 400 furlongs. Indignant at this proceeding, the populace formed a ring round the tribunal of Pilate, then on a visit to Jerusalem, and besieged him with angry clamour. (176) He, foreseeing the tumult, had interspersed among the crowd a troop of his soldiers, armed but disguised in civilian dress, with orders not to use their swords, but to beat any rioters with cudgels. He now from his tribunal gave the agreed signal. (177) Large numbers of the Jews perished, some from the blows which they received, others trodden to death by their companions in the ensuing flight. Cowed by the fate of the victims, the multitude was reduced to silence.[18]

Before analysing each text in detail, it will be useful to set these two events in the context of the narrative as a whole. The *Jewish War* begins by narrating the rise and fall of the Hasmonaean dynasty, describing the reigns of the later Hasmonaean kings as a period of turbulence and instability which gradually gave rise to a period of repressive peace from 32 BCE onwards under Herod I.[19] With this king's death fresh disturbances arose and the country was

[18] Taken from Thackeray, *Jewish*, vol. 2, pp. 389–93.
[19] 1.364.

plunged into virtual anarchy, eventually being forcibly put down by Varus.[20] Following the reprehensible reign of Archelaus and the arrival of embassies conveying the complaints of the people, Augustus decided to unite Judaea to the Empire. The *War* stresses that this annexation was at the request of the people themselves and is portrayed as a concession to them from the Emperor.[21] Of the next thirty-one years, until Agrippa I's reign (41–4), Josephus reports very little. Only two of the seven prefects governing Judaea during this time are mentioned: Coponius, the first governor, and Pilate. Although he relates the rise of Judas the Galilean under Coponius and two incidents involving Pilate, the general impression is that these were relatively stable years when the majority of the population were content with Roman rule. It is only much later in the more detailed description of Felix's governorship that we hear of the rise of brigands ($\lambda\eta\sigma\tau\alpha\acute{\iota}$), and the emergence of *sicarii*, deceivers and impostors ($\pi\lambda\acute{\alpha}\nu\omega\iota$ $\gamma\grave{\alpha}\rho$ $\check{\alpha}\nu\theta\rho\omega\pi\omega\iota$).[22] The relative tranquillity of the first phase of direct Roman rule is reinforced by the fact that the largest part of Josephus' narrative at this point is dedicated to a description of 'Jewish philosophies' ($\phi\iota\lambda\omicron\sigma\omicron\phi\epsilon\tilde{\iota}\tau\alpha\iota$): the Pharisees, Sadducees and Essenes.[23] Josephus' narratives concerning Pilate therefore belong to the *Jewish War*'s relatively harmonious picture of Judaea between Archelaus' deposition and the accession of Gaius Caligula and Agrippa I.[24]

Rhetorical themes within the two stories

Appearing at a time of relative peace and set within a narrative which describes surrounding events only in their barest outline, the two incidents occurring during Pilate's governorship may strike the reader as rather odd. Pilate is introduced abruptly with no extraneous biographical detail except the mere fact that he was 'governor of Judaea' (even the title $\dot{\epsilon}\pi\acute{\iota}\tau\rho\omicron\pi\omicron\varsigma$ is vague[25]); there is no mention of the length of his rule or his departure from the province. The emphasis is not on Pilate's governorship but on the two stories themselves. A closer look at them shows that they have two common characteristics.

First, they have the same structure built around cause and

---

[20] 2.1–79. [21] 2.117 [22] 2.253–65. [23] 2.119–66.
[24] For a historical evaluation of Josephus' account here see pp. 1–4.
[25] His title was 'prefect' ($\check{\epsilon}\pi\alpha\rho\chi\omicron\varsigma$); see pp. 11–12.

effect:[26] an action of Pilate provokes the people; this causes a Jewish reaction which in turn necessitates a counter-reaction from Pilate. Such a scheme is developed furthest in the episode of the standards. Throughout the narrative we are continually presented with a series of actions and reactions between the two actors in the drama, Pilate and the people, each dependent on the previous response.

Second, in both narratives the emphasis is not so much on Pilate's *initial action* as the *Jewish reaction* and what effect this produces on the Roman prefect. In both, Pilate's initial offence is described briefly and serves primarily as a catalyst which sparks off the Jewish reaction. In the first we are told only that Pilate brought in the standards by night. Josephus is not interested in telling us why Pilate brought new standards into Jerusalem or upon whose authority he was acting. Similarly in the second narrative we are told that Pilate caused offence by using Temple money to build an aqueduct; but many important details such as why Pilate used this money and how he acquired it are absent. These details, especially those to do with the *Corbonas*, would presumably have been equally mystifying to Josephus' contemporary non-Jewish readers as they are to a modern reader. At other points in his narrative Josephus explains Jewish customs and religious sensitivities to his audience;[27] that he does not do so here again implies that the details of Pilate's 'crimes' are not of paramount importance to him. What is significant is the Jewish reaction. This is clear from the opening sentence of the aqueduct narrative: 'On a later occasion he provoked a fresh uproar . . . ' (μετὰ δὲ ταῦτα ταραχὴν ἑτέραν ἐκίνει . . .); it is clearly the Jewish protest in response to Pilate's action which is the focus of attention.

Josephus relates two actions of Pilate which led to two different Jewish reactions. In the first, the Jews are entirely peaceful and passive; they go to Caesarea and, without aggression, implore Pilate to remove the standards; even after five days and nights they refrain from violence, accepting death rather than the violation of their laws. Pilate, astonished by their religious devotion, accepted

---

[26] Also noticed by Lémonon, *Pilate*, p. 146. For a similar evaluation of Josephus' rhetoric in the *War* to that outlined here see Krieger, 'Pontius', pp. 67–9.

[27] For example, in 1.270 he explains why Antigonus lacerated Hyrcanus' ears; at 1.477 he explains that polygamy is permitted by Jewish custom; at 1.650 that it is unlawful to put images or busts in the Temple; see also 2.42, 456 and 6.425.

their arguments and removed the standards. Through this narrative, Josephus indicates that a passive demonstration showing
respect for and submission to the governor can achieve its aim. The
reaction occasioned by the aqueduct, however, is completely
different. The people show aggression towards Pilate, they
surround his tribunal, 'besiege him with angry clamour'
(περιστάντες τὸ βῆμα κατεβόων) and a massacre ensues. The final
line is heavily dramatic: the severity of the Roman troops and their
large number of victims reduced the multitude to silence. Clearly an
angry protest will not succeed and can only end in bloodshed and
disaster.

It is no coincidence that these two events together illustrate the
most important purpose of the *War*: opposition in the form of
riots or angry tumults is useless, for Rome is far too strong. Only
a passive, respectful protest can hope to succeed. Josephus uses a
similar technique when he juxtaposes two incidents from the
governorship of Cumanus; one involving a violent protest, the
other non-militant.[28] Later the moral of these pairs of stories is
given verbal expression by Agrippa: even if a governor rules badly
'the powers that be should be conciliated by flattery, not irritated
. . . there is nothing to check blows like submission and the
resignation of the wronged victim puts the wrongdoer to
confusion'.[29]

The two incidents in Pilate's governorship, coming at a time of
relative peace, seem therefore to highlight the two options open to
all subjects of the Roman Empire: either accept Roman rule peacefully and its governors will show consideration or resort to violence
and risk certain annihilation at the hands of Roman troops.

The next clash between Jews and Rome in the *War* concerns
Gaius' statue.[30] Here, as with the standards, the people make their
appeal to the Roman representative peacefully, offering to die
rather than transgress their laws. Petronius, like Pilate earlier, was
astounded by their behaviour and, by his resolve to delay the
erection of the statue, the demonstration succeeded. In this incident
the people seem to have learned from the episodes in Pilate's
administration. The affair of the aqueduct, however, remains as a

---

[28] 2.223–7, 2.228–31. In all, Josephus describes three incidents which occurred
under Cumanus' governorship. The third describes a conflict between Galileans and
Samaritans which, due to his tardiness in dealing with the problem, led to Cumanus'
banishment (2.232–45).

[29] 2.350–1.   [30] 2.184–203.

warning against more aggressive action and it is this policy, rather than the successful peaceful protests, which is eventually employed by members of the war party with disastrous results for the nation.

The characterization of Pilate in the *War*

In view of the rhetorical effect to which Josephus puts his two incidents involving Pilate, it is no surprise that the prefect is described only briefly with no general word on his administration as a whole. Similarly, Josephus gives us no portrayal of Pilate's character; there are no charges or allegations made against him as there are with other Roman governors in the *War*.[31] This implies that Pilate's actions serve merely as catalysts within the story and that Josephus, looking back on events, did not regard his governorship as excessively harsh.

Despite Josephus' lack of interest, it is possible to piece together some picture of the Pilate with whom he presents us. He is said to have brought the standards into Jerusalem 'by night and under cover' (νύκτωρ κεκαλυμμένας). Josephus has used the reference to night earlier in his work;[32] the phrase clearly indicates the perpetration of a crime, or something which would shock others were it performed in daylight. Josephus shows his readers not only that Pilate's introduction of iconic standards was against the Law (which is made explicit at § 170) but also that Pilate *knew* his actions would cause offence and so took precautions to ensure that his installation of the standards was not seen by the people and to present them with a *fait accompli* the following morning. No motives are given for Pilate's conduct, either to incriminate or to exonerate him, and it is left to the reader to form his or her own conclusions. The overriding impression, however, is one of insensitivity; Pilate's conduct was not blatant but combined a certain amount of stealth with secrecy and involved a disregard for the religious feelings of those under his rule.

Similarly at Caesarea, Pilate is not moved by the pleas of the

---

[31] Josephus wrote the *War* under Flavian patronage, yet he has no qualms about portraying Albinus (2.272–6), Florus (2.277–404) and other Roman generals in a poor light, suggesting that Pilate would have come under similar criticism had it been necessary. Other characters such as Bacchides (1.35–6), Scaurus (1.132) and Sabinus (2.16–19) who play a smaller role than Pilate are subjected to a moral judgement. The allegations made against Pilate's character by Philo in *Embassy* 299–305, discussed in the previous chapter, are completely absent.

[32] 1.229, 437. See also John 13.30.

people to uphold their ancestral laws and refuses to remove the standards. He shows either patience or stubbornness in allowing the people to remain motionless outside his house for five days and nights. It is the reaction of the people which Josephus wants to highlight at this point rather than the psychology of Pilate, but it would make sense within the narrative to see the governor expecting the people to tire of their demonstration and simply waiting for them to accept the standards and go home. The endurance of the Jews is, however, stronger than the governor had bargained for and on the sixth day he resolves to end the matter. Here again he betrays the same lack of openness as he did with the introduction of the standards: he takes his seat on the tribunal with the apparent real intention of answering the people, but he has no intention of discussing the matter and instead gives his soldiers a prearranged signal to surround the multitude. An important point is that the soldiers have not yet drawn their swords, though Josephus states that they were armed (§ 172); Pilate's intention was to intimidate the people into acceptance by a sudden display of troops rather than engage in battle at this stage. These tactics are used elsewhere in the *War* by other Roman commanders attempting to minimize bloodshed by frightening their opponents into surrender.[33] Yet such intimidation only produced silence in the multitude and Pilate goes one step further, this time threatening to execute the people unless they accepted Caesar's standards. So far the matter has been entirely in Pilate's hands: he has attempted to dispel the crowd by three means, first ignoring them, then intimidating them and finally threatening them. He has remained completely firm in his conviction that the people must accept the symbols of imperial Rome, not even entering into a discussion of the matter. The Jewish demonstration appeared to have little chance of success. But suddenly the situation changes and the reader learns that the Jews do have the ability to change events, that a passive willingness to die and trust in God can save both them and their ancestral laws. Pilate is 'overcome with astonishment at such intense religious zeal' (ὑπερθαυμάσας δὲ ὁ Πιλᾶτος τὸ τῆς δεισιδαιμονίας ἄκρατον) in the same way that Pompey was filled with admiration for Jewish devotion during the siege of Jerusalem and that Petronius will later be filled with astonishment

---

[33] For example, Vespasian at the Galilean frontier (3.127) and at Jotapata (3.146) and Titus before Jerusalem (5.348–55).

and pity at the sight of the Jewish multitude ready to die rather than accept Gaius' statue.[34] As a result he commands that the standards be immediately removed from Jerusalem.

For Josephus, Pilate's behaviour here is no more a sign of 'weakness' than Petronius' determination to defend Jewish interests is a show of 'treason'. It was a Roman prefect's duty to preserve law and order in his province. Pilate had maintained his defiant position on the standards for as long as he was able but he drew the line at the massacre of large numbers of passive unarmed protesters. In this case the symbols of Rome and personal pride were sacrificed in favour of peace in the province. The verb is active (κελεύει); Pilate still retains some command of the situation. This is the first incident concerning Pilate that Josephus narrates and the affair gives the impression of a new governor testing public opinion, seeing how far the Jewish people would go in defiance of their ancestral religion. Pilate backed down in this case; he is not so stubborn or self-willed that he will not heed public opinion and his amazement at Jewish willingness to die for their religion means that, for the moment, he will uphold their laws in the interests of preserving the peace.

In the second episode, Pilate is said to have 'provoked a fresh uproar' (ταραχὴν ἑτέραν ἐκίνει, 2.175); this, however, is a description of the *result* of his actions, not his deliberate *intention*. It is not the construction of the aqueduct itself which seems to cause offence – Herod's building of one in Laodicea on Sea earns him praise from Josephus (1.422) – but the fact that he completely uses up (ἐξαναλίσκων) the Temple treasure. Josephus passes no comment on the legality of this act but it is clear from the sequel that the anger of the people was aroused by it. It is also apparent from his prior positioning of troops that, as in the standards incident, Pilate knew that there was a high probability that the people would take offence at his actions. This time he has taken precautionary measures to deal with any disturbance, yet his methods again indicate a concern to avoid unnecessary bloodshed. He does not parade his soldiers in an open display of aggression or intimidation which could provoke the rioting people against Rome, but has his troops dressed in ordinary clothes and mingling with the crowd.

---

[34] 1.148 (Petronius). Much later the Romans will show the same incredulousness at Jewish fortitude when confronted with the mass suicides at Masada (7.402–6). This recurring theme is part of Josephus' aim to enhance the standing and piety of his people in the eyes of his Graeco-Roman contemporaries.

The soldiers are armed but have orders to use only clubs and not their swords; it is only rioters who are to be beaten (§ 176). In this incident it is the people who try to intimidate Pilate by surrounding him 'with angry clamour' (§ 175); only after this does Pilate give his men the agreed signal.

Pilate appears to have acted appropriately in the circumstances;[35] his orders to his men, if inconsistent with the final slaughter, do not appear to have been unduly harsh. The incident involving the aqueduct ends dramatically, describing the silence of the multitude. For Josephus it is a tragic end brought about not solely by Pilate's aggression but by the Jews' own riotous behaviour.

The picture of Pilate which emerges from the *Jewish War* therefore is one of a governor who can be consciously insensitive towards Jewish religious customs when they conflict with the interests of Rome. Yet he does not quickly resort to unnecessary violence, preferring intimidation and threats in the first incident and ordering his men only to use clubs and beat rioters in the second. He takes his commission as provincial governor charged with preserving law and order seriously, in the first episode backing down rather than ordering mass executions and in the second quelling a disturbance with what should have been a minimum of violence. But he is not merely a blunt, insensitive representative of imperial Rome, he can be favourably impressed by Jewish religious devotion and allow this to affect his judgement.

Finally Pilate needs to be placed alongside other Roman governors in the *War*: how does he compare with them? Is he harsher or more lenient? Is there a gradual deterioration in the conduct of Roman officials posted to Judaea in which he takes his place?

Taking the last question first, there does not seem to be a general decline in the administrations of Judaean governors according to the *War*; each governor is judged according to his own merits.[36] Only nine of the fourteen Roman governors are mentioned at all and four of them – Coponius, Fadus, Tiberius Alexander and

---

[35] See Josephus' comment in 2.296 and Cumanus' actions in 2.226–7.

[36] Bilde (*Flavius*, p. 74) suggests that an immediate cause of the revolt in the *War* was the ever poorer administration of Palestine by the Romans which led to the growth of the war party and tensions between Jews and non-Jews.. See also Rajak, *Josephus*, p. 79 and Attridge, 'Josephus', p. 209. Cohen, however, correctly notes that only the procurators Albinus and Festus are seen as external factors in the *War*'s description of the revolt and not a gradual disintegration of governors: cf. *Josephus*, p. 154.

Festus – are referred to only briefly.[37] Judas the Galilean incited his compatriots to revolt under Coponius' administration, but this is not linked with the governor's conduct. The two Roman governors mentioned after Pilate, Fadus and Tiberius Alexander, receive a particularly favourable report: 'by abstaining from all interference with the customs of the country [they] kept the country at peace'.[38] Disturbances broke out under Cumanus but again no blame is attached to the governor for this; in fact, he is eventually banished for refusing to take action quickly enough in disturbances between Galileans and Samaritans.[39] Felix and Festus are credited with attacking impostors and brigands.[40] So far, although Judas founded his fourth philosophy under Coponius and the activity of brigands, *sicarii* and impostors has been steadily mounting from the time of Cumanus to that of Fadus (i.e. 48–62 CE), the *War* lays no charges of mismanagement against the Roman governors.

With Albinus the quality of the Roman procurators changes. His administration 'was of another order', states Josephus: 'there was no villainy which he omitted to practise' and 'from this date were sown in the city the seeds of its impending fall'.[41] Florus, however, made Albinus 'appear by comparison a paragon of virtue' and Josephus specifies in detail his tyranny, his unprecedented cruelty, covetousness and bribery and how he wanted war to cover up his own atrocities.[42] Although Agrippa in his speech (2.345–401) refers generally to the 'insolence of the procurators', the intolerable harshness of Roman ministers and oppressive governors, it is clearly predominantly Florus' governorship which has led the people to revolt rather than a culmination of harsh rule, as the people themselves admit in § 402. 'The same procurator will not remain for ever' argues Agrippa, 'and it is probable that the successors of this one will show greater moderation on taking office' (§ 354). It is thus only the last two procurators, especially Florus, who come under harsh criticism from Josephus in the *War*.

Pilate's governorship belongs to a much earlier phase in Jewish–Roman relations. He is not charged with misgovernment, nor is

---

[37] 2.117–18, 220, 271.

[38] 2.220. Later, in 5.205, we learn that Tiberius Alexander's father was responsible for plating the gates of the Jerusalem Temple. The ex-procurator himself continues to earn Josephus' respect as the loyal friend of Titus (5.45) entrusted with the second watch during the siege of Jerusalem (5.510).

[39] 2.223–45.   [40] 2.247, 253–71.   [41] 2.272–6.

[42] 2.277, 282–3, 295, 308, 331, 340, 532.

there any reference to banditry during his time of office. Josephus' description of Fadus and Tiberius Alexander, quoted above, shows that he measures a governor by his interference with Jewish religious customs. On this score, of course, Pilate fell down twice, but seen in context there is no hint in the *War* that Josephus regarded Pilate's administration as particularly poor, violent or directly playing a part in the breakdown of relations leading to the revolt.

Summary

Josephus uses two events in Pilate's governorship to strengthen the *War*'s foremost rhetorical aim: the insistence that resistance against Rome is futile and only passive acceptance of Roman rule can produce harmony amongst subject peoples. The incident with the standards has close parallels with that of Gaius' statue; on both occasions the Jews achieved their aims by trust in God and without resort to violence. The affair of the aqueduct stands as a warning as to what the outcome will be if the Jews trust instead in aggression and riots, a policy which they eventually follow and which leads to the tragic events culminating in the destruction of the Temple. Although Josephus gives no character sketch as such of Pilate, the governor does display certain characteristics. He can be insensitive towards the people, expecting them to be like other nations and accept the symbols of Rome; yet he can be moved by a religious demonstration and shows himself averse to excessive bloodshed. He is a governor of the Roman Empire intent on preserving law and order in Judaea, taking his place in the *War* alongside the other relatively able governors of the early period of the province.

The *Antiquities of the Jews*

Written almost twenty years after the *Jewish War*, the *Antiquities of the Jews* chronicles the history of the Jewish race (20.259) presenting a record of its ancient and glorious past to the Graeco-Roman world.[43] It may have been designed as a counterpart to the

---

[43] 20.259. *Ant.* 20.267 dates it to the thirteenth year of Domitian's reign and the fifty-sixth year of Josephus' own life (i.e. 93/4 CE).

Roman Antiquities of Dionysius of Halicarnassus written almost a century earlier in 7 BCE.[44] The social and political reasons which necessitated such a task are not hard to reconstruct. In the turbulent years after the Jewish revolt, Jews often found themselves in difficult and dangerous circumstances. Josephus' work was an attempt to counteract pagan hostility towards Judaism and false and malicious rumours concerning its origin.[45] He writes to persuade members of the Empire to revert to their former tolerance, and even respect, towards Judaism. He does this by stressing the antiquity of Judaism and the Hebrew scriptures, by emphasizing the special status of the Law, and cites innumerable decrees and edicts from Roman rulers showing favour towards Judaism.[46] These themes were also present to some extent in the *War* but become dominant in the *Antiquities*. Josephus shows that the revolt and its aftermath were a brief interlude in a history dominated by religious tolerance between Israel and its rulers.

The *causes* of the revolt itself receive a wider analysis in the *Antiquities* than in the *War*. Writing later in the *Antiquities*, Josephus was freer to place the blame on a wider set of circumstances and people. The apologetic aim, however, remains the same: rebellion is not an innate trait of the Jewish nation but was forced on the people by a combination of internal and external factors which left them with no choice. Internally the disruption caused by the 'brigands' was combined with dissension amongst the high priests and aristocracy; King Agrippa also played his part in the decline of the country into revolt.[47] Externally, a rescript of Nero annulling Jewish citizen rights in Caesarea carried the quarrel between Jews and their Greek neighbours further until it eventually kindled the flames of war.[48] Pagan troops from Caesarea and Sebaste were also influential in arousing hostilities.[49] By continually offending against the Jewish Law the Roman governors are im-

---

[44] See Thackeray, *Antiquities*, vol. 4, p. ix. This is also assumed by Feldman, *Antiquities*, vol. 9, p. 529, note c; Cohen, *Josephus*, p. 59; and Rajak, *Josephus*, pp. 48, 89. The work is dedicated to Epaphroditus, 1.6–9 (as are the *Life* and *Contra Apionem*). For the identity of this man, see Thackeray, *Antiquities*, vol. 4, p. xi. This dedication does not necessarily imply that Josephus was no longer under Flavian patronage.

[45] For example, that recorded in 4.265–8 stating that Moses and his followers in Egypt had leprosy.

[46] 1.5, 16, 10.218, 16.31–57 (antiquity); 1.16, 24, 3.223, 11.120–1, 12.45–50, 18.266–8 (Law); 14.185–9, 16.174 (decrees).

[47] 20.179–81, 213 (high priests); 20.216–18 (Agrippa).

[48] 20.184   [49] 19.366.

plicated in the rise of brigandage and play a much more significant part in the country's descent into revolt in the *Antiquities* than in the *War*. In this way, Josephus shows that the Jewish people were led into the revolt by forces outside their control.[50]

No account of Judaism could be simply historical or political; it had at the same time to be theological and religious. Behind the *Antiquities* lies the firm Jewish principle that God guides his people throughout history in accordance with his Law. Linked with this is the conviction that the Jews should passively put their trust in God and not attempt to alter his divine plan by resorting to arms. The accounts of Gaius' statue and Pilate's standards illustrate this, as in the *War*. But more dominant throughout the narrative is a strong OT or Deuteronomistic conception of guilt and fate in which the pious are rewarded whilst the unrighteous who do not obey God's Law are punished. This was present in the *War* to a limited extent but becomes a fundamental theme in the present work.[51]

In the introduction (1.14), Josephus states that the lesson to be drawn from *Antiquities* is that

> men who conform to the will of God, and do not venture to transgress laws that have been excellently laid down, prosper in all things beyond belief, and for their reward are offered by God felicity; whereas, in proportion as they depart from the strict observance of these laws, things (else) practicable become impracticable, and whatever imaginary good thing they strive to do ends in irretrievable disasters.

Moses too stresses that God 'grants to such as follow Him a life of bliss, but involves in dire calamities those who step outside the path of virtue'.[52] Many characters are praised for their piety and righteousness towards God and are rewarded by long lives and prosperity.[53] Those who transgress the Law, however, do not escape punishment. The Sodomites were condemned to destruction, Saul's reign was cut short because he neglected God and Solomon died

---

[50] Cohen, *Josephus*, p. 155.

[51] For example, *JW* 1.81–4, 4.297, 7.32.

[52] *Ant.* 1.20. See also 2.28, 107, 6.307, 8.314, 18.127–9.

[53] For example, Abraham (1.256), Isaac (1.346), Jacob (2.196), Moses (4.177, 312–31), Joshua (4.117–19), Gideon (5.232), Asa (8.314), Jehoshaphat (8.393–4), Hyrcanus (13.299–300), Zamaris (17.29–31) and Izates of Adiabene (20.46–8).

ingloriously for his abandonment of God's laws.[54] Agrippa accepted his acclamation as a god and was struck down by divine vengeance.[55] Haman plotted the destruction of the whole Jewish race and deserved his ironically just end, as did Antiochus Epiphanes and the Emperor Gaius.[56] There are many other examples of people suffering because of their contempt for the Jewish Law. Not only individual characters but the whole Jewish nation is warned that afflictions would come upon it should it transgress God's Law.[57]

Josephus' *Antiquities* therefore extols the long and distinguished history of his race and the importance of its divine Law: these facts, long recognized and held in esteem by pagan overlords, should commend Judaism to Josephus' pagan readers. The Jewish nation is under God's protection and anyone who shows insolence and impiety towards its laws, whether a Jew or pagan, risks divine vengeance.

Pilate in the *Antiquities of the Jews*

The *Antiquities* contains four narratives involving Pilate. The first two – the standards and the aqueduct – were also found in the *War*. These are followed by the execution of Jesus, 'a wise man', and an incident involving Samaritans which culminated in Pilate's departure to Rome on the orders of Vitellius. These last events have no parallel in the *War*. The texts are as follows:

> (18.55) Now Pilate, the procurator of Judaea, when he brought his army from Caesarea and removed it to winter quarters in Jerusalem, took a bold step in subversion of the Jewish practices, by introducing into the city the busts of the Emperor that were attached to the military standards, for our Law forbids the making of images. (56) It was for this reason that the previous procurators, when they entered the city, used standards that had no such ornaments. Pilate was the first to bring the images into Jerusalem and set them up, doing it without the knowledge of

---

[54] 1.194–5, 202–3 (Sodomites); 6.104, 141–51, 334–6, 378 (Saul); 8.190–8 (Solomon).

[55] 19.343–52.

[56] 11.209–69 (Haman); 12.248–359 (Antiochus); 18.306, 19.1–113 (Gaius).

[57] For example, 4.319–40, 5.179–80, 185, 200, 6.305, 8.314.

the people, for he entered at night. (57) But when the people discovered it, they went in a throng to Caesarea and for many days entreated him to take away the images. He refused to yield, since to do so would be an outrage to the Emperor; however, since they did not cease entreating him, on the sixth day he secretly armed and placed his troops in position, while he himself came to the speaker's stand. This had been constructed in the stadium, which provided concealment for the army that lay in wait. (58) When the Jews again engaged in supplication, at a pre-arranged signal he surrounded them with his soldiers and threatened to punish them at once with death if they did not put an end to their tumult and return to their own places. (59) But they, casting themselves prostrate and baring their throats, declared that they had gladly welcomed death rather than make bold to transgress the wise provisions of the laws. Pilate, astonished at the strength of their devotion to the laws, straightway removed the images from Jerusalem and brought them back to Caesarea.

(18.60) He spent money from the sacred treasury in the construction of an aqueduct to bring water into Jerusalem, intercepting the source of the stream at a distance of 200 furlongs. The Jews did not acquiesce in the operations that this involved; and tens of thousands of men assembled and cried out against him, bidding him relinquish his promotion of such designs. Some too even hurled insults and abuse of the sort that a throng will commonly engage in. (61) He thereupon ordered a large number of soldiers to be dressed in Jewish garments, under which they carried clubs, and he sent them off this way and that, thus surrounding the Jews, whom he ordered to withdraw. When the Jews were in full torrent of abuse he gave his soldiers the prearranged signal. (62) They, however, inflicted much harder blows than Pilate had ordered, punishing alike both those who were rioting and those who were not. But the Jews showed no faint-heartedness; and so, caught unarmed, as they were, by men delivering a prepared attack, many of them actually were slain on the spot, while some withdrew disabled by blows. Thus ended the uprising.

(18.63) About this time there lived Jesus, a wise man . . .
(64) When Pilate, upon hearing him accused by men of the
highest standing amongst us, had condemned him to be
crucified, those who had in the first place come to love him
did not give up their affection for him . . .

(18.85) The Samaritan nation too was not exempt from
disturbance. For a man who made light of mendacity and
in all his designs catered to the mob, rallied them, bidding
them go in a body with him to Mount Gerizim, which in
their belief is the most sacred of mountains. He assured
them that on their arrival he would show them the sacred
vessels which were buried there, where Moses had depos-
ited them. (86) His hearers, viewing this tale as plausible,
appeared in arms. They posted themselves in a certain
village named Tirathana, and, as they planned to climb the
mountain in a great multitude, they welcomed to their
ranks the new arrivals who kept coming. (87) But before
they could ascend, Pilate blocked their projected route up
the mountain with a detachment of cavalry and heavy-
armed infantry, who in an encounter with the firstcomers
in the village slew some in a pitched battle and put the
others to flight. Many prisoners were taken, of whom
Pilate put to death the principal leaders and those who
were most influential among the fugitives.

(18.88) When the uprising had been quelled, the council
of the Samaritans went to Vitellius, a man of consular rank
who was governor of Syria, and charged Pilate with the
slaughter of the victims. For, they said, it was not as rebels
against the Romans but as refugees from the persecution
of Pilate that they had met in Tirathana. (89) Vitellius
thereupon dispatched Marcellus, one of his friends, to take
charge of the administration of Judaea, and ordered Pilate
to return to Rome to give the Emperor his account of the
matters with which he was charged by the Samaritans. And
so Pilate, after having spent ten years in Judaea, hurried to
Rome in obedience to the orders of Vitellius, since he could
not refuse. But before he reached Rome Tiberius had
already passed away.[58]

[58] Taken from Feldman, *Antiquities*, vol. 9, pp. 43–51, 61–5.

The references to Pilate in the *Antiquities* occur in book 18, a section which parallels book 2 of the *War* but with a great deal of extra material, either in the form of fuller details or additional stories. Josephus gives a fuller description of the early prefects and lists the four high priests deposed by Gratus.[59] Pilate is first referred to in 18.35 as Gratus' successor but a description of Antipas' building of Tiberias, Parthian affairs and the death of Germanicus intervene before the events of Pilate's governorship are returned to in 18.55. The narrative at this point, therefore, is not focused exclusively on Judaean affairs as was the case in the parallel section of the *War*.[60]

The report concerning Pilate is structured as part of a series of five disturbances (θόρυβοι) or events which broke out simulta-neously amongst Jews in Judaea and Rome and amongst the Samaritans. The first three occurred in Judaea – Pilate's introduc-tion of standards, his building of the aqueduct, and the disturbance connected with Jesus. Next, Josephus turns his attention to Rome, first narrating a scandal involving Isis worship and then 'another outrage' (ἕτερόν τι δεινὸν) – Tiberius' expulsion of all the Jews from the city.[61] The final disturbance describes how Pilate put

[59] 18.29–35. Preserving a record of the line of high priests who served during a length of 2,000 years was one of Josephus' aims (20.261); see a similar list in 10.151–3.

[60] *Antiquities* devotes a considerable amount of space to important events outside Palestine, in the Empire and Parthia: for example, 18.39–52 (Parthian wars), 18.53–4 (the death of Germanicus), 18.96–105 (clash between Rome and Parthia). One reason for this may be because of the size and importance of the Jewish community in Babylonia, which was now subject to the Parthians; see Feldman, *Antiquities*, vol. 4, pp. 32–3, note b. Cohen (Josephus, p. 59) less convincingly regards these events as 'extraneous', inserted only in order to provide enough material for the Dionysian twenty books. For a detailed analysis of the way in which Josephus structures his material in the *Antiquities* see Schwartz 'Pilate's Appoint-ment', pp. 185–98.

[61] The expulsion of both Jews and adherents of Egyptian cults under Tiberius is similarly linked by Tacitus, *Ann.* 2.85; if both did occur at the same time, this would explain why Josephus connects these two stories. Suetonius, *Tib.* 36 and Dio Cassius 57.18.5a also mention the expulsion of Jews from Rome. The reason appears to have been because the Jews were too active in proselytism; see Feldman, *Antiquities*, vol. 9, pp. 60–1, note a. The expulsion appears to have occurred in 19 CE (Tacitus, *Ann.* 2.85), not sometime between 26 and 36 as Josephus' narrative implies (18.65). The majority of scholars assume that Josephus is simply mistaken in his chronology at this point. Smallwood, for example, suggests his dating is occasioned by the recollection of Sejanus' hostility towards the Jews at this time ('Some Notes', p. 326); yet the whole assertion of Sejanus' anti-Semitism is suspect; see above, p. 23, note 122. Schwartz argues for the chronological accuracy of this reference: following Eisler he suggests that Pilate came to office in 19 ('Pilate's Appointment', pp. 182–201); see p. 1, note 1 above for further discussion. It may be, however, that

down a Samaritan uprising which led to Vitellius' intervention and the prefect's dismissal.[62]

Rhetorical themes behind the Pilate narratives in the *Antiquities*

The verbal similarities between *Antiquities* 18–20 and its earlier parallel (*JW* 2.117–18, 167–279) are extraordinarily insignificant, suggesting that Josephus was not simply adding extra details to his previous account but has completely rewritten the entire section giving certain themes a different emphasis.[63] The incidents involving the standards and the aqueduct are far from duplicates of their parallels in the *War*; both contain various additions and reductions which give a different slant to the portrayal of Pilate. A comparison of both incidents in the *Antiquities* and the *War* reveals several important changes.

First, the events of Pilate's administration are not introduced so abruptly in the *Antiquities* as they were in the *War*. The precise times of his arrival and departure are given along with the length of his governorship;[64] the whole of Pilate's contact with Judaea is therefore described much more fully in the *Antiquities*. Similarly, in the second work there is a greater interest in Pilate and his actions; the *War* described Pilate's introduction of the iconic standards in just over three lines (of the Loeb edition), whereas the *Antiquities* narrates it in eleven.[65] The strong sequence of cause and effect which was so much a feature of the account in the *War* has been minimized in the *Antiquities*, suggesting that the actions and reactions of the central characters are no longer of primary significance. Related to this, the

Josephus has deliberately left his record of the Jewish expulsion from Rome until Pilate's time so that he can group all his 'disturbance stories' together, giving a much stronger effect of attacks on Jews breaking out simultaneously throughout the Empire than would have been achieved by inserting the story in its correct chronological place.

[62] Pilate is referred to again briefly in 18.177, a passage mentioning only that Gratus and Pilate were the only governors appointed to Judaea under Tiberius.

[63] This has been demonstrated by Cohen, *Josephus*, pp. 58–65. He writes, 'the natural assumption of continual and detailed consultation of BJ by AJ is unjustified' (p. 65).

[64] 18.35, 89. For Eisler's view that these dates were due to later Christian interpolators in the time of Maximin Daia see p. 1, note 1 above.

[65] By moving up the phrase 'for our law forbids the making of images' in *Antiquities*, Josephus has made it into an enlargement upon Pilate's crime rather than an explanation of the people's outrage. Krieger finds similar rhetoric at work in the *Antiquities* as that outlined here; see 'Pilatus', pp. 69–74.

Jewish reactions are no longer highlighted: the initial Jewish reaction which took nine lines to describe in the *War* has been shortened to three in the *Antiquities*. The Jewish activities in Caesarea have also been condensed and cease to give the impression of almost inhuman passivity: the Jews do not remain motionless around Pilate's house but continually entreat him to remove the standards in what is described as a 'tumult' (θορυβεῖν). The cumulative effect of these details is that it is no longer the Jewish reaction which primarily engages the reader's attention. Although the Jewish willingness to die rather than to transgress ancestral Law is still a dominant motif, Pilate himself has become much more important, both his activities and motivation. This ties up with the interest in the *Antiquities* not only in national history but in the personal histories of individuals who played a part in shaping the nation's fortunes.[66] In this incident therefore Josephus shows an interest in Pilate as a Roman governor. In particular his attitude to the Jewish Law is important; an attitude which, in common with other characters in the *Antiquities*, will ultimately determine his fate.

The Jewish reaction has similarly been toned down in the story of the aqueduct in the *Antiquities*. Josephus admits that some 'hurled insults and abuse' (λοιδορίᾳ χρώμενοι ὕβριζον), though he tempers this by adding that it was only the sort of thing in which throngs commonly engage. Section 62 makes it clear that not all were rioting. Faced with the ensuing massacre, Josephus states, the Jews 'showed no faint-heartedness'. They were 'caught unarmed' whilst their opponents were 'delivering a prepared attack'. Some were slain on the spot; others withdrew because of their injuries. There is no dramatic ending describing people trodden to death by their compatriots in the ensuing flight as in the *War*. All the dead and injured are victims of the aggression of the troops, an aggression which apparently overstepped Pilate's intentions (§ 62).

These alterations mean that the central feature of this story in the *Antiquities* is not so much Pilate's crime or the Jewish protest, but the attitude of the Jews faced with a vicious attack from the pagan auxiliary troops. This fits in with an apologetic tendency within the *Antiquities*: Josephus regards the harshness and bias of the non-Jewish troops at the governors' disposal as one of the contributing factors in the revolt. This particular incident gives the first indication

---

[66] For example, the stories of King Izates of Adiabene and his mother Helena (20.17–48) or the death of Gaius (19.113).

of future friction between the troops and the people under direct Roman rule.[67] Second, the courage of the Jewish people faced with such brutality is praised, thereby fulfilling the *Antiquities'* major apologetic aim of commending the nation to Josephus' readers.

Pilate has retreated from significance by the end of the incident. He plays an important role in initiating the conflict by appropriating Temple funds but he quickly recedes to allow the fortitude of the Jews and aggression of the troops to take centre stage. Little attention is paid to Pilate's character here: his actions serve primarily to illustrate Josephus' apologetic interests concerning the Jewish people and the Roman troops.

The third episode, involving 'Jesus, a wise man', or the *Testimonium Flavianum*, has no parallel in the *War*. Unfortunately the whole passage appears to have suffered at the hands of later Christian interpolators and the original wording of this section is now lost.[68] Given the context, the original text probably recorded another disturbance, this time focusing on Jesus or his followers after his death. Whatever the original, the present text adds little to the picture of Pilate in the *Antiquities*. The centre of attention is Jesus and his followers; Pilate is referred to only briefly.

The final story centres on a Samaritan disturbance, again an event which has no parallel in the *War*. The central elements in this event are the activities of the Samaritans and their unnamed leader, a man 'who made light of mendacity and in all his designs catered to the mob' (18.85). Throughout the *Antiquities* the Samaritans receive a poor press – the land of Samaria is constantly seen as the place of apostate Jews and Law-breakers.[69] In the present scene,

---

[67] See later 19.356–66, especially § 366 where Josephus explicitly states that these troops were a source of great disasters to the Jews and later in Florus' time sowed the seeds of war. Also 20.176.

[68] On this passage, its problems and possible solutions, see Bammel, 'Testimonium' and Baras, 'Testimonium'. Bibliography in Feldman, *Antiquities*, vol. 9, pp. 573–5.

[69] See especially 11.306, 340–6. For Josephus' description of their origins see 9.288–91. After the Jewish return from the Babylonian exile, the Samaritans attempted to hinder the reconstruction of the Jerusalem Temple (11.19–30, 83–103) and at first refused to pay tribute for sacrifices in Jerusalem (12.156). The Samaritan temple was built in the time of Alexander the Great, with a 'Law-breaker', Manasses, as its high priest (11.306). According to Josephus, the Samaritans were quick to dedicate this temple to Zeus Hellenios in the time of Antiochus Epiphanes (12.257–64). During a dispute between Jews and Samaritans over which temple had been built according to Mosaic laws, King Ptolemy Philometor decided in favour of the one in Jerusalem. The Samaritan temple was eventually destroyed by Hyrcanus (13.254–6).

despite Josephus' slanderous characterization of its leader, the project initially sounds like a relatively harmless religious expedition. Yet the people appear in arms, assemble at a village and accept many new arrivals. The exact intentions of the Samaritans therefore, including what they planned to do with the vessels once they had found them, become more sinister. That the gathering did in fact have political implications is half admitted by the Samaritan council in front of Vitellius in the sequel (18.88). This event confirms the already established picture in the *Antiquities* of the Samaritans as a devious, untrustworthy and self-seeking nation. This negative description is probably linked with Josephus' praise of his own Jewish nation and a reflection of contemporary Jewish prejudices against their northern neighbours.[70]

Pilate again retreats into the background in this incident: he is depicted as a competent Roman governor putting down a messianic gathering which threatened to disrupt law and order without undue force and executing its leaders.

The Samaritan disturbance contains a sequel describing Pilate's return to Rome. Although this is linked chronologically to the Samaritan incident, it is also a sequel to Pilate's administration generally and his actions with the standards in particular. It is only in the standards incident that the *Antiquities* pays much attention to Pilate himself; there he is portrayed as bent on destroying the Jewish Law by his innovative attempt to introduce standards into Jerusalem. Throughout the last three incidents Pilate has receded into the background whilst other issues or apologetic aims come to the fore. Yet the narrative of the *Antiquities* has repeatedly stressed that an unpleasant fate awaits those who attempt to tamper with the Jewish Law. It is only now, ordered to Rome by Vitellius, that Pilate is called to account for his crimes, not primarily against the Samaritans but against Jewish ancestral customs. There is an interesting textual variant in § 89 which reads Ἰουδαῖοι for Σαμαρεῖται.[71] This would have Pilate sent to account to the Emperor regarding matters with which he was charged by the *Jews*. Although this does not fit the context and clearly it is the Samaritans who are meant, the textual variant gives the correct 'theological sense'. For Josephus it is because of his crimes against

---

[70] On an anti-Samaritan polemic within Judaism see Haacker 'Samaritan'; Montgomery, *Samaritans*, p. 156. See also Matt. 10.5–6, Luke 9.51–6, 10.30–7 (Good Samaritan), 17.11–9.

[71] MS, MWE Lat; see Feldman, *Antiquities*, vol. 9, p. 64, note 1.

the Jewish nation and its Law that Pilate loses his position and only incidentally because of a dispute with the Samaritans.

The council (βουλή) of the Samaritans complained to Vitellius, the legate of Syria, about Pilate's slaughter of Samaritans at Mount Gerizim. They declared that 'it was not as rebels against the Romans but as refugees from the persecution (ὕβρεως) of Pilate that they had met in Tirathana' (§ 88). Throughout Josephus' narrative, the Samaritans have been portrayed as self-seeking and duplicitous. There is therefore no reason to suggest that Josephus sees their present words as the real explanation behind the uprising, or expects his readers to do so. Yet the reference to ὕβρις is significant; the word is often used in Jewish literature of one who will incur God's wrath and suffer divine retribution.[72] Its use recalls Pilate's outrage against the Law and the disruption caused by the standards, an act which leaves Pilate liable to 'disaster' and 'calamity'.[73]

Vitellius, like other Syrian legates in the *Antiquities*, is portrayed positively; they provide a contrast to the harsh and intolerant governors of Judaea.[74] Without further investigation he dispatches Marcellus to Judaea and orders Pilate to Rome to account for himself before Tiberius. This Pilate had no option but to obey and hurried to Rome. The subsequent fate of Pilate is left untold. Josephus notes only that Pilate reached Rome to find Tiberius already dead. Gaius, his successor, 'devised countless attacks upon the *equites*' (to which social group Pilate belonged), 'he deprived [them] of their privileges and expelled them from Rome or put them to death and robbed them of their wealth' (19.3). Whatever happened to Pilate, he did not return to Judaea. His dismissal fits into the *Antiquities'* picture of the judgement which catches up with all those who act against the Jewish Law. The description of Pilate's administration in the *Antiquities* therefore highlights many important rhetorical themes in the work as a whole. Most prevalent is the interest in personal histories and the divine punishment to which the impious are exposed. The courage and devotion to ancestral Law of the Jewish nation is also emphasized, as is the part played by pagan troops in the breakdown of Jewish–Roman relations and Josephus' negative portrayal of the Samaritans.

---

[72] See above, p. 31.
[73] 1.14 and 1.20 cited above, pp. 64–5.
[74] Kreiger, 'Pilatus', p. 74.

The characterization of Pilate in the *Antiquities*

Since Pilate retreats to some extent from a central position in the *Antiquities*' accounts of the aqueduct, Jesus and the Samaritans, we should expect to find his character described most fully in the first incident, that concerning his introduction of standards into Jerusalem. In this event Pilate himself comes to the fore and his character and motivation are described.

Most importantly he is shown as acting against the Jewish Law and subverting Jewish practices (ἐπὶ καταλύσει τῶν νομίμων τῶν Ἰουδαϊκῶν ἐφρόνησε, § 55). That his offence against the Jewish Law was conscious and premeditated is shown by the use of the verb φρονέω, which suggests 'meaning/intending to do something', and by the fact that he set them up at night, without the knowledge of the people (§ 56). Clearly he was aware of the important step which he was undertaking. Josephus stresses that 'our Law forbids the making of images', an assertion which his narrative has stressed on many occasions.[75] He also emphasizes the novelty of Pilate's innovation: 'the previous procurators, when they entered the city, used standards that had no such ornaments. Pilate was the first to bring the images into Jerusalem and set them up'. Pilate in the *Antiquities* therefore consciously and deliberately breaks the Jewish Law by introducing standards containing effigies of Caesar into Jerusalem, an act which no previous governor had dared to do.

By introducing the standards Pilate is compared unfavourably with preceding governors and aligns himself with other characters who attempted to profane or destroy (καταλύω) the Jewish Law such as Antiochus Epiphanes, Herod I or, later, the people of Dora who attempted to place Caesar's statue in the synagogue.[76]

In the *Antiquities*, Pilate gives a reason for his refusal to remove the standards: 'to do so would be an outrage (ὕβρις) to the Emperor' (§ 57). Although Josephus does not condemn due honour being shown to the Emperor, it must not impinge upon or supersede honour shown to God and his laws.[77] The rest of the narrative

---

[75]   For example, 3.91, 8.190–8, 15.274, 329, 17.151, 18.121–2, 19.300–11.

[76]   Antiochus (12.322), Herod (15.274, 281, 388, 16.1), the opponents of the Jews in Ionia (16.37), the people of Dora (19.301). The verb καταλύω is most often used in Josephus to refer to the overthrow of empires, for example, 2.348, 10.30, 74, 108, 113, 208, 248, 11.335, 337, 12.1, 19.173 (Julius Caesar destroying democracy).

[77]   See Josephus' comments on Herod I's reign (15.328) and Petronius' tension between following the orders of Gaius and respecting Jewish customs (18.265–8).

concerning the standards in the *Antiquities* describes a clash between Pilate's stubborn and aggressive determination to honour Caesar, irrespective of Jewish sensitivities, and the determination of the Jews not to allow the governor to jeopardize the peace of the nation by transgressing the Law. Pagan innovations could involve the whole nation and not just the perpetrator in divine retribution and so it was worth suffering, even dying, in an attempt to prevent them.[78] By their calm trust in God the Jews demonstrate the supremacy of their ancestral religion.

Pilate makes no attempt to reason with the crowd; although he takes the magisterial seat (βῆμα, § 57), Josephus records no attempt at dialogue. Instead the prefect has already concealed troops in the stadium. There is no gradual escalation of intimidation in the *Antiquities'* account such as was the case in the *War*. Pilate resorts to outright aggression faster, surrounding the crowd with his troops and threatening them with death.

In exactly the same way as in the *War*, Pilate is astonished at the strength of Jewish devotion to their laws. Yet the effect of the change in Pilate is intensified in the *Antiquities'* account. The man who would have subverted Jewish practices and put down Jewish resistance by force is suddenly astounded by the strength of Jewish religious feeling. The active verb (ἐπανεκόμισεν) almost gives the impression that Pilate, in his amazement and haste to rectify his actions, removed the standards himself.[79]

Yet Pilate's amazement at the people's devotion is short-lived; in the very next episode he again openly treats Jewish religious sensitivities with contempt by his use of Temple funds for the aqueduct. Here, however, he appears in a better, or at least more neutral, light than in the *War*. He is said to have spent (ἔπραξεν) money from the sacred treasury, rather than using it up entirely as the *War* suggests. In the *Antiquities* it is the sight of the angry mob which induces Pilate to send in his troops, whereas in the *War* they were already in position, implying that Pilate had expected trouble. Again in the *Antiquities* Pilate gives the people a chance to withdraw after he has secretly stationed his men, whilst such an offer was absent from the *War*. Pilate's harshness here has been toned down to point up the brutality of his troops.

In the following two narratives, Pilate is faced with two uprisings

---

[78] See 15.280–91.
[79] In *JW* 2.174, Pilate gives orders for the removal of the standards.

not directly caused by his own actions. Acting on accusations formulated by 'men of the highest standing amongst us' (τῶν πρώτων ἀνδρῶν παρ' ἡμῖν), Pilate condemned Jesus to crucifixion (§ 64). The governor appears to be competently putting down some kind of uprising by executing its leader. He handles the Samaritan uprising in a similar way. Given the armed nature of the gathering it is hardly surprising that Pilate takes preventative measures, blocking the projected route to the mountain summit with a detachment of cavalry and heavy-armed infantry (ἱππέων τε πομπῇ καὶ ὁπλιτῶν); whether the prefect himself is actually present is not clear. This time the troops are not accused of over-aggression; they slay some and put others to flight. Pilate's subsequent response, however, does seem rather heavy handed: not only does he execute the leaders of the uprising but he takes the opportunity to rid himself of some of the more influential amongst the fugitives.

Although Pilate is portrayed as a reasonably competent governor, unwilling to use an undue amount of force in maintaining peace in his province in the last two episodes, his dominant characterization in the *Antiquities* derives from the first episode where he is shown as deliberately acting against the Jewish Law.

Finally, how does Pilate compare with other Roman governors in the *Antiquities*? As noted earlier, the Judaean governors play an important part in the gradual disintegration of the country into revolt. They are implicated in the rise of brigandage in the *Antiquities* to a far greater extent than in the *War*. In particular, none is said to have abstained from interfering with the country's laws. Cuspius Fadus attempted to compel the people to hand the high priestly vestments over to Roman custody, whilst Tiberius Alexander (a former Jew) is charged with not standing by the religious practices of his people.[80] Cumanus too receives a poorer report: he is said to have incited the people and accepted bribery.[81] Felix unlawfully married a Jewess named Drusilla.[82] Already

[80] 20.6–9 (Fadus); 20.100 (Alexander). Compare the description of these two men in *JW* 2.220.
[81] 20.105–12, 118–25. Josephus correspondingly paints a better picture of the Jewish crowd during his time of office. In the first incident (20.105–12) he omits their stone-throwing and in the dispute between the Samaritans and Jews he neglects to mention the massacre of Samaritans by Jews recorded in *JW* 2.235. This gives the impression that Cumanus' attacks were less provoked.
[82] 20.141–4.

during his governorship matters were going from bad to worse with the land infested with brigands and impostors. The governor added to the general deterioration by bribing the *sicarii* to have the high priest Jonathan murdered: when this act went unpunished, the brigands slaughtered indiscriminantly with 'perfect impunity'. Josephus sees a link, even at this relatively early stage, between the impious acts of the brigands, left to run riot by Felix, and God's bringing the Romans to purify the city.[83] Eventually, Felix's administration had sunk to such a level of corruption that it was 'as if no one was in charge of the city'.[84] On his arrival Festus found the city still devastated by brigands. He ordered the Jews to pull down a wall which they had built to prevent the activity of the Temple priests being seen from Agrippa's palace but was prevented by Nero who on this occasion upheld the wishes of the Jews.[85]

The only procurator who is described in better terms in the *Antiquities* is Albinus. Although he is said to have released many prisoners 'for a personal consideration' before he left, so infesting the land with brigands, in general his character is not described in such negative terms as in the *Jewish War* (2.272–6). Perhaps this is because in the *War* Josephus places the blame only on the last two governors, Albinus' governorship therefore has to herald a sudden deterioration in Jewish–Roman relations. Josephus does not record any specific incidents from Albinus' time to substantiate his claims in the *War*, instead making only generalized allegations. In the *Antiquities*, however, Albinus' procuratorship takes its place after other corrupt governors and when conditions have already deteriorated substantially. There is therefore not the same need to place a great deal of blame on Albinus' character in particular and Josephus is content to relate only a couple of incidents involving the procurator. He is followed by Florus who receives the same condemnation in the *Antiquities* as in the *War*: 'it was Florus who constrained us to take up war with the Romans'.[86]

Pilate's term of office therefore plays a much more important role in the *Antiquities* than in the *War*. He is the first of a succession of Roman governors who, by disregarding the Jewish Law, help to push the country towards open revolt and so incur God's wrath upon the nation.

[83] 20.160–6.   [84] 20.180   [85] 20.185–7, 193–6.   [86] 20.252–7.

Summary

The governorship of Pilate illustrates many rhetorical aims of the *Antiquities*. Jewish religious devotion and endurance are stressed in the first two episodes; the part played by Roman troops in the deterioration of conditions leading to the revolt is emphasized in the aqueduct affair; and the generally negative picture of the Samaritans is sustained in Josephus' description of their uprising. The characterization of Pilate itself merges with an important apologetic interest of the *Antiquities*, the interest in personal history and the relationship between guilt and fate, particularly in relation to the Jewish Law. Pilate is portrayed as setting himself up against that Law. Despite his generally competent handling of different situations throughout his governorship it is this attitude which ultimately determines his fate and leads to his removal from the province.

The historical events

Despite his strong personal and nationalistic interests, Josephus aimed at historical accuracy throughout his narratives.[87] Modern archaeology has confirmed the veracity of many of Josephus' descriptions of places and buildings whilst research into his use of sources suggests that he adhered closely to their substance and main contents.[88] As long as Josephus' theological and rhetorical tendencies are borne in mind, it should thus be possible to reconstruct something of the historical events behind his narrative.

[87] See his claims in *JW* 1.3, 16, 7.455 and *Ant.* 20.157.

[88] For a survey of modern research into Josephus' value as a historian see especially Bilde, *Flavius*, pp. 191–200. What sources were at Josephus' disposal for his description of Pilate's administration is uncertain. The *War* appears to be based only on personal recollection at this point (see *JW* 1.18). The narrative of Nicolas of Damascus upon which the lengthy description of Herod I is based appears to end with the accession of Archelaus in 2.111: cf. Thackeray, *Jewish*, vol. 2, p. 364, note a. In the *Antiquities* Josephus (and his assistants) rely on a great many more sources, ranging from scripture to official edicts and lists of high priests. Winter (Trial, p. 74, note 7) suggests that details of what occurred in Judaea under Pilate were derived from a written source, 'some sort of chronology composed by a contemporary of Pilate'. Yet such a written source is not necessary – Josephus would presumably have heard stories relating to Pilate's governorship from his family and older contemporaries when he was in Judaea and Galilee. For a survey of modern investigations displaying Josephus' careful use of his sources see Bilde, *Flavius*, pp. 98–9.

The standards

Date

Due to its position at the beginning of the account of Pilate's administration in both *War* and *Antiquities*, the prefect's introduction of troops with iconic standards into Jerusalem is generally assumed to have occurred early on in his term of office.[89] Although there is no direct evidence linking it to Pilate's first year (i.e. 26), his behaviour does give the impression of a new governor testing public opinion and the incident probably happened in the first winter of his term as Judaean governor.

Pilate's actions

Josephus describes the objects of offence in differing ways in the two books. In *Jewish War* 2.169 Pilate introduces 'effigies of Caesar (εἰκόνας) which are called standards (σημαῖαι)'; in § 174 the standards (σημαῖαι) are removed. In *Antiquities* 18.55, however, it is the busts of Caesar (προτομὰς Καίσαρος) attached to the standards (σημαῖαι) which cause offence; in § 57 the people ask Pilate to remove the images (εἰκόνας) and in § 59 it is the images (εἰκόνας) which are removed. Despite the differences in terminology, C. H. Kraeling, in his important article on the subject, identifies these as iconic *signa* belonging to an infantry cohort.[90]

A squadron's standards were both sacred and necessary; they identified the unit and expressed its allegiance to the state and its religion. It would have been unthinkable for a governor to bring in a detachment without its standards or to dictate what adornments these should bear.[91] Pilate must therefore have introduced an entirely new cohort into Jerusalem either to supplement, or to replace, the existing force in the city. This new cohort, perhaps as a sign of honour, had standards which contained images of the Emperor and had not previously been deployed in Jerusalem by Pilate's predecessors (*Ant.* 18.56). The Jewish request that the

---

[89] See Kraeling, 'Episode', pp. 282–3; Feldman, *Antiquities*, vol. 9, p. 42 note e and Smallwood, *Jews*, p. 161.

[90] Kraeling, 'Episode', pp. 269–73.

[91] On standards belonging to auxiliary troops see Kraeling, 'Episode'; Spiedel, 'Roman Army', pp. 224–32; Watson, *Roman Soldier*, pp. 129–31; Webster, *Roman Imperial*, pp. 136–48; Maxfield, *Military Decorations*, pp. 218–34.

standards be removed was synonymous with a request for the removal of the whole unit.[92]

A more difficult question is: Why did Pilate introduce these particular troops? Josephus' answer in the *Antiquities*, of course, is that Pilate deliberately acted to subvert Jewish customs. Yet the *War* gives no indication of this intention and it would be difficult to imagine a provincial governor, however harsh, deliberately initiating his administration with such a provocative move, one which, in the inevitable public discontent, could only jeopardize his own position. S. G. F. Brandon suggests that such a departure from the practice of previous governors could only have come from those who appointed Pilate; yet if this were the case it is surprising that he was apparently able to issue orders to withdraw the troops without prior consultation with his authorities.[93] As military prefect of Judaea, Pilate would presumably have full authority to deploy troops where he wanted.

An important consideration in interpreting Pilate's actions here is that Josephus, writing as a Jew, lays particular emphasis on the *images* whilst Pilate, as a Roman prefect, was in all probability interested only in *troops*. The governor's decision to alter the garrison would have been determined by practical military considerations.[94] The decision to send in one particular unit could quite easily have been made before the new governor realized, or before it was pointed out to him, that this particular squadron could not be used in Jerusalem because its standards were offensive to the people. It might have appeared absurdly oversensitive to the Roman prefect that standards which were perfectly acceptable in Caesarea were not tolerated in Jerusalem and that certain standards would be allowed whilst others would not. Irritation that such religious scruples hindered his free deployment of troops may have led to Pilate's determination that the Jerusalemites would have to accept whatever troops he, as their prefect, decided to use. There may also have been an element of bringing Judaea into line with

[92] Later, in *Ant.* 18.120–2, the Jewish leaders complain to Vitellius about the images (εἰκόνας) on the standards belonging to his troops. His solution is similarly not to remove the offending *images* but to order the *whole army* to take a different route.

[93] Brandon, *Jesus*, p. 69. The six days at Caesarea (during the winter according to *Antiquities*) would not have been long enough to contact either the Emperor or the Syrian legate. Brandon raises Sejanus as a possibility for the instruction but admits that it is impossible to identify the ultimate source of responsibility.

[94] Kraeling, 'Episode', p. 295.

other provinces, none of which dictated to the governor on military matters or refused to accept imperial portraits.[95] Pilate therefore placed his free use of troops above considering the religious sensitivities of his people. He probably thought that the expedient of bringing the troops in under cover of night would be enough to avert demonstrations: the people, faced with the garrison and its offending standards already installed, would have to accept matters.[96]

Offending against the Jewish Law, then, was not Pilate's prime intention,[97] though his actions do show arrogance and contempt towards the people and their customs, linked with an underestimation of the strength of their religious feeling. Anxious to take no nonsense from the people, Pilate's actions seem designed to establish from the start both his own superior position in the province and that of the Empire which he served.

The Jewish objection

This demonstration of the superiority of Rome may shed some light on the Jewish objection. Ostensibly, of course, Josephus has taken pains in both accounts to explain that the people were concerned only with the presence of offensive images in Jerusalem; once these had been removed they were quite content.[98] Yet in all probability this represents only half the story. All Roman standards, whether iconic or not, were objects of worship and sacred to

[95] McGing links Pilate's behaviour here with his coins on which he changed existing policy by introducing types which were new to Judaea but well known in the rest of the Empire: cf. 'Pontius', p. 434. On his coins, however, Pilate showed a concern to combine both Roman and Jewish symbols, one on each side. The introduction of iconic standards shows no attempt to compromise with Jewish feelings. The coins date from after this incident (28–31) and perhaps reflect lessons learnt from the encounter. The Jewish people would not object to Roman aniconic symbols as long as they did not feel that their own religious/national identity was being compromised.

[96] The fact that Pilate was in Caesarea at the time of the change of troops and did not come to Jerusalem illustrates both that he did not want to draw undue public attention to the change of guard and also that he probably did not expect a great deal of public unrest.

[97] As Smallwood (Jews, p. 161) notes, there is no hint, even in *Antiquities*, that Pilate deliberately tried to introduce Emperor worship into the city.

[98] In *Antiquities* Josephus states that the Law forbids the making of images (εἰκόνων ποίησιν); in the *War* it is the erection of an image in Jerusalem (ἐν τῇ πόλει δείκηλον) which is not allowed.

the unit which they represented.[99] This cultic importance could surely not have escaped the observation of the Jewish people, accustomed to the presence of Roman troops in their land for several decades.[100] The permanent garrison housed in the Antonia fortress in Jerusalem would have been religiously offensive due to the worship of the standards and also politically and nationalistically objectionable in that they were a permanent reminder of Israel's subjugation to a foreign power. This was probably always the case, ever since the days of Coponius. In general, however, the people were powerless to alter the situation: to demand the removal of the standards, and with them the troops, would at best have had no effect on the Romans for whom the Jerusalem garrison was vital in the effective policing of the nation, especially during festivals, and could at worst be construed as resisting Roman policy in the province. Hitherto the people had no alternative but to accept the Roman garrison. But with Pilate's introduction of iconic standards the situation changed in the Jews' favour. Now they had a specific grievance to bring against the troops in the Antonia: their standards contravened the Jewish law banning images, a law which had been respected by previous Roman governors. In practice, as we have seen elsewhere, first-century Judaism tended to be selective and flexible regarding what offended against the second commandment.[101] The extreme anti-iconic tendency within Judaism to which Josephus' writings attest may be a reflection of resurgent nationalism in the early days of the revolt and not a dominant feature of conditions forty years previously. But iconic standards positioned

---

[99] On the cultic nature of standards see Tertullian *Apol* 16.8; Pliny *NH* 13.3(4).23; Dionysius of Halicarnassus 6.45.2 and Tacitus *Ann.* 1.39.7, 2.17.2. Roman troops sacrificed to their standards after the capture of Jerusalem, *JW* 6.316. Josephus is our only source for such a practice; its purpose was presumably to demonstrate the supremacy of the gods of the cohort over Yahweh, as was the case with the setting up of standards on the walls at Jerusalem (6.403). For a fuller discussion on standards see Kraeling, 'Episode', pp. 275–6.

[100] Ibid., p. 281, and Smallwood, *Jews*, p. 161, suggest that it was the iconic standards which made the people realize that all such *signa* were objects of worship. However, it seems incredible that the nature and significance of these standards were unknown to people familiar with experiences and stories of Roman military expeditions for almost a century.

[101] C. Roth ('Ordinance', pp. 170–1) argues that there is no contemporary evidence for the pre-war period to suggest that there was a complete and effective ban on non-human effigies for decorative purposes. Gutmann ('Second Commandment', p. 174), too, argues that a rigidly and uniformly anti-iconic attitude throughout biblical and Hellenistic-Roman times 'remains a myth'. See also Goodenough, *Jewish Symbols*, vols. 1–13 and Lémonon, *Pilate*, pp. 151–2.

in close proximity to the Temple and used in pagan cultic worship would undoubtedly have been religiously offensive to many.[102] The people would also have been united by the threat that previously safeguarded rights were being infringed by a new Roman governor: not only were the hated pagan troops and their standards still in the Antonia fortress, but now their cultic objects contained images of the Emperor. The toleration extended to their Law could be used by the people as a front for demands which, though certainly accommodating an important religious dimension, also had a nationalistic element. The appeal to the Law was therefore, at least to some extent, a cover for a more political demand regarding the removal of the troops. Writing an apology for Judaism to subjects of the Empire, Josephus has naturally covered up the political aspect of the affair.[103]

Events at Caesarea

Josephus' presentation of the Jewish demonstration is obviously heavily coloured by his apologetic aims. J. McLaren is doubtless correct in assuming that the protest was not as spontaneous as Josephus relates; certain individuals would have been involved in its organization and the crowd would have aired their grievances through spokesmen.[104] Possibly the chief priests and aristocracy were involved. Nor was it in all probability as completely passive as Josephus would have us believe (as Pilate's use of the word θορυβεῖν in fact betrays), though there is no reason to see a resort to arms. The people seem to have engaged in a relatively quiet protest in Caesarea, putting their case before the governor for six days.

Quite how far Pilate was aware of the various motives making up

[102] As a contravention of the laws of Exod. 20.4 and Deut. 5.8. The fact that later tradition magnified the event into an attack on the *Temple* underlines the sense of violation which the people must have felt at the outrageous introduction of the standards. See in particular Eusebius, *Chron.* 19, *D.E.* 8.2, 122–3; Origen, *In Matt.* 17.25 and Jerome, *In Matt* 24.15. *Megillat Taanit* may also refer to this incident when it records that on 3 Kislev (Nov/Dec) 'the images were removed from the Temple court'. See Smallwood, *Jews*, pp. 161–2, note 62 and Zeitlin, *Megillat Taanit*, pp. 239, 244, 259–61.

[103] See Gutmann ('Second Commandment', p. 170) who cites *Against Apion* 2.6.

[104] McLaren, *Power*, p. 84. He, however, regards this incident as identical with that described by Philo, *Embassy* 299–305. The spokesmen would therefore have been the four Herodians. For further discussion on the identification of the two accounts see p. 39, note 67.

the Jewish demand is difficult to judge. Possibly he was aware of the political and nationalistic elements in the request. This might underlie his protest (recorded only in *Ant.* 18.57) that the removal of the standards would be an act of dishonour or outrage to the Emperor. For a Roman military commander to allow his subjects to dictate which troops he could station in the province's ancient capital would indeed be an insult to the *imperium* invested in him by the Emperor. This sense of outrage would be heightened all the more when the dispute concerned images of the Emperor himself and troops which had possibly gained the honour of imperial effigies by military distinction.[105] Yet a provincial governor would presumably be equally anxious not to inaugurate his governorship by a breach of a national law which was generally tolerated by Rome. The Jewish delegation had a strong case: they could appeal to their scriptures for support of the law prohibiting the worship of images. Pilate was in a difficult situation. Was he to insist on his own right to deploy freely any military unit in the ancient capital, or was he to uphold Rome's policy of toleration regarding ethnic religions? The first major incident in the career of any new ruler serves as the basis for relations between the ruler and the people in the ensuing administration. Pilate began with a demonstration of disregard for the ancestral customs of the Jews and precedents set by previous governors. Yet the people seem to have been equally anxious to show the new governor that they would not tolerate such action when it clearly offended against their Law.

Josephus' accounts give the impression that Pilate stubbornly sat out the Jewish demonstration, waiting for the people to tire and disperse. But the time may have been spent more profitably: Jewish deputies may have explained their religious objections to the standards to the governor whilst he reviewed the situation and what the practical implications of removing the troops would be.

[105] Later in his administration Pilate was faced with a similar problem concerning the gilded shields, narrated by Philo. In that case, too, he protested that the removal of the shields would be an insult to the Emperor. But there the people demanded the removal of shields which had been set up specifically in honour of Caesar; by removing the shields Pilate ran a very real risk of appearing to dishonour the Emperor. It was thus necessary in that case to involve the Emperor in the decision to remove the shields, particularly in the dangerous political climate of the early 30s. In the case of the standards, however, it would be extremely unlikely that Pilate used troops whose standards contained images of the Emperor in order to honour him: practical military questions would have been to the fore when picking the troops. It was therefore safe for Pilate to remove the troops without prior consultation with Tiberius.

Eventually he seems to have decided on a test of public opinion, intimidating the people with his troops to see how far they were prepared to go in upholding their laws. Impressed by their determination not to allow the new governor to contravene their laws and, if the demonstration was anything like the scale Josephus describes, perhaps annoyed that the people were neglecting their work, Pilate ordered the removal of the unit from Jerusalem.[106] The depth of Jewish religious and nationalistic feeling, which he had seriously underestimated, was brought home to him by their restrained protest. In this first clash with the people, Pilate probably realized that their determination matched his own. However, he eventually puts law and order in the province above personal pride: he shows enough flexibility to rescind his orders and replace the troops.[107] Self-interested motives may also have played their part: it would not have looked good in Rome if one of Pilate's first acts as governor was to massacre unarmed people.

The aqueduct

Pilate's crime

The building of an aqueduct to provide Jerusalem and its Temple with a constant water supply sounds like a perfectly commendable endeavour. The relevant passages in the *War* and the *Antiquities* give the impression that it was not so much the aqueduct itself that caused offence but something connected with it. The *Antiquities* rather vaguely notes that the people 'did not acquiesce in the operations which this involved' (οἱ δ᾽οὐκ ἠγάπων τοῖς ἀμφὶ τὸ ὕδωρ δρωμένοις, § 60). The 'operations' here could refer either to Pilate's use of the Temple money or to the actual construction of the aqueduct. The *War* may throw some important light on this. Here Pilate not only 'spent' money from the treasury as in the *Antiquities* but he 'used up' (ἐξαναλίσκων) the money on an aqueduct of 400 furlongs;[108] the people were 'indignant at this proceeding' (πρὸς τοῦτο τοῦ πλήθους ἀγανάκτησις ἦν). The im-

[106] E. P. Sanders (*Judaism*, p. 284), sees an attitude throughout Judaism from Hasmonaean times to Bar Kochba expressing willingness to die rather than transgress ancestral Law, for example, *Test. of Moses* 9.6; Philo, *Hypothetica* 6.9.
[107] McLaren (*Power*, p. 83), also sees Pilate's actions here as a sign of flexibility. McGing ('Pontius', p. 429) sees it as a sign of 'weakness, a willingness to give in'.
[108] In the *Antiquities* the distance is given as 200 furlongs. For two possible archaeological remains of Pilate's aqueduct see Lémonon, *Pilate*, pp. 168–70.

plication in the *War* is that it was not the construction of the aqueduct which caused offence but Pilate's misuse of Temple funds, the fact that he had 'used up' or completely drained the available resources. These funds, known as *Corbonas*, were primarily used for sacrificial purposes.[109]

How did Pilate obtain the money? Although the administration of the treasury lay essentially in the hands of the priests,[110] during Roman rule there was a certain amount of political supervision by the governor.[111] Even so, if Pilate had taken Temple funds by force, Josephus' account would doubtless have been written in a completely different way, expressing his horror that a pagan governor had violated the Temple. Pilate must therefore have had the co-operation (whether voluntary or coerced) of the Temple authorities.

Some explanation may be thrown on the proceedings by m.Shek 4.2 which allows the use of surplus money from the treasury to be used for 'all the city's needs'. The dating of this ruling is uncertain but it is possible that it, or a similar earlier ruling, was in force in the first century. If this was the case then Pilate's use of the surplus for improving the city's water supply would presumably have been permitted. The Temple treasurers would have handed over the surplus from their funds to pay for the new aqueduct. Whilst the *War*'s use of the verb ἐξαναλίσκω may be over-exaggerated, problems seem to have arisen when Pilate began to demand more than the surplus for his venture. Building projects are notorious for requiring more money than initially expected; perhaps the aqueduct began to require more and more funds which Pilate continued to demand from the Temple treasurers, eventually using up more than the allowable surplus and draining the supplies for the daily sacrifices. Perhaps, too, Pilate began to take his use of the money

---

[109] For the composition of the Temple treasury, which included gold, silver, materials, priests' garments and huge sums of money, see Schürer, *History*, vol. 2, pp. 279–84.

[110] The money was administered by treasurers known as γαζοφυλάκες (*Ant.* 15.408, 18.93) drawn from amongst the priests. See Schürer, *History*, vol. 2, p. 281 and Lémonon, *Pilate*, p. 167. Lémonon (ibid., p. 168) also thinks Pilate worked alongside the priests, as does McGing ('Pontius', p. 429). The treasury consisted of the half-shekel annual tax payable by every male Jew over 20 (Exod. 30.14–5), not only from Palestine but all over the Empire (*Ant.* 14.215, 16.163, *Embassy* 156), and also gifts. See Lémonon (ibid. p. 165) for further details.

[111] Schürer, *History*, vol. 2, pp. 283–4. In *Ant.* 20.15 besides the right to name high priests, Herod of Chalcis received authority over the Temple and the holy vessels. Schürer (ibid., p. 284) suggests this authority previously lay with the Roman governors: 'as in the administration of the treasury, so in the completion of the Temple buildings the priestly and political powers worked together'.

for granted, demanding and expecting that the priests would hand it over to him and treating it as his own *fiscus* rather than sacred money from the holy Temple.[112]

The Jewish objection

Unlike the incident with the standards, the Jewish objection here does not appear to have been spontaneous. The people wait for Pilate to visit Jerusalem before voicing their grievances. The aqueduct appears to have been already under way, if not already completed, when the riot breaks out. The occasion of Pilate's visit may have been a feast or even the opening of the aqueduct. The nature of the Jewish objection described by Josephus fits well with Pilate's conjectured 'crime' outlined above. Resentment at the prefect's use of the Temple funds took some time to brew. Some may never have been happy about the arrangement from the start, unwilling to see sacred money being handed over to a pagan governor; others may have accepted the arrangement initially but as Pilate demanded more than simply the surplus they became disillusioned and angry. Some may have been ready to jump at any chance to engage in anti-Roman riots; others may have favoured the arrangement, thinking that it was better to use surplus Temple money rather than be required to pay a new tax for the undertaking. Gradually, however, many of the people seem to have become irritated at what appeared to be Pilate's continual use, even control, of their treasury. If his use of the money went so far as to requisition resources reserved for the sacrifices, then this too would have been a serious ground for complaint.

How widespread was Jewish resentment and hostility towards Pilate's undertaking? The *War* gives the impression that a great number (τὸ πλῆθος) joined forces to surround Pilate and make their grievances known. The *Antiquities*, however, gives the impression that not all were involved in the riot; only some hurled insults and abuse, and in § 62 there is a reference to those who were not rioting. Yet both these accounts may have been influenced by

---

[112] This is suggested by Lémonon who also thinks the fact that the high priestly vestments were in Roman control added to the hostility. The Roman governor would appear not to be content with controlling the use of the vestments but also treating the Temple treasury as his own private funds. He also suggests that Pilate's initiation of the affair may have caused offence and that his decision would have left the priests with very little chance to object: cf. *Pilate*, p. 168.

Josephus' particular apologetic aims: the *War* illustrating the disastrous effects when large numbers of people turn to rioting; the *Antiquities* (in an attempt to glorify the nation) exonerating some of the people involved and stressing that they were unarmed. Neither statement can therefore be taken at face value.

Two features of the story, however, suggest that the account in the *Antiquities* may be a more accurate reflection of the historical situation. First, the 'crime' itself. It would be readily understandable if the people were divided over the extent to which they saw Pilate's behaviour as an infringement of their Law or native rights. The same division of the community appears to have occurred later in the differing attitudes towards the shields set up by Pilate in his residence in Jerusalem.[113] Second, Pilate's methods of dealing with the problem (§ 2.176). If the prefect had been met with large-scale rioting the obvious course of action would be to bring in his troops and intimidate the people into submission. Sending 'plain-clothes men' into such a situation could have been disastrous: once a soldier had exposed which side he was on by clubbing a rioter, he would be open to attack from the surrounding Jews. On a large scale, Pilate would be sending his men into a potentially highly dangerous situation. It seems more likely that this was a large crowd in which only a more extreme element were rioting. In this case, Pilate's policing actions would make sense.[114] A large display of troops to intimidate the people would be out of place in such a scene; but disguised troops who could unobtrusively move through the crowd and deal with troublemakers without causing undue panic would be perfect. Although a large crowd had gathered about the governor, therefore, not everyone was rioting.[115]

The 'plain-clothes men' with their clubs raise one more question: Did Pilate expect trouble, knowing that he had caused offence by his use of treasury funds? Even if his use of the money was justified and relations with the Temple authorities were initially perfectly cordial, he would in all likelihood gradually become aware that resentment at his excessive use of the fund was building up. Pilate may not have expected a mass protest, but the men were necessary for any hostility which might break out. The governor here shows a

---

[113] See above, pp. 42–3.

[114] Brandon (*Jesus*, p. 76, note 3) similarly sees Pilate's actions as having more in common with a police rather than a military operation.

[115] McLaren (*Power*, p. 86) also sees a split in the reaction of various Jews to the building project, though he bases his arguments on *Ant.* 18.62.

reluctance to use an excessive amount of force, though his methods led to panic amongst the people.

This incident demonstrates a certain degree of co-operation between Pilate and the Jewish religious authorities. The aqueduct would have been beneficial not only to the inhabitants of Jerusalem but also for the Temple; possibly it was initially designed as a joint venture to promote good relations between the governor and the people. But the increasing debts incurred by the project and perhaps an overbearing, demanding manner from Pilate eventually led to opposition.[116] The precise date of this event is unknown; according to Josephus' chronology it must have occurred between 26 CE and the death of Jesus (generally assumed to have been in either 30 or 33).

The execution of Jesus

The *Testimonium Flavianum* adds little to our picture of the historical Pilate. The governor has only the messianic leader executed, not his followers. Probably Pilate thought that by executing the ringleader the disturbance would die down. Again, this shows a dislike of excessive violence. As earlier in the aqueduct incident, Pilate is shown working closely with the Jewish hierarchy.[117]

The Samaritan uprising and Pilate's return to Rome

The Samaritan uprising

Before assessing Pilate's actions it is necessary to consider exactly what the Samaritan disturbance involved.[118] Central to Samaritan thought was the idea that Mount Gerizim was Israel's one true sanctuary;[119] it was the only place where sacrifice was acceptable

[116] For another building project connected with Pilate see the description of his Tiberiéum in Caesarea, p. 12 above.

[117] A fuller historical discussion of this particular event will be reserved until after the gospel accounts.

[118] For Samaritan theology see especially MacDonald, *Theology*; Montgomery, *Samaritans*; Haacker, 'Samaritan'; Bowman 'Early Samaritan', pp. 63–72.

[119] This comprised the tenth Samaritan commandment. Although the mountain is only referred to twice in the Pentateuch, the Samaritans found scores of implicit references to it and its status as Israel's true cultic centre.

and prayers and praise efficacious. Even after Hyrcanus destroyed the Samaritan temple the beliefs associated with the mountain continued. It was equated with Bethel, the gateway to heaven; many of the patriarchs were believed to have their tombs on or near the mountain. The *Samaritan Chronicles* assert that God hid the ark of the covenant and sacred cultic vessels in a cave on Mount Gerizim at a time of divine disfavour inaugurated by the wicked priest Eli.[120] Samaritan eschatology centred upon a figure known as the Taheb whose function was to act as a restorer or revealer of the truth. He was seen as the prophet like Moses referred to in Deuteronomy 18.18 (or sometimes *Moses redivivus*) in contrast to the Davidic Messiah of Judaea.[121] This figure was expected to reveal the ark and the vessels on Gerizim in preparation for true worship on the mountain and the inauguration of a period of peace and prosperity for the Samaritan nation.[122]

Josephus' description of Samaritan activities in Tirathana[123] have obvious parallels with such expectations. The unnamed Samaritan seems to have posed as the expected Taheb and persuaded the people that he could reveal the ark and restore true worship to the mountain.

Although bereft of a sanctuary, the Samaritan high priest and priesthood continued to sacrifice on Mount Gerizim in the first century. Each year the people climbed the mountain three times to celebrate the three great pilgrimage feasts: Tabernacles, Passover and Weeks.[124] It is possible that the first-century 'Taheb' appeared before one of these established feasts. Or, perhaps more probably, he may have appeared shortly before the Day of Atonement (10th Tishri), the most important Samaritan feast and the day on which the Taheb was to make a proper atonement for Israel and to

[120] This is also attested in the fourth-century Samaritan work *Memar Markah* 77b. The belief is probably much older and in all likelihood lies behind the passage in Josephus; see Montgomery, *Samaritans*, p. 239. A corresponding Jewish belief is to be found in 2 Macc. 2.4–8. For a brief survey of Samaritan literature see Anderson, 'Samaritans', pp. 945–6.

[121] See John 4.25 and Collins, 'Hidden', on the Taheb and the traditions behind the hidden vessels.

[122] The biblical warrant for this was found in Deut. 27.2–3; MacDonald, *Theology*, p. 330.

[123] Montgomery locates this as modern Tire, 4m S.W. of Shechem: cf. *Samaritans*, p. 146, note 15.

[124] See Bowman ,'Pilgrimage', pp. 17–28. Only every seven years were all the people expected to appear before God; generally only selected groups attended.

establish the period of divine favour.[125] Although this new age was to be one of peace, the Samaritans may have expected opposition in their ascent of the mountain and so were armed.[126] Some texts envisage an eschatological war between the Taheb and Israel's enemies before the restoration of true worship. If such a view were current in the first century this would provide an additional, and more ominous, necessity for the arms.

But such a 'religious' movement would inevitably lead to repercussions on a political level. A Roman governor could not allow such a potentially dangerous movement to escalate. Pilate was therefore acting well within his rights as the protector of Roman law and order in the province by intervening in the situation. As B. C. McGing notes: 'a Roman governor who did not deal with the situation firmly would be failing seriously in his duty'.[127] Pilate's actions do not seem unnecessarily severe. According to Josephus he sent in 'a detachment of cavalry and heavy-armed infantry'; they are not sent to the village but to block the path up the mountain (§ 87). The aim was not to massacre the people but simply to stop their intended course of action. Nor does the military intervention appear particularly harsh.[128] Certainly Josephus does not mention huge losses; his note that some were killed in a pitched battle whilst the others fled gives the impression that the majority were put to flight. Of the remaining prisoners, Pilate put to death the leaders and most influential people; here again he was well within his rights as provincial governor to judge and execute anyone threatening the stability of the province. This incident must have occurred in 36 CE, possibly just prior to the Day of Atonement celebrated in September. This would allow time for Vitellius' decision to send Pilate to Rome and the prefect's arrival in the city shortly after March 37.[129]

---

[125] See MacDonald, *Theology*, p. 267; Bowman, 'Early Samaritan', p. 63.

[126] MacDonald, *Theology*, p. 363. Later, during the revolt (67 CE), large numbers of Samaritans again assembled on Mount Gerizim ready for a conflict with Rome, giving way only when the water supply ran out. This assembly may also have been messianically and nationalistically inspired.

[127] McGing, 'Pilate', p. 433.

[128] There does not seem to be any justification for Lémonon's comment that the soldiers behaved as brutally here as in the aqueduct affair. Besides, the alleged brutality of the soldiers in the latter may owe more to Josephus' apologetic than to historical reality, *Pilate*, p. 237.

[129] For the date of Pilate's return to Rome see p. 1 above.

Pilate's departure

The council (βουλή)[130] of the Samaritans complained to Vitellius, the legate of Syria, about Pilate's handling of the Mount Gerizim affair. The legate would be the first, and most obvious, arbitrator when dissension arose between the governor of Judaea and the people.[131] The Samaritans alleged that they assembled not as rebels against Rome but as refugees from Pilate's persecution. This supports the suggestion that they were about to embark on a messianic trek with the unnamed Samaritan as Moses at their head; the messianic aspect (and so the potential threat to Rome) has been carefully omitted.

Josephus gives the impression that Vitellius dispatched Marcellus and sent Pilate to Rome immediately. It is perhaps more likely that some exchange between Pilate and the legate occurred. Pilate would obviously have given his side of the story, how the uprising had appeared to threaten Roman stability in that part of the province and how he felt it was necessary to quell it; the Samaritans would have stressed the religious nature of their protest, charging Pilate with ruling unbearably harshly. Vitellius wisely decided to refer the case to the Emperor: later Quadratus, faced with contradictory stories from Jews, Samaritans and Cumanus similarly decided to send the governor and representatives from the two nations to Claudius.[132] There is no indication that Vitellius thought that Pilate was to blame; he may have simply wanted both sides to have a hearing at the highest level so that no repercussions could ensue, especially when one of the issues at stake was the quality of rule by a Roman official. In any case, Vitellius was not competent either to dismiss Pilate or to appoint a successor.[133]

What would have happened to Pilate if Tiberius' death had not intervened before his return to Rome is unknown: the Samaritans had maintained good relations with the Romans and the Emperor respected the religious traditions of ethnic groups.[134] As J. P. Lémonon has argued, however, the fact that Gaius did not reap-

---

[130] On the Samaritan council see Montgomery, *Samaritans*, pp. 87–8.

[131] See p. 5 above.

[132] *Ant.* 20.132, *JW* 2.244.

[133] On Marcellus/Marullus see above, p. 8, note 42.

[134] They had not revolted after Herod I's death and were subsequently remitted a quarter of their tribute (*JW* 2.96, *Ant.* 17.319). The political value of Samaria was appreciated not only by Herod I but also by Rome; the district acted as a firm foothold in the province. See Montgomery, *Samaritans*, p. 82.

point Pilate does not necessarily indicate an unfavourable outcome
to his trial. After a governorship of ten years and with the accession
of a new Emperor it was the obvious time for Pilate to accept a new
commission.[135]

Conclusion

In the *Jewish War*, Josephus presents us with a relatively able yet
insensitive governor of the Roman Empire. Two incidents during
his rule underscore the major rhetorical argument of the whole
work: a nation's peace and harmony depends upon quiet acceptance of Roman rule, not violent uprising. Pilate is described in
more detail in the *Antiquities* and in much harsher terms. Although
he governs with a certain degree of competency, he sets himself
against the Jewish Law and is eventually sent back to Rome by
Vitellius to answer for his crimes. Pilate, along with other Roman
governors in this work, plays his part in the gradual decline of
Jewish society into revolt.

The historical reconstructions of the events behind Josephus'
stories, however, show a governor intent on inaugurating his
government with a firm hand, reluctant to take any nonsense from
the people he is to govern. Yet at the same time he can show
flexibility and an ability to stand down in the interests of preserving
peace. He seems to have been able to work alongside the priestly
authorities with Caiaphas at the head: the aqueduct may have been
a joint venture, Jewish and Roman authorities working together to
the benefit of the people of Jerusalem. Faced with potentially
difficult political events, the earlier ones at a time when the
protection afforded by the Syrian legate was missing, Pilate appears
to fulfil his duty of effectively maintaining Roman order in the
province without recourse to undue aggression.

---

[135] Lémonon, *Pilate*, p. 238. McGing also makes the same point: cf. 'Pontius',
p. 434.

4

PILATE IN MARK'S GOSPEL

With Mark's gospel we move from Jewish literature to our
earliest surviving reference to Pilate in a Christian gospel.[1] The
work itself gives no specific date and there have been various
attempts to fit the contents of the gospel to known historical
events. At the earliest end of the spectrum a date shortly before
Gaius' assassination has been suggested (41 CE)[2] or, on the basis
of possible Qumran fragments, just prior to 50 CE.[3] The majority
of scholars, however, date the gospel some time between 60 and
70 CE; more specifically, opinion is divided between whether it
was written shortly before or shortly after the fall of Jerusalem.[4]
The place of composition is no less disputed with hypotheses
ranging from Jerusalem,[5] Alexandria,[6] Antioch,[7] Galilee[8] to

[1] In what follows I am assuming the priority of Mark. Other early Christian
references to Pilate occur in Acts 3.13, 4.27, 13.28 (by allusion) and 1 Tim. 6.13.
Curiously, Paul never mentions Pilate in any of his genuine letters, even in 1 Cor.
15.3 where a reference might have been expected.
[2] Torrey, taking 13.14 to be Gaius' statue, cited by V. Taylor, *Gospel*, p. 31.
[3] O'Callaghan, 'Papiros', pp. 91–100; against this view see Benoit, 'Note',
pp. 321–4.
[4] Those who date it before 70 include Cranfield, *Mark*, pp. 3–8; Lane, *Gospel*,
pp. 17–21; V. Taylor, *Gospel*, pp. 31–2; Schweizer, *Mark*, p. 25; Nineham, *Gospel*,
pp. 41–2; Hengel, *Studies*, pp. 1–30; Kee, *Community*, p. 100–1; Martin, *Mark*,
pp. 51–83; Best, *Mark*, p. 35; Gundry, *Mark*, pp. 1041–5. Those dating it after 70
include Hooker, *Gospel*, pp. 5–8; Brandon, *Jesus*, pp. 221–82; Kelber, *Kingdom*, p. 1.
[5] Suggested by Wellhausen, cited by Rawlinson, *Gospel*, p. xxx. This particular
view has not won any wide acceptance.
[6] Chrysostom linked the gospel with Egypt (*Hom. in Matt.* 1) though this may be
a mistaken inference from Eusebius *EH* 2.16.
[7] This may be more probable than Alexandria but no ancient writers connect the
gospel with Syria. The fact that Mark translates Aramaic words for his audience
does not necessarily go against an Antiochean origin (so Best, *Mark*, p. 35) since the
majority of city-dwellers would presumably have spoken Greek rather than
Aramaic. The explanation that two λεπτὰ make up a *quadrans* (12.42), however,
would be meaningless in the Eastern provinces since the latter coin was only used in
the West.
[8] This view is especially associated with Marxsen (*Evangelist*, pp. 54–116) who

Rome,[9] the last representing the majority view. Early church tradition is virtually unanimous in its assertion that the gospel was written in Rome shortly after Peter and Paul perished in the Neronian persecution of 64.[10] Since the contents of the gospel seem to support the traditional view of its provenance,[11] the following discussion assumes that Mark was writing for a predominantly gentile Christian audience in Rome after the persecution of 64 but before the fall of Jerusalem. It will be argued that the picture of Pilate which emerges from this gospel would be particularly appropriate for a community which had recently suffered such misery and humiliation at the hands of imperial command.

Pontius Pilate appears twice in Mark's gospel. In 15.1–15 he directs the Roman proceedings against Jesus and later, in 15.43–5, he grants Jesus' corpse to Joseph of Arimathea. Both references are to be found in what is generally referred to as Mark's 'passion narrative', that is, 14.1–16.8.

Mark's passion narrative

The self-sufficiency and narrative continuity which distinguish this section of the gospel from the previous groups of generally rather isolated pericopae was noticed by the form critics of the early

suggested that the gospel was an exhortation to Jerusalem Christians to flee to Pella in the early stages of the siege of Jerusalem with the promise that the expected parousia would take place there. But apart from the fact that a gospel appears to be entirely the wrong literary form for such a straightforward and urgent message (and the facts that Pella is in Peraea and the author of the gospel often appears to be ignorant of Palestinian geography), the endurance of the gospel and references within the text to continuance and growth of the gentile Christian community suggest that it was not originally composed as a 'flysheet' for Jerusalem Christians promising an imminent parousia. A rejection of Marxsen's theory, however, does not necessarily mean a rejection of Galilee; see, for example, Kelber, *Kingdom*, pp. 129–47 and Myers, *Binding*, p. 41. Kee (*Community*, pp. 101–3) suggests Southern Syria. However, these theories meet with the same three difficulties as Antioch (see p. 94, note 7 above). Other scholars suggest that the gospel was written in a large city of the Roman Empire but do not specifically link it with Rome: see Hooker, *Gospel*, pp. 5–8 and Anderson, *Gospel*, pp. 26–9.

[9] Those in favour of Rome include Cranfield, Lane, V. Taylor, Schweizer, Nineham, Rawlinson, Hengel, Brandon, Matera, Best and Gundry.

[10] Irenaeus, *Adv.Haer.* 3.1.1; Anti-Marcionite Prologue and Papias, quoted in Eusebius *EH* 6.14.6 and 3.39.15; Clement of Alexandria, *Hypotyposes* 6. See Hengel, *Studies*, pp. 2–6. Tradition also associates Mark's gospel with Peter and its author as the John Mark known to us from Acts 12.12. For varying analyses of these traditions compare Hengel with Niederwimmer, 'Johannes Markus', pp. 172–88.

[11] See, for example, Hengel's analysis, ibid., pp. 7–30.

twentieth century.[12] They suggested that the passion story was the first of the traditions associated with Jesus to become a continuous narrative. This had several points to recommend it: the similarity of the passion accounts in both the Markan and the Johannine traditions suggested that the precise sequence of events had become established relatively early on;[13] the speeches in Acts (which may reflect early preaching) are dominated by Jesus' death and resurrection;[14] most of Paul's references to the cross are found in what sound like earlier formulaic passages (e.g. 1 Cor. 15.3–7); finally, meditation upon and questions raised by the paradox of a crucified Christ would have necessitated an early coherent passion account.[15] Although they were willing to allow certain Markan additions,[16] the earlier form critics regarded Mark 14.1–16.8 as a continuous narrative held together by specific references to times and places and with largely independent existence before its incorporation into Mark.[17] Modifications of this view held by more recent upholders of a form-critical approach are mainly a question of degree: all are agreed that some primitive narrative lies behind the Markan passion story; the dispute centres around how similar this was to what we now have in Mark.[18]

[12] In particular Dibelius, *Die Formgeschicht*; Schmidt, *Der Rahmen*; V. Taylor, *Formation* (1935), especially pp. 44–62.

[13] See Lührmann, *Markusevangelium*, pp. 227–8 for a table of similarities. However, as Lührmann points out, although the passion accounts in both Mark and John appear surprisingly similar when a brief list of topics is compiled, this disguises the fact that the traditions associated with each topic are frequently completely different (as a comparison of the Markan Sanhedrin trial with that in John will show) (p. 228). Furthermore, several of the events could hardly have happened in any other order – the arrest had to come before the trial which had to come before the crucifixion, etc. It is also possible that John was aware of Mark's account; see, for example, Donahue 'Pre-Markan', pp. 9–10 and pp. 165–6 below.

[14] For example, Acts 2.22–36, 3.17–26, 4.8–12.

[15] In 1 Cor. 1.23 Paul asserts that the cross was a stumbling block to the Jews and folly to the Gentiles. The events surrounding such a humiliating death would have quickly demanded interpretation.

[16] For instance, both Dibelius and Schmidt saw the anointing episode in Mark 14.3–9 as an insertion into the account, as was also the priest's plot (14.1b–2), the treachery of Judas (14.10–1) and the reference to the betrayer (14.17–21).

[17] Bussmann (*Synoptische Studien*, vol. 3, pp. 180–91) went so far as to suggest that Paul's use of κατὰ τὰς γραφας (1 Cor. 15.3–4) refers to a well-known written account of Jesus' passion and death. As V. Taylor points out, however, this could equally well be a vague OT allusion or a collection of testimonies from scripture: cf. *Formation*, pp. 48–50.

[18] At one end of the spectrum, Pesch sees a virtually unchanged text going back to the very first years after the events: cf. *Markusevangelium*, vol. 2, pp. 1–27. Nineham similarly thinks that a continuous narrative, itself made out of isolated stories, came into being fairly early on and that Mark relied on this though he felt no hesitation in

Modern approaches to the passion narrative, however, have tended to move away from the constraints of such an approach. Rather than attempting to reconstruct Mark's purpose and theology by trying to uncover a tradition which he has altered and into which he has made insertions, scholars engaged in literary and structuralist analyses of the gospel have concentrated on the way the author of Mark orders and presents his material to the reader, and the recurrence of theological and polemical themes in the work as a whole.[19] In terms of language and theology, the passion narrative is an integral part of the finished gospel.[20] This has led to a greater emphasis on Mark as a creative author, not slavishly reproducing earlier tradition but selecting events and presenting them in a particular way to his readers.

Although Mark was certainly using earlier traditions, the following analysis will not attempt to uncover these in the case of the Roman trial. Instead, Pilate's role will be assessed in the context of the gospel as a whole; that is, the characterization and meaning taken on by the Roman prefect as a result of Mark's skilful arrangement and presentation of his material.

Context

Chapters 1 to 12 of Mark's gospel describe Jesus' teaching and ministry over a period of about one year. The narrative unfolds

adding to it: cf. *Gospel*, p. 365. Knox divided the passion narrative into two sources, a 'disciples source' and a 'twelve source'. His hypothesis was that Mark had both sources in front of him and simply conflated the two accounts into one: cf. *Sources*, pp. 115–47. V. Taylor (*Gospel*, p. 658) also thought Mark used two sources, suggesting that it was possible to discern a non-Semitic summary narrative underlying the passion account whose 'unity, continuity and stark realism mark it as a primitive complex'. This Roman passion account, which in itself may be composite, was then expanded by Mark with the aid of various additions of a strong Semitic character. Bultmann (*History*, pp. 275–84) argued that the passion account developed from simple kerygmatic statements such as are found in the speeches in Acts or cast in prophetic form in Mark 8.31, 9.31 and 10.33–4. This simple account was developed at various stages, partly by the addition of earlier stories and partly by the reforming of the existing narrative. In particular, the whole narrative was worked over at some point by the addition of OT motifs supplying prophetic proofs of God's will in the crucifixion. An exception to this general view is Linnemann (*Studien*) who rejected any kind of pre-Markan passion account, regarding Mark as a collector of independent reports. For a much fuller survey of form-critical approaches to Mark's passion narrative see Donahue, 'Pre-Markan', pp. 1–16.

[19] Ibid., pp. 16–20; Kee, *Community*; Malbon, *Narrative*; Myers, *Binding*; van Iersel, *Reading*; Belo, *Materialist*; Best, *Mark*.

[20] On the homogeneity of the Greek style of Mark see Neirynck, *Duality*, p. 37.

quickly as Jesus and his disciples move from one geographical location to another; many short pericopae are joined by the characteristically Markan word εὐθύς, 'immediately', giving a feeling of speed and intensity. In 8.27–10.52 the group embark on the journey to Jerusalem. Here Jesus' preaching and teaching culminate with a long eschatological discourse to his disciples, warning them of tribulation to come and portents of the end (chapter 13).

These chapters give the impression that events are speeding towards a decisive goal. With chapters 14 to 16 that goal has been reached: the pace of the narrative is slowed down considerably; the rather vague εὐθύς has given way to specific indications of time, every hour now becoming important in the description of Jesus' death and resurrection.[21] This is not a new theme; it has been carefully prepared for by the previous narrative and becomes especially prominent after events at Caesarea Philippi (9.2–13). Jesus himself has pointed to it, both by means of three explicit statements (8.31, 9.31, 10.33–4) and by references to the suffering of the Son of Man (9.12), giving up his life as a ransom for many (10.45) and the parable of the tenants in the vineyard (12.1–12). The narrator has also hinted at impending disaster through the reference to the plot of the Pharisees and Herodians (3.6), 'Judas Iscariot, who betrayed him' (3.19) and the death of John the Baptist (6.17–29).[22] Mark's Jewish readers might also have seen similarities between the passion story and Jewish court tales about the wise man who is persecuted then rescued, vindicated and exalted to a high position, such as the Joseph narratives in Genesis 37–50, and the accounts in Daniel and Esther.[23]

The passion account has therefore not only been carefully prepared for in the preceding narrative but forms its climax. In the final three chapters the author of the gospel takes his time to describe in careful detail the events of the last two days of Jesus' earthly life and those of the following Sunday morning.

---

[21] For example, 14.1, 12, 17, 15.1, 25, 33–4, 42, 16.1–2.

[22] See also Lightfoot on chapter 13 as a parallel to the passion (*Gospel*, p. 55).

[23] None of these, of course, descends to the depths of degradation or achieves the exaltation accorded to Jesus by the gospel story. See Nickelsburg, 'Genre', pp. 153–84.

Markan themes culminating in the passion narrative

In the same way that Jesus' death and resurrection have already been hinted at throughout the earlier part of the gospel, several other significant Markan themes find their culmination in the passion narrative. Some of these have inevitably had an influence on the way in which Pilate has been portrayed and for that reason will be outlined briefly at this point.

(1)   An important theme throughout the whole gospel is that of the antagonism of the Jewish leadership. As early as 3.2 the Pharisees were alert to any accusations which they might bring against Jesus and by 3.6 they have taken council with the Herodians to destroy him. After the cleansing of the Temple the chief priests become involved and, with the scribes, seek a way to eliminate Jesus on the grounds that he was too popular with the crowds (11.18). With Judas' offer to betray his master in chapter 14, the plots of the chief priests become reality (14.1–2, 10–11). Mark spares no effort in his denigration of these leaders: not only are they plotters, schemers and sinners (14.41), but their court convenes with the sole intention of finding evidence against Jesus which would warrant his death (14.55). When Jesus' pronouncement in verse 62 leads to his condemnation on a charge of blasphemy,[24] it is apparently members of the council who spit on him, cover his face, strike him and demand that he prophesy to them (v. 65) – hardly suitable behaviour for responsible members of a court. Throughout the trial Mark has emphasized the complicity of the *whole council* (14.53, 55, 64, 15.1); the findings of the court are unanimous and not one member speaks out at any time in Jesus' defence.[25]

(2)   Another characteristic which is particularly prominent in the passion account is the frequent use of scriptural references or allusions to OT themes, showing Christ's death to be in accordance with the will of God. In particular the LXX of Isaiah 53.12 appears to lie behind the Markan use of $\pi\alpha\rho\alpha$-$\delta\acute{\iota}\delta\omega\mu\iota$ in the passion predictions of 9.31, 10.33 and 14.21.

---

[24] See below, pp. 105–6.
[25] Later, in 15.42–6, this bleak picture is dispelled slightly when we learn that at least one member of the council – Joseph of Arimathea – was sympathetic towards Jesus.

Allusions to the suffering servant of Deutero-Isaiah are also common, as are references to the psalms.[26]

The need for reflection upon Jesus' suffering and death was obvious: crucifixion was a shameful and humiliating death (Deut. 21.22–3)[27] and belief in a Messiah who was not only rejected by his own people but who was also crucified by the representative of a foreign power was 'a stumbling block to Jews and folly to Gentiles' (1 Cor. 1.23). The disturbing events of Jesus' last days therefore needed to be interpreted in the light of scriptural references and shown to be actually in accordance with God's will. Such Christian reflection would have begun at an early stage and it is unlikely that Mark was responsible for all the allusions. Probably he made use of existing scriptural 'proof texts'; possibly he added others himself. What is important is that Mark retained them and incorporated them into his finished gospel. Together with Jesus' repeated predictions of his death, they show that all the events of Jesus' ministry, most notably his shameful death and resurrection, were in accordance with God's plan (9.12, 14.21, 49).

Within the Roman trial scene, scriptural motifs appear to be especially present in 15.1–5. In particular, these verses show several parallels with the suffering servant motif of Isaiah 52–3. Examples are the silence in Isaiah 53.7,[28] wonder in Isaiah 52.15[29] and handing over in Isaiah 53.12.[30] A curious fact about 15.6–15, however, is that, unlike the rest of the passion narrative, these verses show no discernible trace of scriptural references whatsoever.[31] This may suggest that this particular section owes more to the evangelist himself than other parts of the narrative and that other themes were uppermost in Mark's presentation at this point.

(3) One of these themes may have been kingship. This is important in the passion narrative as a whole but comes into special

---

[26] For example, Pss. 34, 41.9, 42.6, 11, 43.5, 69.21, 109.25 and, especially in connection with the crucifixion, Ps. 22.1, 7, 18. See Lindars, *Apologetic*, pp. 88–110.

[27] See Hengel, *Crucifixion*.

[28] οὐκ ἀνοίγει τὸ στόμα αὐτοῦ, . . . οὕτως οὐκ ἀνοίγει τὸ στόμα (also Pss. 38.13, 14, 39.9, Od. Sol. 31.8, T. Ben. 5.4).

[29] οὕτω θαυμάσονται ἔθνη πολλά.

[30] παρεδόθη εἰς θάνατον. See further van Iersel, *Reading*, p. 191.

[31] Lohse (*Mark's Witness*, p. 78) lists scriptural allusions in the passion narrative but has none at all for this section. Lindars similarly lists no references, cited by Donahue, 'Pre-Markan', p. 4.

prominence during the Roman trial. Throughout 15.2–32 Jesus is referred to as the national king six times, yet the title is never elsewhere used of him.[32] The preceding chapters of the gospel have referred to Jesus as Christ, Holy One of God, Beloved Son, Son of David or Son of God.[33] Never before has anyone referred to Jesus as King, yet it is the charge against Jesus inscribed above the cross (15.26) and in chapter 15 Mark concentrates on this theme, defining in what sense Jesus really was the King of Israel. Chapter 15.1–15 highlights the Roman governor's perception of messiahship in terms of a political king in opposition to Caesar, a perception which Mark has already shown to be false.[34]

(4) Linked to kingship and forming its counterpart within the passion narrative is the theme of mockery. Jesus is subjected to a brutal, or at best undignified, mockery three times throughout the narrative: after his Jewish trial at the hands of the council members he is told to 'prophesy', is spat upon and struck (14.65); after the Roman trial he receives an even more humiliating treatment at the hands of the Roman soldiers who mock him as 'King of the Jews' (15.16–20); even on the cross the passers-by, chief priests and his fellow prisoners mock him, taunting him to come down from the cross if he is the Christ, the King of Israel (15.29–32).[35] This mockery in Mark is linked to a fundamental misunderstanding, both by Jews and Romans, regarding Jesus' messiahship. He does not fit traditional messianic specifications and so is rejected.[36]

Behind the mockery, however, lies a bitter irony: the actors in the drama unconsciously speak the truth, a truth which

[32] 15.2, 9, 12, 17, 26 and 32. If Jesus' entry into Jerusalem was a re-enactment of Zech. 9.9, then the theme of kingship, though not openly declared by the bystanders, is implicit here; see France, *Divine*, p. 87.

[33] 1.1, 8.29, 12.35, 14.61 (Christ); 1.24 (Holy One of God); 1.11, 9.7 (Beloved Son); 10.46–8, 12.35 (Son of David); and 1.1, 3.11 (Son of God).

[34] Jesus' answer to the tribute question in 12.13–17 shows that his policy was one of quiet acquiescence towards his Roman overlords; political and divine authority need not necessarily conflict as long as God received his due. His answer would no doubt have seemed a deplorable compromise to any of Mark's readers with a more nationalistic outlook (see Paul's letter to Rome 13.1–7: had there been some dispute over the authority of pagan rulers a decade before Mark was written?). On these verses in Mark see Bruce, 'Render', pp. 249–63; Dunn, 'Caesar', pp. 269–70 and Haacker, 'Kaisertribut'.

[35] Like the rest of the passion, this mockery was predicted by Jesus, 9.12, 10.34.

[36] On the central role of irony and misunderstanding in the Markan passion narrative see Juel, *Messiah*, pp. 47–52 and Nickelsburg, 'Genre', p. 172.

exposes their lack of perception. Jesus' Jewish adversaries mockingly tell him to prophesy and, if he is the Christ, to come down from the cross. The reader, however, knows that Jesus *is* endowed with prophetic insight;[37] but he is more than a prophet, he really is the Christ, the King of Israel, even υἱός Θεοῦ.[38] Far from coming down from the cross to save himself he remains there as a ransom for all people.[39] Similarly, the mockery at the hands of the soldiers centres upon the absurdity of the kingly claims of the scourged figure before them. To pagan troops (whether in the 30s or the late 60s CE), the 'King of the Jews' would be none other than the Emperor himself and it is as someone setting himself up against the kingship of Caesar that Jesus is ridiculed and abused.[40] Clearly such a worldly, political interpretation is at variance with Jesus' true identity, yet the soldiers unconsciously point to the truth.

The mockery from Jesus' opponents, his own humiliation and Mark's irony culminate in the title on the cross. Above the tortured body of a man dying of crucifixion Pilate affixes a *titulus* reading Ὁ βασιλεὺς τῶν Ἰουδαίων (15.26). The Roman governor's mockery here of Jesus and, indirectly, the Jewish nation, is self-evident.[41] In view of this, it would not be surprising also to find an element of mockery at the prefect's court.

(5) A final Markan theme which has relevance for the trial before Pilate is that of rejection. One of the deepest tragedies of

---

[37] For example, the passion predictions 8.31, 9.31, 10.33–4; the eschatological predictions of chapter 13; Jesus' knowledge of the colt (11.1–6) and the upper room (14.12–16).
[38] See p. 101, note 33, above.   [39] 10.45, 14.24.
[40] In the Greek-speaking world the Emperor was often referred to as βασιλεὺς (see p. 106, note 58 below). Many features of the mockery in 15.16–20 are reminiscent of the Emperor. The robe itself was in imperial purple (Rev. 17.4, 18.16; Virgil, *Georg.* II.495; Josephus, *JW* 7). The crown of thorns does not seem to have been used as an instrument of torture but to mimic the radiate crowns worn by 'divine' Hellenistic rulers (Barrett, *St John*, p. 540; Brown, *Gospel*, p. 875), or the imperial wreath. Χαῖρε mimics the *Ave Caesar* used to address the Emperor.
[41] Mark does not specifically state here that Pilate was responsible for the title (compare John 19.19), but his readers would surely assume that it was he who communicated the official charge to the executioners. Unlike John's gospel, where the chief priests sense the mockery directed towards their own nation and ask Pilate to alter the title (John 19.21–2), the inscription in Mark seems to incite the chief priests and bystanders to further mockery in an attempt to disassociate themselves from Jesus completely.

Mark's gospel is that Jesus is abandoned not only by the Jewish leadership but even by his closest followers in his hour of need and he goes to his death almost completely alone. In 14.27 this isolation was predicted by Jesus: 'You will all fall away; for it is written, "I will strike the shepherd, and the sheep will be scattered"'. In verse 50 of the same chapter the disciples all flee after Jesus' arrest and in verses 51–2 the young man runs away naked rather than stand by Jesus. Peter denies his master in 14.66–72, ironically at the same time as Jesus admits his true identity before the council.[42] Those who were crucified with Jesus in 15.32 revile him and in Jesus' dramatic cry at 15.34 even God has apparently forsaken him. The only people who do not desert him are women from Galilee and Jerusalem who watch the crucifixion from a distance (15.40–1) and, later, Joseph of Arimathea who courageously asks Pilate for permission to bury the body (15.42–6). In Mark's description of the Roman trial it is the once openly friendly crowd who forsake Jesus, abandoning him completely and demanding his execution.

With these five themes in mind – the antagonism of the Jewish leadership, the need to show that Jesus' death was in accordance with God's will, the importance of redefining kingship, mockery and rejection – we shall now turn to the Roman trial in Mark's gospel and consider the picture of Pilate emerging from it.

The characterization of Pilate in Mark

The majority of scholars regard the Pilate of Mark's gospel as a weakling, convinced of Jesus' innocence, vainly engaging in successive attempts to release him but forced to go along with the wishes of the chief priests and the crowd.[43] S. G. F. Brandon remarks that

---

[42] The dove-tailing of the two stories in chapter 14.53–72 indicates that they occur simultaneously.

[43] For example, V. Taylor (*Gospel*, p. 579): 'Mark gives an . . . objective account, not hiding the weakness of Pilate, but showing plainly that he did not believe the accusation of the priests to be valid'. Gnilka (*Evangelium*, p. 305) too writes: 'Pilatus wird als Schwächling gezeichnet' ('Pilate is portrayed as a weakling'). Best (*Temptation*, p. 96) asserts that the trial before Pilate underlines the hostility of the Jews in that it shows Pilate making some attempt to save him, while Cole (*Mark*, p. 232) writes: 'for he stands self-revealed as he attempts in vain, first to avoid the issue, and then to escape responsibility for the decision'. Van Iersel (*Reading*, p. 179) asserts

Pilate 'acted as a veritable weakling, devoid alike of dignity, efficiency and spirit'.[44] D. E. Nineham sums up the views of many when he asserts: 'most commentators think we should allow for some idealization in St Mark's account, arising out of the Christian desire to exculpate the Romans and put responsibility on the Jews'.[45] Alternatively, he is seen as not taking the case seriously, wishing to release Jesus if only to spite his Jewish antagonists.[46] However, there are several indications within Mark's portrayal of the Roman trial which indicate that, read in a first-century context, Pilate is not to be understood as a weak impotent figure but rather as an astute governor who handles a potentially difficult case with a certain amount of mockery and at the same time a great deal of political shrewdness. The following discussion will show that the representative of Rome in Mark's gospel is not exculpated but plays a full part in the events leading to Jesus' execution.

The handing over to Pilate (15.1)

In Mark's portrayal, the hearing before Pilate takes place after a formal trial before a Jewish Sanhedrin (14.53, 55–65). Although the bias of the proceedings is stressed, Jesus clearly stands before a Jewish court facing a capital offence; a court which, however corrupt, did have the power to come to a legal decision. Witnesses are called, a unanimous verdict is reached and Jesus is condemned on a charge of blasphemy (v. 64). It was presumably this decision which was reiterated the following morning at the consultation (συμβούλιον) of the Sanhedrin (15.1).[47] The elaborate naming of the parties constituting the council not only stresses the complicity of the whole Jewish leadership but also emphasizes the official character of the act, as does legal terminology such as δέω, ἀποφέρω and παραδίδωμι.[48]

An important result of the morning meeting of the Sanhedrin is that Jesus is now 'bound' (δήσαντες). No such binding took place at Jesus' arrest, a fact perfectly in keeping with general procedure

---

that Pilate 'is persuaded against his will to approve and confirm the punishment'. See also Benoit, *Passion*, p. 137; Nicklesburg, 'Genre', p. 165; Pesch, *Markusevangelium*, vol. 2, p. 459; Burkill, *Mysterious*, p. 294.

[44] Brandon, *Jesus*, p. 261.   [45] Nineham, *Gospel*, p. 413.

[46] For example, Piper, 'God's', p. 179. Lane suggests that Pilate's efforts to rescue Jesus were due to his 'anti-Semitic bias', though he gives no evidence to support this claim: cf. *Gospel*, p. 555.

[47] Bammel, 'Trial', p. 415; Pesch, *Markusevangelium*, vol. 2, p. 456.   [48] Ibid.

since the binding of a person only under accusation would have been unusual.[49] The consultation of verse 1a, which would have summed up the findings of the previous evening's inquiries, 'constituted an act that had its procedural consequences'.[50] Jesus' legal status has now changed: he has been condemned to death, is bound and now handed over to Pilate as a culprit.

Pilate is introduced abruptly in verse 1 with no description of his official title. Presumably his role in Jesus' death, and perhaps also something of his character, were sufficiently well known to Mark's audience to necessitate no further means of identification other than his name.[51] Mark's narrative gives no indication as to *why* Jesus has to be handed over to Pilate. The implication seems to be that the Jewish death sentence has to be ratified by the Roman prefect and carried out by his troops.[52] The construction καὶ εὐθὺς πρωῖ gives a feeling of speed to the proceedings; the Jewish authorities are anxious to have Jesus executed as soon as possible.[53]

The hearing before Pilate (15.2–15)

In Mark's portrayal, the Jewish court condemned Jesus for his exalted claims in 14.62. When asked by the high priest if he was the Messiah, Jesus answered, 'I am, and you will see the Son of Man seated at the right hand of the Almighty and coming with the clouds of heaven'. This, Mark tells us, immediately led to a

[49] Bammel, 'Trial', p. 415. In John's gospel, however, Jesus is bound immediately at his arrest and remains so throughout the night (John 18.12, 24).

[50] Ibid., 'Trial', p. 415. Though commenting on the historicity of the Markan narrative at this point, Bammel's observations are still relevant for a literary understanding of the Markan text.

[51] See Hengel, *Studies*, p. 9. The omission of Pilate's title coupled with the fact that Caiaphas is never mentioned by name led Pesch to suggest the existence of a very old main source for the gospel which originated in or before 37 CE when both Pilate and Caiaphas were deposed: cf. *Markusevangelium*, vol. 2, p. 21. This is unnecessary since Pilate's name was very quickly associated with the crucifixion and would doubtless be familiar to Mark's readers.

[52] For the historical uncertainty over the Jewish right of capital punishment at this period, see above, pp. 15–16. The historical problems raised by the evangelists' presentations will be discussed below, pp. 196–202.

[53] Though common throughout the rest of the gospel, the word εὐθύς is used only four times throughout the passion narrative. In all cases the word is associated with the immediate fulfilment of prophecy. In 14.41–2 Jesus tells the three disciples in Gethsemane that the hour has come and εὐθύς in verse 43 Judas arrives and in verse 45 kisses him. After Peter's denial, the cock crows εὐθύς (14.72), reminding the reader of Jesus' prediction in 14.30. Here, in 15.1, Jesus' general predictions regarding the passion are hurrying on towards their fulfilment.

unanimous charge of blasphemy (v. 64).[54] Pilate's question in 15.2 is not a new, political charge but goes back to the findings of the Jewish court, in particular to the central questions of Jesus' messiahship and status: 'Are you the King of the Jews?' The Roman governor is not interested in the religious meaning of messiahship but only in any political repercussions such a claim might have. His question therefore focuses on the political implications of the Jewish charge, in an attempt to gauge how far he might present a threat to Roman stability in the province.[55]

The title 'King of the Jews' (ὁ βασιλεὺς τῶν Ἰουδαίων) is used in Mark's gospel only by Pilate and his soldiers.[56] The phrase 'of the Jews' indicates that the speaker is not a Jew himself; when the Jewish chief priests mock Jesus on the cross they refer to him as 'King of Israel' (15.32).[57] In a first-century Roman province the title would take on particularly dangerous connotations: anyone claiming any kind of kingship would run the risk of appearing to challenge the divine rule of Caesar.[58] Mark's readers would doubtlessly know of other kingly claimants who had been executed for

---

[54] Strobel (following P. Billerbeck) suggests that the blasphemy consisted of referring to himself as the Son of Man and the claim that he would sit at the right hand of the Almighty, a position which would put him above the high priest and his court and deeply insulted the whole Torah-based structure of society: cf. *Stunde*, pp. 92–3. It is also possible, however, that the charge is anachronistic and that Mark has retrojected contemporary disputes over the person of Jesus in church-synagogue disputes of his own day back into Jesus' trial; see Burkill, *Mysterious*, p. 289. For fuller discussions of the Jewish charge see Gundry, *Mark*, pp. 891–922 and Brown, *Death*, pp. 429–60, 627–35.

[55] Many commentators understand the σύ in Pilate's question as contemptuous, indicating the governor's incredulity that messianic accusations have been levelled at such a prisoner (e.g. Pesch, *Markusevangelium*, vol. 2, p. 457). But the σύ may not necessarily be emphatic and so cannot be pushed as any indication of Pilate's surprise: Moulton and Turner (*Grammar*, vol. 3, p. 37) doubt the emphatic nature of σύ here. It parallels the σύ in the question of the high priest in 14.61.

[56] 15.2, 9, 12, 18, 26.

[57] It is clear from 15.31–2 that King of the Jews = King of Israel = Messiah.

[58] As Jason and others found out by proclaiming Jesus' messiahship in Thessalonica (Acts 17.7). Their Jewish opponents charged them with 'acting against the decrees of Caesar, saying that there is *another king*, Jesus'. There is evidence that the later Hasmonaean rulers assumed the title βασιλεὺς τῶν Ἰουδαίων. Alexander Jannaeus (103–76 BCE) appears to have been the first to refer to himself as βασιλεὺς on his coins (Schürer, *History*, vol. 1, p. 227). According to Josephus (*Ant.* 14.36 citing Strabo of Cappadocia), this same monarch sent a gift to Pompey which bore an inscription reading Ἀλεξάνδρου τοῦ τῶν Ἰουδαίων βασιλέως. Herod I is similarly referred to as ὁ τῶν Ἰουδαίων βασιλές by Josephus (*Ant.* 16.311). Brown (*Gospel*, p. 851) may be correct in his suggestion that the title may have been 'kept alive during the Roman governorship as a designation for the expected liberator'.

their aspirations.[59] The precariousness of Jesus' position would be only too apparent.

Faced with such a loaded question, Jesus' reply takes on extreme importance yet the precise meaning of Σὺ λέγεις is difficult to determine. Some scholars have taken it as a denial;[60] others as a full admission,[61] though if that is the case, it is difficult to see why the chief priests supply further charges and why Jesus is not sentenced immediately. The majority of commentators have understood the reply somewhere between these two extremes: it is 'evasive',[62] 'non-committal'[63] or, with V. Taylor, 'it is an affirmative which implies that the speaker would put things differently'.[64] Pilate has completely misunderstood Jesus' messiahship in terms of political or materialistic kingship. Jesus will not deny his messiahship, yet neither will he accept the Roman's distortion of it. Before the Jewish council Jesus admitted that he was 'the Christ, the Son of the Blessed' but immediately went on to redefine his identity in terms of the 'Son of Man' (14.62), a title which was less easily misinterpreted in a military or political sense.[65] Jesus makes no such redefinition before Pilate; the Roman's misunderstanding of Jesus' kingship will continue to dominate the passion narrative until the crucifixion.

Without waiting for Pilate's response, Jesus' opponents accuse him of many things (πολλά), again emphasizing their desire to see him convicted. To these, Jesus is silent (v. 4). The possible LXX

[59] Josephus records several royal pretenders in the turbulent years after Herod I's death: Judas the son of Ezekias (*Ant.* 17.271–2); a slave named Simon (17.273–7); the shepherd Athrongaeus (*JW* 2.60–5). In *Ant.* 17.285 he writes: 'Anyone might make himself king as the head of a band of rebels whom he fell in with, and then would press on to the destruction of the community, causing trouble to few Romans and then only to a small degree but bringing the greatest slaughter upon their own people'. Such kingly impersonators when caught were dealt with severely by the Romans (17.276). See Hengel, *Zealots*, pp. 290–302 and Horsley and Hanson, *Bandits*, pp. 88–127.
[60] Pesch argues that it is a question which amounts to a denial, and that Pilate's use of ὃν λέγετε in verse 12 also suggests that Jesus has denied kingship: cf. *Markusevangelium*, p. 457.
[61] For example, Piper, 'God's', p. 179 and Cole, *Mark*, p. 233.
[62] Van Iersel, *Reading*, p. 179.   [63] Branscomb, *Gospel*, p. 287.
[64] V. Taylor, *Gospel*, p. 579.
[65] It was probably an understandable unease with the insurrectionary connotations associated with the title 'King of the Jews' which deterred the early Christians from using it to describe Jesus. Apart from the Johannine writings and the synoptic passion accounts, where its meaning is refined and qualified, it is scarcely used elsewhere in the NT. See Burkill, 'St Mark's', p. 166 and Cullmann, *Christology*, pp. 220–2.

background to this feature has already been discussed, but in the Markan narrative the silence of Jesus also serves to emphasize dramatically his one reply. It gives Jesus an added sense of dignity, and, in the light of Jesus' silence in the face of false witnesses in 14.60, it suggests that the many accusations of the priests are also false.

Faced with the prisoner's silence, Pilate asks Jesus if he has anything to say in his defence. Under Roman criminal law, an accused person who made no response to the charges was counted in the same way as if he had pleaded guilty. If he put up no defence, the hearing would be over and Jesus would automatically be convicted; a fact of which Mark's readers would presumably have been aware.[66] Yet Jesus within Mark's narrative refuses to plead his own case and his silence is said to amaze Pilate (v. 5). Throughout the gospel Mark has repeatedly emphasized the amazement of those witnessing the miracles or hearing his authoritative teaching but 'stresses equally, if not more, the failure of the crowd and of the disciples to understand them'.[67] Of the various verbs used to express this amazement (θαυμάζω, θαμβέομαι, ἐκπλήσσομαι, ἐξίστημι), the verb which is used here in verse 5, θαυμάζω, appears to be used of those least perceptive of Jesus' identity.[68] We should probably not read a deep religious significance into Pilate's attitude at this point;[69] the verb denotes no more than ordinary wonder or

[66] Garnsey, 'LEX IULIA', p. 173 and Sherwin-White, *Roman*, p. 25.

[67] Best, *Mark*, p. 60. For other references to amazement see 1.22, 27 (the verb here may even imply alarm; see Lane, *Gospel*, p. 76), 2.12 (where the Pharisees are also amazed along with the crowd), 6.2 (where Jesus' countrymen are said to be astonished but then take offence at him), 7.37, 10.24 and 26 (where the disciples are amazed but quickly show by their questions that they do not understand), 10.32, 11.18.

[68] It is used in 5.20 of those in the Decapolis hearing Legion's teaching; in 6.6 it is used to describe Jesus' amazement at the disbelief of his countrymen. The final two uses of the verb are of Pilate: in the present context and again at 15.44 where the governor wonders if Jesus is already dead or not. A related verb, ἐκθαυμάζω is used in 12.17 to describe the reaction of the Pharisees and Herodians to Jesus' answer over paying taxes to Caesar; these two groups continue to be antagonistic towards Jesus.

[69] Many scholars have read a religious connotation into 15.5, virtually making Pilate a witness to the divinity of the man before him, for instance, 'Es zeigt das Aussergewöhnliche, Gottliche an' ('It indicates the unusual, the divine') (Gnilka, *Evangelium*, p. 300); 'It may suggest a superstitious dread' (S. E. Johnson, *Commentary*, p. 247). See also Pesch, *Markusevangelium*, vol. 2, p. 458. Nineham asserts that the verb θαυμάζω has 'profound religious connotations in the gospel': cf. *Gospel*, p. 412. In contrast see Gundry (*Mark*, p. 933), who asserts that the word does not imply that Pilate has a sense of Jesus' divine power.

bewilderment at a man facing a death sentence who will not defend himself. The Roman governor is amazed at Jesus but, like others in the story, has no perception of his significance.

With verses 6–7 the narrator momentarily moves away from the main action to supply his readers with two pieces of background information: the existence of the Passover amnesty and an introduction to an important character in the trial, Barabbas.

In verse 8 the story continues. The people come up (ἀναβάς)[70] to Pilate's praetorium and ask him to honour his usual custom of releasing one prisoner to them at the feast. Mark's account implies that the amnesty was a custom which either Pilate had introduced himself or had inherited from his predecessors and seen no reason to discontinue.[71] Either way, it shows that Pilate was willing to please the people and anxious to avert trouble at a festival where spirits might be high and the city crowded to bursting. Any of Mark's readers familiar with Jewish practices would recognize the significance of releasing a prisoner at Passover, a feast itself celebrating release from slavery in Egypt; others would see it as a conciliatory gesture. It is noteworthy, however, that it is not Pilate who makes an offer to release Jesus on the basis of what he has heard in 15.1–5, but the *crowd* who initiates the discussion. Mark states simply that the crowds 'began to ask Pilate as he was wont to do for them' (ἤρξατο αἰτεῖσθαι καθὼς ἐποίει αὐτοῖς). As yet there is no indication which prisoner the people will choose. The reader is aware of the existence of Barabbas but there is no indication that the crowd is particularly sympathetic towards him. If anything, the appearance of the crowd and the practice of releasing a prisoner would appear to look good for Jesus. With relatively few exceptions, the Jewish crowds have been spontaneous and enthusiastic supporters of Jesus from the very first;[72] there is no indication that they have turned against him now.

Pilate does decide to link Jesus' fate with the release of a prisoner,

---

[70] Since the governor's tribunal was usually on a raised dais (*JW* 2.301) the use of ἀναβάς here may symbolically imply that the crowd is coming up to judge.

[71] Although the article is absent, it is clearly *the* feast (i.e. Passover) which is meant by κατὰ δὲ ἑορτήν (V. Taylor, *Gospel*, p. 580). The imperfect ἀπέλυεν implies a customary act.

[72] In 1.28 Jesus achieves instant popularity, his fame spreading around the whole region of Galilee. This popularity continues in 1.32, 37, 45, 2.2, 13, 3.7–8, 20, 4.1, 5.21, 24, 6.33, 34–44, 54–6, 8.1–10, 34, 9.14 and 10.1 (in Judaea), 11.18, 12.12, 37 (around Jerusalem). The only places where Jesus was not enthusiastically accepted was in the country of the Gerasenes (5.17) and his own country (6.1–6).

but in a particularly calculating way. His offer in verse 9 needs to be understood in the light of the explanatory comment in verse 10 – 'For he perceived that it was out of envy (διὰ φθόνον) that the chief priests had delivered him up'. What in Mark's presentation would cause the chief priests to be *envious* of Jesus? Disputes over religious matters alone might arouse a certain amount of resentment, even hostility, between a popular leader and the priestly aristocracy but the only thing which would arouse *envy* amongst the chief priests would surely be if Jesus' teaching threatened their own privileged position and if he was winning a greater influence over the people than they had themselves. This is exactly the picture with which Mark presents us. He clearly shows the reader that the religious authorities did not enjoy great repect amongst the people, that Jesus was extremely popular with the crowds, and that the chief priests were consequently fearful of an uprising.[73] Within the present narrative, Pilate realizes that the chief priests have their own motives for handing Jesus over: they are not guided by loyalty to Rome, but primarily out of fear for their own position. Far from proving Jesus' innocence,[74] however, this recognition would convince Pilate that Jesus ought to be handled with the utmost thoroughness. The case of a possible messianic leader whose influence over the people worried the priests to the extent that they were willing to hand him over to the representative of Rome was not to be dismissed lightly;[75] particularly when the prisoner had already claimed to be the Messiah (14.62), spoke of a 'kingdom',[76] and refused to say anything further in his own defence.

Pilate's question at this point in the narrative is a test of public support.[77] The crowd has asked for the release of a prisoner and Pilate offers them their 'king': 'Do you want me to release for you

---

[73] In 1.22 the people declare that the scribes teach without authority, in contrast to Jesus. Examples of the chief priests' fear of an uprising can be found at 11.18, 12.12, 14.2. Gundry suggests that the chief priests were envious of Jesus because the crowds regarded him as their king (*Mark*, p. 927). On the various religious authorities referred to here see Kingsbury, *Conflict*, pp. 14–21 and Cook, *Mark's Treatment*.

[74] There does not seem to be any justification for Hendrickx's comment on verse 10, 'he is therefore depicted as aware of the innocence of Jesus' (*Passion*, p. 65); see also Hooker, *Gospel*, p. 369.

[75] On a different level, the use of φθόνος negates the whole findings of the Sanhedrin in 14.53–65. The sentence of a judge who is motivated by envy is worthless (Lührmann, *Markusevangelium*, p. 256).

[76] For example, 4.11, 26, 30, 10.14, 15, 23, 24, 25.

[77] For a similar interpretation at this point see Gundry, *Mark*, pp. 926–7.

the King of the Jews?' The tone of the question is mocking. The
Jews are an occupied people, they can have no king. But it is
primarily a challenge: who will support this messianic leader? The
supporters of messianic uprisings suffered along with their leaders;
anyone openly supporting Jesus would suffer the same fate.[78] This
explains why the crowd in Mark's gospel disassociates itself from
Jesus and allows the chief priests to influence it into shouting for
Barabbas (v. 12).[79] The verb ἀνασείω, 'to stir up', unfavourably
underlines the actions of the chief priests who prey on the people in
their weakness.[80] There is no contradiction between the previous
support of the crowd and its present rejection of Jesus: in the same
way that Peter abandoned Jesus when the pressure was too much
(14.66–72), the crowd too abandons Jesus under political pressure.
It is perhaps significant that Peter's denial of Jesus has been inserted
directly preceding the trial before Pilate (14.66–72); all Jesus'
supporters are deserting him.

Far from being a tool in the hands of the chief priests and crowd
in these verses, Pilate is very much in control. He recognizes the
self-interest in the actions of the chief priests but also realizes that
Jesus is a potential threat to law and order. When the people ask
for his usual favour, he skilfully and ominously highlights the
political charge resting on Jesus, and the people are scared into
backing the candidate of the chief priests (v. 11). But who exactly
was Barabbas? Mark's description of this character is extremely
oddly constructed: 'And among/in the midst of the rebels in
prison, who had committed murder in the insurrection, there was a
man called Barabbas' (ἦν δὲ ὁ λεγόμενος Βαραββᾶς μετὰ τῶν

[78] The suggestion that the use of the term 'King of the Jews' was an attempt to
enlist the patriotic feelings of the multitude on the side of the prisoner does not seem
to take enough account of the dangerous connotations which the title would arouse
in the first century; see for example Pesch, *Markusevangelium*, vol. 2, p. 464. Cole
(*Mark*, p. 235) accepts that the title stirs up the bitterness of the crowd but attributes
this to a lack of political shrewdness in Pilate.
[79] Mark does not specifically say that ὁ ὄχλος here was the same crowd/s which
earlier heard Jesus gladly. Yet since the phrase is nearly always used in Mark of
those who accept and support Jesus (the exception being at 14.43), it would be
difficult not to read such overtones here. There is certainly no hint that this is an
entirely different pro-Barabbas crowd which has gathered to demand the release of
its hero (as, for example, France, *Divine*, p. 87; Meyer, *Ursprung*, vol. 1, p. 195 and
Rawlinson, *Gospel*, p. 195). The rejection by ὁ ὄχλος here is not anti-Jewish but is
part of the general theme of rejection running through Mark's passion narrative
(referred to above, pp. 102–3).
[80] All the more so if the verb has the nuance 'to lead astray' as in Isa. 36.18,
Pesch, *Markusevangelium*, vol. 2, p. 465. See Bornkamm, *TDNT*, vol. 7, pp. 98–200.

στασιαστῶν δεδεμένος οἵτινες ἐν τῇ στάσει φόνον πεποιήκεισαν. Unless Mark is being extremely careless, he seems to be carefully distinguishing between Barabbas and those who have committed murder during an obviously well-known insurrection.[81] Had the evangelist wanted to link Barabbas himself with murder and insurrectionary activity a more obvious expression would have been something like 'one of the rebels . . .' (εἷς τῶν στασιαστῶν).[82] Thus Mark's report fixes the *time* of Barabbas' imprisonment but does not specify his crime, nor how far legal proceedings had progressed against him. Pilate's attempt to gauge support for Jesus, therefore, has not necessarily lost him a dangerous political prisoner. The references to 'the rebels' and 'the insurrection' in connection with Barabbas, however, tar him with an insurrectionary brush, further discrediting the choice of the chief priests.[83]

Had the Markan Pilate regarded Jesus as innocent and wished to release him, now would have been the obvious time. Having discovered that the crowd are not willing to stand up for Jesus, Pilate could have dismissed them and released both Barabbas and Jesus as a double gesture of Roman good will at the festival. Yet he does not do this. In fact nothing in Pilate's previous behaviour has given any hint that the governor does regard Jesus as innocent. He

---

[81] Possibly Mark's readers would be familiar with the occasion of an insurrection under Pilate; exactly what this involved and whether it was identical with any of the tumults related in Josephus is unknown.

[82] Winter, *Trial*, p. 97. A. Menzies, cited by Rawlinson (*Gospel*, p. 228) suggested that Barabbas had become accidentally connected with the rioters. Pesch suggests that the strange formulation may suggest that Barabbas was innocent, *Markusevangelium*, pp. 462–3.

[83] The scene with Barabbas may illustrate a deeper theological point. The actual phrase ὁ λεγόμενος Βαραββᾶς is odd: although ὁ λεγόμενος can introduce a proper name, it is normally preceded by a personal name and followed by a descriptive title (e.g. Matt. 1.16, 4.18, 10.2, 27.17, 22). Certain codices and minuscules give the name as Barrabas, which would mean 'son of a/the teacher', but this reading is 'not probable' (V. Taylor, *Gospel*, p. 581). Although Bar Abba is occasionally found in the Talmud as a designation for some of the rabbis (ibid., p. 581, Gnilka, *Evangelium*, p. 301, note 30), the most natural meaning of Barabbas is 'son of a/the father'. Ironically the crowd, stirred up by the chief priests, reject the true Son of the Father in favour of another 'son of the father' who has somehow become mixed up in insurrectionary activity. The people are looking for a 'Son of the Father' as their leader but misunderstand the nature of his role and mistakenly choose the wrong one. There is also the beginning of a second theological theme here, one which will be developed further in Matt. 27.17: out of Jesus' death comes the release of another. The vague name Barabbas is true of all people and so Jesus' death liberates everyone, 10.45, 14.24 (see van Iersel, *Reading*, pp. 180–1, who however presses the point too far: Jesus is not put to death *in place of* Barabbas in Mark; it is only in Matthew that an explicit choice between the two men is offered).

has shown amazement that the prisoner will not speak on his own behalf against his Jewish accusers; yet Jesus has come before the governor condemned by a Jewish court after admitting his messiahship. Mark's readers would know that unless strong evidence to dispute the charge was forthcoming any Roman governor, in the interests of law and order, would have no choice but to convict a man making such claims.

But the Markan Pilate is in a delicate position. The evangelist has pointed out several times that the events of Jesus' last hours occur at the feast of Passover (14.1, 12, 15.6). The feast celebrated liberation from slavery in Egypt and, at a time of Roman domination, messianic hopes might be expected to be at their height. The chief priests have already expressed their fears that to arrest Jesus and kill him during the feast might provoke a tumult of the people (14.2). Similarly here, although the people have publicly sided with Barabbas against Jesus in front of Pilate, a heavy-handed approach could provoke rioting later, especially in view of Jesus' popularity. The dilemma confronting the Markan Pilate was therefore how to deal with Jesus without disturbing the peace. The governor hits upon an ingenious solution: he swops roles, putting the people in the position of judge and asking them what should be done with Jesus. The voice of the people, though not sufficient to decide the outcome of a trial, was valued by Rome in determining the political feasibility of a verdict.[84] If the crowd itself could be made to acquiesce in Jesus' execution then there could be no danger of later displays of discontent against Roman harshness. Pilate puts the people on the spot, issuing a direct challenge to their political allegiance: 'What then shall I do with the man whom you call the King of the Jews?'

Whatever their historicity, such tactics would not be unknown or uncommon to Mark's readers. Two examples from Josephus may help to illustrate the way in which Mark's first-century readers might have understood Pilate's actions here. The first occurs in *Ant.* 13.288–96. The envy of the Jews, particularly the Pharisees, had been aroused against the Jewish King Hyrcanus because of his successes and those of his sons (§ 288). At a feast a Pharisee named Eleazar said that if the King wished to be righteous he should give up the high priesthood and be content with governing the people (§ 291), a remark which provoked the other Pharisees

---

[84] Bammel, 'Trial', p. 431.

to indignation and Hyrcanus to fury. A Sadducee named Jonathan persuaded Hyrcanus that all the Pharisees were of that opinion, urging the King that this would become clear if he were to ask them what punishment Eleazar deserved. Hyrcanus followed this advice, saying that 'he would be convinced that the slanderous statement had not been made with their approval if they fixed a penalty commensurate with the crime' (§ 294). Unfortunately for those Pharisees concerned, they thought that death was too harsh a penalty and suggested stripes and chains (§ 294). Their leniency angered Hyrcanus who assumed that the man had slandered him with their approval and from that time onwards sided with the Sadducees.

The second narrative, *Antiquities* 17.155–64 comes in the reign of Herod I. After his eagle had been pulled down from above the Temple and hacked to pieces, Herod summoned the Jewish officials to the amphitheatre, telling them how much he had done for the nation and that pulling down the eagle was sacrilege. 'Because of his savage state and out of fear that in his fury he might avenge himself upon them, those present said that the things had been done without their consent, *and it seemed to them that the perpetrators should not be exempted from punishment*' (§ 164, my emphasis). Because the Jewish officials had been quick to condemn those responsible, Herod dealt mildly with the officials themselves. In the parallel description in *Jewish War* 1.654–5 the people are summoned and ask Herod to deal only with the perpetrators. In both these stories a group of people is forced to pass a judgement on a crime; this is then used by the Jewish ruler to assess their complicity in the affair. Furthermore, in the second example, the Jewish officials under Herod could hardly have later complained at the King's harshness towards those who pulled down the eagle since they themselves had sanctioned such treatment and were only too pleased to be able to escape the slur of complicity and resulting punishment themselves. In neither of these examples is the behaviour of the ruler a sign of weakness: it is rather a deliberate challenge to the allegiance of their subjects, an attempt to make them part of the decision which they then have no alternative but to accept.

Pilate's question has exactly the same motivation: it is an attempt to test the allegiance of the people and to force them to become part of the decision, thereby implicating themselves.[85] It is also

---

[85] Hendrickx argues that a Roman governor would not be likely to ask the people

cleverly constructed to achieve the Roman prefect's ends: 'Then what shall I do/do you want me to do with [the man whom *you call*][86] the King of the Jews?' (Τί οὖν [θέλετε] ποιήσω [ὃν λέγετε] τὸν βασιλέα τῶν Ἰουδαίων;) verse 12. Again Pilate is using the potentially dangerous political title; there may also be a hint of the Roman's scorn for the futile messianic expectations of a subject people. But this time, by the use of ὃν λέγετε, he has personalized it: by their reply the Jewish crowd will reveal whether they really do accept Jesus as *their* King or not. The word θέλετε stresses that the decision rests with the crowd, they must take responsibility for the consequences of their judgement.[87] If Pilate had asked, 'What shall I do with the one you call the religious teacher?', the possible answers would have been much wider. In response to Pilate's actual question, however, the people had no choice unless they too wanted to be implicated in insurrectionary activity, or at best be seen as supporting a kingly aspirant. Like the Pharisees at Hyrcanus' banquet, the severity of the punishment demanded by the people will illustrate how far they are from siding with the prisoner. The people are cornered; they know what penalty Rome inflicts on political agitators and they accordingly cry out for the crucifixion of Jesus (v. 13). Like the disciples earlier, fear and weakness lead the crowd to abandon Jesus.

Next, the Markan Pilate seems to step back momentarily from his former challenging position, now asking: 'Why, what evil has he done?' (Τί γὰρ ἐποίησεν κακόν;), (v. 14).[88] This last question is heavily ironic in that Mark's Roman governor seems to be more open to Jesus' innocence, even at this late stage, than the crowd.

---

what to do with an accused prisoner, *Passion*, p. 65. This seems to be too literal a reading of the text. We would not expect either John Hyrcanus or Herod I to ask their subjects' opinions regarding legal issues, but the examples from Josephus show them asking those opinions for political effect. In all these cases, the actual historicity of the events is of secondary importance to the effect which the narrator wishes to produce.

[86] This seems to be the natural reading of ὃν λέγετε.

[87] The readings θέλετε and ὃν λέγετε are uncertain (both C ratings in the UBS 4th Edition). The witnesses for their omission are fairly weighty (ℵ B C W for omission of θέλετε; A D W for omission of ὃν λέγετε) and it is perhaps easier to see why these phrases should have been added to the text (possibly from Matt. 27.22) rather than removed. If not original they certainly fit the sense of the question which would then read simply 'What then shall I do with the King of the Jews?'

[88] Mark shows a distinct liking for groups of threes: three questions here, Jesus is mocked three times, three passion predictions, three sleeping disciples in Gethsemane, Jesus' threefold return, three women at the tomb, etc.; see Burkill, 'Mark's', p. 256 and Petersen, 'Composition', pp. 185–217.

Although portrayed as a strong political manipulator throughout this scene, Mark's Roman is clearly not as hostile towards Jesus as his compatriots and their leaders. It is almost as if Mark has used Pilate to hold up the proceedings for a moment, asking the people to think about what they are doing. They, however, refuse to answer, shouting all the more for crucifixion. Mark's readers are surely intended to realize that Jesus has not done any evil and so the crowd cannot reply to Pilate's question.

The Roman governor is now in a strong position: as a messianic claimant, Jesus had to be removed but the major obstacle, public outrage, has now been eliminated. The people could hardly riot over someone whose death they had demanded. Verse 15 is therefore full of Markan irony: Pilate is satisfying the demands of the crowd, but these are demands which he has engineered and which suit his own purposes.[89]

Pilate sends Jesus to be flogged (φραγελλόω).[90] This could be administered as a punishment in its own right[91] or, as here, was the usual preliminary to crucifixion.[92] Mark's readers would be well aware of the horrors of this degrading torture. No further details are necessary; the evangelist is not interested in rousing support for Jesus by emphasising the extent to which he was physically abused. After having Jesus scourged, Pilate hands him over to crucifixion. The word παρέδωκεν in 15.15 echoes that in 15.1 and is reminiscent of the passion predictions in 9.31 and 10.33–4. Pilate has performed his role in Jesus' passion and now passes him on to the next stage on his way to Calvary.

[89] No death sentence is necessary in Mark's account since this has already been pronounced by the Jewish council in 14.64; see Gnilka, *Evangelium*, p. 303.

[90] This appears to be the Latinized version of the verb μαστιγόω, the usual Greek word for 'flogging' or 'scourging' found throughout Josephus' writings and used in John 19.1; see Barrett, *St John*, p. 539 and pp. 182–3 below.

[91] For instance, the case of Jesus ben Ananias who was scourged by Albinus before being released (*JW* 6.300–9). Fear of the lash is expressed in *JW* 6.143. On several occasions during the Jewish revolt, according to Josephus, it was used to produce terror in the compatriots of the one scourged (e.g. *JW* 2.612, 7.200, *Life* 147). Jewish usage limited flogging to forty strokes, in practice thirty-nine (2 Cor. 11.24, Deut. 25.3); the Romans, however, had no limit and people often died under the torture (*JW* 7.373; Eusebius, *EH* 4.5.4). It was a punishment from which Roman citizens, as with crucifixion, were exempt (Acts 22.25).

[92] See Josephus, *JW* 2.306, 308, 449, 5.449, 7.200–2; Livy, *History of Rome* 1.26, 33.36; Philo, *In Flaccum* 72; Seneca, *Ad Marciam* 26.3; Apuleius, *Metamorphoses* 8; Dionysius of Halicarnassus 7.69. Whether the scourging took place before the crucifixion, on the way to the place of execution or actually on the cross varied.

Conclusion

Pilate in Mark's gospel is not a weak governor, bowing to public pressure and the demands of the chief priesthood. Instead he is a skilful politician, manipulating the crowd to avoid a potentially difficult situation, and is a strong representative of imperial interests. Although Mark clearly lays primary guilt for Jesus' death upon the Jewish leadership, Pilate is not exonerated. He plays a vital part in the chain of events leading to the crucifixion and shares the guilt involved therein. This is perfectly in keeping with the third passion prediction in which there is no hint that Jesus' gentile judge will be favourably disposed towards him: 'the Son of Man will be delivered to the chief priests and the scribes, and they will condemn him to death, and deliver him to the Gentiles; and they will mock him and spit upon him and scourge him, and kill him; and after three days he will rise' (10.33–4). At his death not only is Jesus deserted by his closest supporters but the whole political world of first-century Palestine, both Jewish and Roman, have sided against him. The Jewish leadership have arrested and condemned him but Pilate sends Jesus for crucifixion.

This portrayal of Pilate serves two major functions within the Markan narrative. The first ties in with persecution, an important background to the gospel. Verse 4.17 speaks of followers of Jesus who fall away 'when tribulation or persecution arises'; 8.34–8 counsels disciples to take up their cross and promises that those losing their lives for Jesus and the gospel will be rewarded; 10.30 speaks of persecutions now, 'in this time'.[93] Even more clearly, 13.9–13 refers to followers of Jesus being delivered up to councils, beaten in synagogues, standing before governors and kings and family members betraying one another to death. Rather than an apocalyptic warning of future persecutions, this passage appears to be referring to a present reality. As M. Hengel writes: 'Is it not obvious that here Mark has in mind those cruel events of 64, when there was the first mass killing of Christians? . . . The emphatic theology of suffering and the cross in the gospel has its very specific *Sitz im Leben* here'.[94] Mark is writing for people who have been

---

[93] The two storms at sea may also illustrate the way in which Jesus rescues his community in persecution (4.35–41, 6.45–52). See generally van Iersel, 'Persecuted Community?'.

[94] Hengel, *Studies*, p. 24. The primary texts describing Nero's persecution are: Tacitus, *Ann.* 15.44; Suetonius, *Nero* 16; Eusebius, *EH* 2.25 and Sulpicius Severus,

hated, betrayed, seen their friends persecuted and are in fear for their own lives.[95]

One of the aims of Mark's work was surely to strengthen such people, to show them that Jesus predicted persecution and difficulties. The story of Peter's denial and subsequent restoration (14.7) shows that there can be forgiveness even for those who have denied Jesus and the parables of growth and Christian community illustrate the continuance of Christianity beyond present troubles. Into this framework Mark's picture of Jesus' hearing before Pilate fits perfectly. To have shown Jesus standing before a weak, impotent governor determined to release him would have been far removed from the experiences of Mark's readers, some of whom may have experienced the harsh reality of a Roman hearing themselves. But to portray the Roman governor in a strong position, preying on the fears and weaknesses of the people, would have far more contemporary relevance. Although Jesus' Roman trial is not a model for Mark's readers (they are after all to proclaim what the Spirit tells them rather than keep silent, 13.9), it does present a credible picture of his strength and courage at the hands of a harsh Roman governor. Mark shows that discipleship may involve persecution and harsh treatment by Rome but this was not only foretold but also endured by Jesus in his earthly life.

Mark's Jewish and Roman hearings together illustrate a second crucial point for earliest Christianity: although crucified as an insurrectionary, Jesus was innocent of all charges and goes voluntarily to his death as the righteous one of God. Mark shows that neither the Jewish nor the Roman hearing held any weight. The Jewish judges were motivated by envy and a desire to be rid of Jesus; they were men who would stoop to childish mockery of their victim. The Roman hearing, though before a harshly manipulative and shrewd governor, was based on a misunderstanding of the

---

Chronicle 2.29 (the latter, writing in the fifth century, was heavily dependent upon Tacitus for his account).

[95] Tertullian's reference to an *institutionem Neronianum* (*Ad Nationes* 1.7, *Apol.* 5) and Severus' rather vague reference to edicts (*Chron.* 2.29.3) have led some scholars to suggest the existence of an edict of Nero (or at latest Domitian) forbidding the practice of Christianity anywhere in the Empire. However, no inscription referring to it has ever been found, nor does Pliny appear to be aware of such an edict (*Ep.* 10.96/7) and Tertullian's phrase may simply mean 'the practice adopted by Nero' (Ste Croix, 'Why Were?', p. 14). Yet even if no formal edict outlawing Christianity was passed by Nero, the Christian community in Rome would still feel in a vulnerable position and might fear further persecutions. See Hengel, *Studies*, p. 24 and Best, *Mark*, p. 52.

nature of kingship. Mark's Jewish court presented Jesus to the governor as one condemned for his messianic claims; claims which Pilate interpreted as threatening Roman stability and interests. It is also significant that Pilate only confirmed the existing sentence; he did not initiate it. Rome had not previously had any reason to arrest Jesus as a political activist but simply acted on the Jewish findings. The reader, however, knows that Pilate is mistaken in his acceptance of the Jewish condemnation and that Jesus was not claiming an earthly political kingship, involving territorial conquest and a threat to Roman order in the province, as the Roman governor supposed. This would be an important apologetic point for first-century Christians accused by their opponents of following a failed Jewish revolutionary who met a shameful end on a Roman cross.

Several scholars have seen the account of the hearing before Pilate as an apology for the crucifixion, but Mark does not achieve his purpose by emphasizing the *weakness* of Pilate as they suppose.[96] S. G. F. Brandon in particular admits that the traditional reading of Pilate in this scene portrays him as impossibly weak and stupid and is forced to conclude that Mark wrote for 'simple-minded' people. Mark's handling of his material is much more sophisticated than this: he presents the reader with a credible representative of Roman rule, whilst skilfully arranging the narrative on two levels. Jesus stands before Pilate in silence; the governor's misunderstanding of his kingly identity sends him to his death. The reader, however, recognizes that Jesus is innocent. Although Jesus was crucified as an insurrectionary, Mark's gospel shows that the execution was based on envy and misunderstanding: Christians followed the innocent Son of Man who gave his life as a ransom for many (10.45), not a failed political leader.[97]

[96] For example, Brandon, *Jesus*, pp. 256–64; Nineham, *Gospel*, p. 411–12 and Gundry, *Mark*, p. 13.
[97] A historical appraisal of the Roman trial of Jesus will be left until after the characterization of Pilate has been examined in all four gospels (see pp. 196–202 below).

5

PILATE IN MATTHEW'S GOSPEL

With Matthew's gospel we are dealing with a book written for a different early Christian readership in another location and facing its own particular set of problems. Virtually all scholars are agreed that Matthew, like Mark, was composed in an urban environment, possibly with a fairly wealthy readership in mind.[1] The location has traditionally been at Antioch, the capital of the province of Syria and the fourth largest city in the Roman Empire.[2] In favour of Antioch is the city's Greek-speaking gentile character together with its large Jewish population; the long existence of Christianity in the city (since the 30s according to Acts 11.19–26); and the fact that Matthew's gospel seems to have been known and possibly quoted in the early second century by Ignatius, the bishop of Antioch.[3] Although this is still a widely held view,[4] a growing number of

---

[1] In favour of an urban environment is the fact that the word πόλις occurs twenty-six times in Matthew, compared to eight times in Mark, suggesting that Matthew had a particular interest in city life. See Kingsbury, 'Conclusion', p. 264. In support of the wealthy status of some of the members of Matthew's community is the fact that the evangelist seems less concerned for the poor than does either Mark or Luke: for example, where Luke has 'Blessed are the poor', Matthew either added or felt no need to alter 'Blessed are the poor *in spirit*' (both are probably dependent upon the same source, Q: Matt. 5.3, Luke 6.20). Matthew also contains several references to money and it is striking that he always uses higher denominations than those found in Mark or Luke: compare, for instance, Matt. 25.14 with Luke 19.11–7. The reference in 10.9 to 'gold' is absent from both Mark and Luke. See Kilpatrick, *Origins*, p. 124.

[2] For a vivid description of city life in Antioch at the time see Stark, 'Antioch', pp. 189–210.

[3] Schoedel suggests that Ignatius knew and quoted the same tradition as Matthew but that he did not have access to the gospel of Matthew in written form: cf. 'Ignatius', pp. 175–6. Conversely Meier argues that four texts from Ignatius' letters are clearly dependent on Matthew's gospel – *Sm.* 1.1, *Ph.* 3.1, *Pol.* 2.2 and *Eph.* 19.2–3 (the latter being a midrash on Matthew's 'star of the magi'): cf. 'Matthew', pp. 178–86. See also Massaux, *Influence*, pp. 94–107.

[4] The classic exponent of this view is Streeter, *Four Gospels*, pp. 500–28; more recently see Meier, 'Matthew and Ignatius' and Luz, *Matthew*, pp. 90–2.

scholars suggest that the gospel may have originated much closer to Palestine, possibly in a city of upper Galilee or Syro-Phoenicia.[5] In support of such a location is the close contact it would afford with emerging rabbinic Judaism (a contact for which there is very little evidence at Antioch[6]) and the fact that the gospel must have originated somewhere where Jewish influence was strong enough to bring serious trouble to Christian believers (10.17, 23).[7] Although it is impossible to be certain, this geographical area does make good sense of the pictures both of Judaism and of Pilate which emerge from Matthew and will be taken as the general area of origin in the following discussion.

An important consideration regarding the dating of Matthew's gospel is the precise relationship between the group of Christians to which the author belonged and Judaism. Both the author himself and those for whom he writes appear to be Jewish Christians.[8] Yet

[5] Upholders of this view include Kilpatrick (*Origins*, pp. 133–4) who argues for the Tyrian coastal cities; Hengel (*Judaism*, vol. 1, p. 105) who argues for Palestine; Segal ('Matthew's', pp. 25–9) who, on the basis of Matt. 10.28, argues for a loosely confederated group of congregations in Galilee and Syria between which missionaries were constantly on the move; White ('Crisis', pp. 211–47) who argues for a setting somewhere along a Syro-Phoenician arc stretching from upper Galilee to Coele-Syria; and Dunn (*Partings*, pp. 151–2). Other suggestions include Alexandria (Brandon, *Fall*, p. 221 and Tilborg, *Jewish Leaders*, p. 172); Caesarea (Viviano, 'Where Was?', pp. 182–4); and Transjordan, particularly Pella (Slingerland, 'Transjordanian', pp. 18–28).

[6] The authority of Yavneh took some time before it was recognized in the diaspora. See Segal, 'Matthew's', p. 26 and Dunn, *Partings*, pp. 232, 322, note 6.

[7] Further arguments which are often brought against Antioch are the fact that the author of the gospel seems completely unaware of Paul's letters and his doctrine of righteousness apart from the Law (although the implication of Gal. 2.11–14 is that Paul lost support at Antioch and so abandoned it as a base) and, more importantly, the differences between the Christianity reflected in the gospel and that of Ignatius in his letters (see White, 'Crisis', p. 228). Hengel has shown that the fact that the gospel was written in Greek does not necessarily exclude a Palestinian origin: cf. *Judaism*, vol. 1. Furthermore Matthew has added a reference to Syro-Phoenicia in 4.24 which has no parallel in Mark and has omitted the reference to the Syro-Phoenician woman (Mark 7.26), describing her instead as a 'Canaanite woman' (15.22), possibly because the story might have been offensive to his readers; see Kilpatrick, *Origins*, pp. 132–3.

[8] In contrast to Mark, the author of Matthew's gospel does not need to explain Jewish customs to his readers, as a comparison of Matt. 15.1 with Mark 7.1–4 shows. It is assumed in this discussion that Matthew the tax-collector with whom the gospel is traditionally associated was not the author (against Goodspeed, *Matthew* and Gundry, *Matthew*, pp. 609–22). Papias, cited by Eusebius (*EH* 3.39.16), claimed that Matthew copied oracles in the Hebrew language and that everyone interpreted them as he was able (see also *EH* 5.8.2 and 3.34.5–6). Since the gospel was written in Greek and it is inconceivable that an eyewitness would be so dependent on Mark, it is extremely unlikely that this collection of oracles was our gospel of Matthew; see

throughout the pages of his gospel the author displays an extremely vehement hostility towards non-Christian Jews, especially Pharisees and the Jewish leadership.[9] Although some scholars suggest that this conflict arises because Matthew's community still regards itself as part of Judaism,[10] the majority argue that by this time it had begun to think of itself as distinct and had recently withdrawn from or been expelled by the local synagogue.[11] The continual references to 'their' synagogue and the anti-Jewish tone of the gospel seem to support this suggestion.[12] But it would perhaps be anachronistic to see too rigid a distinction between what was 'inside' and 'outside' Judaism at this point. Matthew's gospel seems to reflect the turbulent times towards the end of the first century when the early church came into conflict with emerging rabbinic Judaism. The two groups still held much in common – culture, tradition, importance of the Law – but were bitterly divided over their interpretation of the Law and the place and significance of Jesus of Nazareth within it. The gospel is generally dated somewhere between 80 and 90 CE.[13]

Throughout this chapter, then, it will be assumed that Matthew's gospel was probably written in Galilee or lower Syria in the penultimate decade of the first century and reflects the growing crisis between the Jewish synagogue and the early Christian communities in the restructuring of Jewish society following the fall of Jerusalem.

Luz, *Matthew*, pp. 93–5 for a fuller discussion of the author's identity. Meier goes against the prevailing view in his suggestion that the author of Matthew's gospel was a gentile: cf. 'Matthew', pp. 625–7.

[9] See, for example, 21.28–32, 33–46, 22.1–10, chapter 23, 27.25. It is also clear from the gospel that Matthew's readers are suffering persecution at Jewish hands; see 5.10–11, 44, 10.17–8, 23, 28, 32–3, 39, 13.21, 24.9–10 and Hare, *Theme*.

[10] For example, Segal ('Matthew's', p. 31) who claims that 'in spite of their Christian confession, Matthean Christians are within the spectrum of Jewish Law observance. What they oppose is Pharisaic interpretation of the Law and their claim of authority to interpret the laws'. See also Dunn, *Partings*, pp. 151–6, 213–5.

[11] For example, Gundry, 'Responsive', pp. 62–7 and Stanton, *Gospel*, pp. 113–281.

[12] For example, the contrast between 'their synagogue' and 'my church' in 16.18 or 21.43.

[13] There are several reasons for this dating. If the gospel was written after Mark's as most scholars suppose (see below, p. 123), then it cannot be earlier than c. 65 CE. Jerusalem already seems to have fallen (21.43, 27.25). If 27.24–7 refers to the Jewish poll-tax, then the gospel (or at least the traditions behind it) must date from before 97 when the tax was repealed by Nerva. W. D. Davies suggests that the Sermon on the Mount is a Christian answer to Jamnia, which would put the gospel shortly before or after the turn of the century: cf. *Setting*, pp. 256–315.

The work refers to Pontius Pilate three times. His first and most extensive appearance is during the Roman trial narrative (27.1–26). He is mentioned again in 27.58 when he allows Joseph of Arimathea to take Jesus' body and a third time in 27.62–6 when he grants the chief priests and Pharisees a guard to watch over the tomb.

After briefly considering the context of Matthew's references to Pilate, this chapter will look first at special Matthean concerns within the passion narrative, as indicated by his redaction of Mark, and then go on to look at the characterization of Pilate which emerges from the trial scene.[14]

Matthew's sources

The majority of scholars assume that Matthew's primary source was the gospel of Mark. Into this earlier work he has added 'sayings material' (either written or oral) from at least one other source, Q, which he has in common with Luke, and an amount of material peculiar to his own gospel, including proof texts and legendary sounding stories, known as M (though it is doubtful whether this was a coherent single source).[15]

Although he reorders and abbreviates Mark's material, Matthew generally follows his main source fairly closely.[16] In his account of the Roman trial, however, Matthew has been much freer with Mark's account than usual.[17] He has inserted the story of Judas' suicide between the account of the Sanhedrin's leading Jesus away and his standing before Pilate (27.3–10). He has also added the story of Pilate's wife's dream (27.19), Pilate washing his hands (27.24) and the cry of the Jewish crowd (27.25).[18] The rest of the Markan narrative has also undergone a considerable amount of redaction. We should not be surprised, then, if Matthew's Pilate comes across slightly differently from the Roman prefect in Mark's presentation.

[14] For a fuller account of Matthew's redaction of Mark see Senior, *Passion*.

[15] In favour of Markan priority are, for instance, V. Taylor, *Gospel*, p. 11; Kilpatrick, *Origins*, pp. 8–9; Luz, *Matthew*, pp. 73–6. For a list of those who favour Matthean priority see Luz, ibid., p. 47. There is, however, excessive disagreement amongst scholars regarding the Q hypothesis.

[16] For discussion see Luz, *Matthew*, pp. 46–78.

[17] Schweizer, *Matthew*, p. 506.

[18] For similar legendary sounding Matthean additions to the passion account see 26.52–4, 27.51–4, 62–6, 28.2–4; see also Kilpatrick, *Origins*, p. 49.

It has often been recognized that Matthew's gospel consists of five sections or 'books'. Each contains a narrative followed by a discourse: for example, the Sermon on the Mount (chapters 5–7), the discourse on mission (chapter 10), parables (chapter 13), the discourse on church life and order (chapter 18) and the eschatological discourse (chapters 24–5). This fivefold structure has frequently been compared to the five books of Moses in the Torah, suggesting that Matthew regarded the Christian gospel as a new Torah.[19] The infancy narratives constitute an overture to the gospel, in which the main themes are introduced, whilst the passion narrative forms its climax. Many of the nativity themes are taken up again and reach their culmination in the final three chapters of the gospel.[20] For Matthew the death and resurrection of Jesus together constitute an apocalyptic event in which all prophecy is fulfilled.[21] Israel's leaders have rejected the Messiah, the kingdom is given to others (8.11–12, 21.43) and the age of the church is established (28.16–20). It is in this final dramatic fulfilment of prophecy that Pilate plays his role.

Matthew's special interests reflected in his redaction of Mark 15.1–15

The themes prominent in Mark's presentation of the passion narrative – the antagonism of the Jewish leaders, fulfilment of prophecy, kingship, mockery and rejection – have all been taken over and reused by Matthew in his own account. But he has skilfully blended the Markan text with other material to highlight his own particular concerns within the narrative.

(1)   A striking theme in Matthew's presentation of the Roman trial is that of the responsibility for the death of Jesus. Running throughout the whole scene is the haunting question: On whom did the guilt ultimately lie? Each actor attempts to shift the responsibility away from himself. Judas, in 27.3–5,

---

[19] Such fivefold divisions were not necessarily limited to the Jewish Torah – the Psalms and Irenaeus' *Adversus Haereses* were similarly arranged in five sections. See Meier, 'Matthew', p. 629.

[20] For example, Herod's killing of the infants forms the earliest omen of the crucifixion; the same verb ἀπόλλυμι (to destroy) is used at both 2.13 and 27.1 (and 12.14). The title Christ is also prominent in both sections – 1.1, 16, 18, 2.4 and 27.17, 22 – as are dreams. See Vögtle, *Matthäische Kindheitsgeschichte*, pp. 153–83.

[21] See 26.54–6.

repented when he saw that Jesus had been condemned and vainly attempted to disassociate himself from what was to happen by returning the money to the chief priests and elders. Yet the betrayer could not so easily avoid his share of the guilt surrounding Jesus' death and commits suicide (27.5). Similarly Pilate is warned by his wife not to have anything to do with Jesus ('that righteous man') and, later in the trial, will wash his hands to show symbolically that although he must send the silent prisoner to his death, he will not accept responsibility (v. 24). Primary responsibility for the execution of the Messiah, however, rests in the Matthean narrative with those who accept it – all the people (including the chief priests and elders, πᾶς ὁ λαὸς). The crowd has been completely persuaded of Jesus' guilt by its leaders. Within the context of the narrative the crowd's words in verse 25 – 'his blood be on us and on our children' – are meant to reassure the Roman prefect that Jesus deserves to die. Using a traditional Israelite formula indicating responsibility for a death in the eyes of God,[22] Matthew's crowd attempts to overcome Pilate's hesitation by offering to run the risk of becoming guilty and bearing the consequences itself should Jesus turn out to be innocent.

Yet throughout the entirety of this scene Matthew has underlined the fact that Jesus *is* innocent. The description of the fate of Judas shows that even his betrayer recognized this innocence. Verses 19 and 20, relating the fact that Pilate's wife dreams of the innocence of Jesus, provide a break in the dialogue, almost as if each prisoner has been mustering his forces. What is important here is that whilst the chief priests and elders side with Barabbas, God himself intervenes on behalf of Jesus, declaring that he is a righteous man.[23] Dreams are used frequently in Matthew and are an unquestionable source of divine guidance.[24] Matthew's Christian readers are

[22] For example, Deut. 19.10, Lev. 20.9, Josh. 2.19, 2 Sam. 1.16, Ezek. 18.13, Jer. 26.15 and especially, 2 Sam. 3.28–9. The expression is not a curse but a standard designation of responsibility for a crime and its consequences. See Reventlow, 'Sein Blut', pp. 316–21.
[23] The idea of two sides, one of God, the other belonging to humankind, has previously appeared at another critical point in the narrative (16.23) where, by not accepting the suffering of the Christ, Peter shows himself to be on the side of humanity opposed to God.
[24] 1.20–1, 2.12, 13 and 19–20. Dreams are also one of Yahweh's means of communicating with humans in the OT; see Everts, 'Dreams', p. 231. Dreams are

thus to recognize both Jesus' innocence and also that the
Jewish crowd must bear the consequences of its rejection of
the Messiah.[25] On a different level, the change from ὁ ὄχλος
to ὁ λαὸς in verse 25 may also be significant: the λαὸς for
whom Jesus was sent have now rejected him.[26]

(2) Linked with this theme of responsibility and stemming from
Matthew's own situation with regard to Judaism, is the much
more anti-Jewish tone throughout his Roman trial scene
compared to that of his source. Neither the Jewish leaders nor
their people are spared from Matthew's condemnation. In
27.1 the chief priests and elders of the nation meet together in
order to put Jesus to death.[27] The same group display a
particularly callous lack of interest in justice in 27.4 and incite
the crowd to ask not only for the release of Barabbas, as in
Mark, but also for the condemnation of Jesus in verse 20. In
the second scene involving Pilate, Joseph of Arimathea is not
a member of the Sanhedrin (as in Mark 15.43) but is described
simply as 'a disciple of Jesus' (27.57). Clearly Matthew will
not allow the man who buried Jesus to be an influential Jewish
leader.

The Jewish people themselves are no less implicated in
Jesus' death. The very fact that the elders are clearly described
as the elders *of the people* emphasizes that they act as the

also found in other Graeco-Roman literature, e.g. Valerius Maximus 1.7.2 and Dio
Cassius 44.17.1 (the dream of Julius Caesar's wife).

[25] In view of the impact of the fall of Jerusalem on first-century Jewish thought
(see chapter 3 on Matthew's contemporary Josephus above), it is quite possible that
Matthew and his readers understood the fall of the city as a consequence of the
death of Jesus. See Albright and Mann, *Matthew*, p. 345; Kilpatrick, *Origins*, p. 47;
France, *Matthew*, p. 226; Brown, *Death*, pp. 837–9. For further discussion see also
Przybylski, 'Setting' and Dunn, *Partings*, pp. 154–6.

[26] 1.21, 2.6. The majority of commentators take v. 25 as showing the whole nation
of Israel, the chosen people of God, joining together to accept guilt for Jesus' death
(e.g. Fenton, *Matthew*, p. 436; Gundry, *Matthew*, p. 565; Beare, *Gospel*, p. 531).
Senior (*Passion*, p. 258) takes this even further, suggesting that Matthew's use of
λαός at this point shows that he understands the Jewish rejection of the Messiah as a
'pivotal event in salvation history' (see also Luz, *Theology*, 134–5). Przybylski sees a
contemporary relevance to ὁ λαός here, drawing a parallel between those who
rejected the messiahship of Jesus before Pilate and the Jewish nation of Matthew's
own day who continue to deny that Jesus is the Christ: cf. 'Setting', p. 200. Whilst
these connotations may be present, however, it is probably better not to build up too
much on one word, especially since it is always the Jewish leaders towards whom
Matthew is most critical. As Dunn (*Partings*, p. 155) points out, even after 27.25 'the
people' may still be won over to the gospel as the fears of the Jewish leadership in
27.64 make clear.

[27] ὥστε θανατῶσαι αὐτόν is not found in Mark's account.

representatives of the crowd throughout the narrative (Mark has simply 'elders'). Although Pilate fears a riot in verse 24, the earlier part of the Roman trial in Matthew gives the appearance of being a much more restrained, formal gathering than that found in Mark. The gathering of the crowd is described in verse 17 using the verb συνάγω. The same verb has recently been used to describe assemblies of the Sanhedrin in 26.3 and 26.57. This gives the impression that the crowd has gathered to judge between the two prisoners. In verse 20, the chief priests and elders of the people persuade the crowd to ask for the release of Barabbas and the death of Jesus. R. H. Gundry asserts that Matthew's substitution of 'persuade' (ἔπεισαν) 'lightens the crowd's burden of guilt by making them victims of evil persuasion'.[28] If anything, however, the reverse is the case. Mark's use of the verb 'to stir up' implies that the people are agitated almost to a state of diminished responsibility; Matthew's lighter verb gives the impression of a more reasoned decision: the crowd will make its request in the full knowledge of what it is doing. In response to Pilate's alternatives, the crowd says 'Barabbas' (the verb is εἶπαν).[29] In verse 22 the crowd again proclaims (λέγουσιν) what should be done with Jesus. The addition of πάντες underlines that it is the choice of all the Jews, both the leaders and the people. The change from an aorist imperative (σταύρωσον) to a passive imperative (σταυρωθήτω) – 'Let him be crucified!' – gives the impression that the crowd itself is passing judgement. The verdict is clear and thought through. Only in verse 23 do the proceedings threaten to become out of hand and riotous.

(3)   Another striking element in Matthew's account when compared to that of his source is the emphasis on the *choice* to be made between Jesus and Barabbas and the contrast between the two men. In place of Mark's one-sided 'Do you want me to release to you the King of the Jews?' Matthew has made the choice explicit: 'Whom do you want me to release for you, Jesus Barabbas or Jesus who is called Christ?' Again in verse 21 Pilate asks 'Which of the two . . .?' The parallelism is

[28] Gundry, *Matthew*, p. 562. The verb is again used of the actions of the Jewish leaders in 28.14.

[29] In Mark, the demand of the crowd is lost. We are to assume from the stirring of the crowd in verse 11 and Pilate's question in verse 12 that the crowd actually has demanded the release of Barabbas. Matthew, however, leaves us in no doubt.

heightened by the fact that the two men have the same first name, Jesus,[30] and Barabbas' patronym would also be quite appropriate as a description of Jesus of Nazareth.[31]

Mark's description of Barabbas has been drastically re-worked by Matthew. Most notably his political activity – his possible involvement in an uprising and murder[32] – has been suppressed by Matthew in favour of a much simpler δέσμιον ἐπίσημον, a famous or notorious prisoner. One effect of this contraction is that it does not detract the reader's attention from the theme of choice in the narrative. Another effect is that Barabbas' activity has been completely depoliticized, all hint of insurrectionary activity has been removed. He is simply a well-known prisoner who might quite naturally have supporters amongst the people. Similarly Pilate refers to Jesus not as the politically loaded 'King of the Jews' but as 'Messiah'. The choice in Matthew is therefore no longer between two politically dubious men but one between a famous prisoner and the Christ; that is, it is the religious significance of Jesus which is at stake. The emphasis is not so much on the man chosen but the one rejected: the Messiah.

(4)   Finally, it is this title – Christ – which dominates Matthew's Roman trial narrative rather than the 'King of the Jews' as in Mark. The title is extremely important for Matthew; he is concerned not only with showing that Jesus *is* the Christ but also with illustrating *in what way* Jesus is the Christ. The title is initially equated with the Son of David (1.1) and the King of the Jews (2.1–12), both titles carrying political overtones. It is not used again until chapter 11 where it is redefined in terms of one who heals and saves.[33] A significant stage is reached at 16.16 when Peter acknowledges that Jesus is not only the Christ but that he is 'the son of the living God' (a phrase not found in Mark). It is only 'from this time' (16.21–2) that Jesus

---

[30] Textual support for the reading Ἰησοῦν in verses 16 and 22 is not good. It is omitted by a, A, B, D, L, W, ℵ and most others. Origen, however, remarked in the third century that many copies did not state that Barabbas was also called Jesus. He felt that the omission was probably right since no sinner in the whole of scripture bore the same name as Jesus (*In Matt.* 122). In the light of this reverential attitude, it is more likely that the name Jesus was erased from copies of Matthew than that it was added at a later date and so the reading 'Jesus Barabbas' has been retained in brackets by the UBS Greek Text[4] with a 'C' rating.

[31] See above, p. 112, note 83.

[32] See pp. 111–12 above for a fuller discussion of Barabbas' activity.

[33] See especially 11.2–6 where Jesus cites Isa. 35.5–6 and 61.1.

begins to tell his disciples about his impending sufferings and death and that discipleship involves taking up a cross (16.24).[34] In the Roman trial scene it is Jesus' messiahship which is on trial and which the Jewish crowd, persuaded by its leaders, rejects.

Matthew's presentation, then, though dependent on Mark's, emphasizes a different set of features – in particular the innocence of Jesus, his messiahship and the responsibility of the Jewish crowd and its leaders. Not surprisingly, these dominant motifs have had an effect on the way in which Pilate is portrayed in this gospel. The Matthean Pilate has become only a minor character compared to the central position occupied by the Roman governor in Mark (despite the fact that the Roman trial is twice as long in this gospel), suggesting once again that relations with Judaism were much more important and urgent than relations with Rome for Matthew's community.

The characterization of Pilate in Matthew

Following his source, Matthew records a morning meeting of the Jewish leaders during which Jesus is bound and handed over to the Roman prefect (27.1–2). Pilate is identified not only by his name (as in Mark) but also by a rather vague description of his title – 'the governor' (τῷ ἡγεμόνι).[35] In verse 3 the reader is told that Jesus is now condemned.

After a dramatic aside describing the suicide of Judas (27.3–10), we again return to the Roman trial (v. 11). Matthew continues to follow Mark's narrative closely in the following exchange. Pilate begins by tackling the central political charge: 'Are you the King of the Jews?'.[36] The Matthean Jesus replies ambiguously – 'You say it'

---

[34] On Christ in Matthew see Nolan, *Royal*, especially pp. 145–9 and Kingsbury, *Structure*, pp. 96–8.

[35] Pilate's precise title appears to have been *praefectus* or ἔπαρχος; see above, p. 11.

[36] Jesus is only referred to as 'King of the Jews' in Matthew by gentiles – by the magi in 2.2, by Pilate in this scene, by the soldiers in 27.29, and on the *titulus* above the cross in 27.37. It is redefined as 'King of Israel' by the mocking chief priests, elders and scribes at the cross (27.42). The title King is used by Jesus apparently of himself (as the Son of Man) in the parable of the sheep and the goats (25.31–46). Matthew also traces Jesus' descent through Judah's kings back to David in 1.6 and this Davidic line is repeatedly stressed throughout the gospel – 1.1, 9.27, 12.23, 15.22, 20.30–1, 21.9, 25.31–46. Kingsbury has shown that those who have correctly perceived Jesus as the Son of David in this gospel are those of no social or

(Σὺ λέγεις). He does not deny his kingship nor does he accept the political title as an adequate description of his identity.[37] Matthew stresses Jesus' silence, adding 'he made no answer' (οὐδὲν ἀπεκρίνατο) in verse 12 and repeating that 'he gave him no answer, not even to a single charge' (οὐκ ἀπεκρίθη αὐτῷ πρὸς οὐδὲ ἓν ῥῆμα) in verse 14.[38] Pilate's amazement is similarly highlighted by the addition of the word 'greatly' (λίαν).[39] As in Mark's gospel, Pilate might be amazed at Jesus but, as a Roman judge, he would still be required to send the silent prisoner to his execution.

The next two verses provide the transition to the crowd scene. First the reader is informed of a custom of the governor, presumably established by himself or his predecessors, in which one prisoner could be released at the crowd's request. Verse 16 similarly supplies background detail, explaining that Barabbas was another prisoner in custody at that time.[40]

In verse 17 the crowd gathers to await its annual privilege. Throughout Matthew's gospel the Jewish crowds have generally been portrayed as friendly or neutrally disposed towards Jesus.

---

theological importance (e.g. blind men or the Canaanite woman): cf. 'Son of David', pp. 598–601. Furthermore, any political understanding of this role is reinterpreted by the entry into Jerusalem where Jesus is addressed as 'the humble king' (21.5).

[37] Senior argues that Σὺ λέγεις is the third in a series of questions posed by hostile people (Judas in 26.25 and the high priest in 26.64 – to both of whom Jesus replies Σὺ εἶπας) in which Jesus' reply is ironic, meaning 'You have answered your own question': cf. *Passion*, p. 228. Perhaps we need to draw a distinction between the way in which the readers of the gospel would understand these replies and the way in which the characters within the text understand them. The reader, with all the information provided by Matthew, understands Jesus' reply as a qualified acceptance of the title 'King of the Jews' whilst characters within the story do not. The irony involved in Matthew's use of these two levels of interpretation is obvious: like the high priest earlier, Pilate has unwittingly stumbled on the truth of who Jesus is, though he cannot understand it himself. See Howell, *Matthew's*, p. 241.

[38] In verse 13, since Matthew has already stated that Jesus made no answer, he alters Mark's οὐκ ἀποκρίνῃ οὐδέν to οὐκ ἀκούεις. Πρὸς οὐδὲ ἓν ῥῆμα stresses both Jesus' silence and the many accusations of the Jewish leaders. Ῥῆμα is probably to be translated as 'accusation' rather than its literal meaning 'word' (see 18.16).

[39] Verse 14 also omits Jesus' name, focusing attention on Pilate's reaction. Although θαυμάζω in Mark did not appear to imply any kind of religious wonder, the verb can sometimes have this meaning in Matthew. The verb is used seven times throughout the gospel – 8.10, 27, 9.33, 15.31, 21.20, 22.22 and 27.14. Of these, four appear to have religious overtones – 8.27, 9.33, 15.31 and 21.20; two do not – 8.10 and 22.22 (which is the only use of θαυμάζω besides 27.14 taken from Mark). Perhaps Matthew does want to show his reader Pilate's awe at Jesus, but as the Roman judge he will still condemn him.

[40] The subject of εἶχον, though not stated, is surely the Romans rather than the Jewish authorities.

They generally hold him to be a prophet (21.11, 21.46), even the Son of David (12.23, 21.9, 15),[41] but are far from fully under- standing Jesus' identity as the Christ, still less in terms of Matthew's central christological title, Son of God.[42] Gathered before the governor's tribunal, there is still a chance that the crowd might side with Jesus. Yet throughout his narrative, Matthew has shown the people as lacking in leadership or instruction. Often they are misled by their traditional leaders and are censured by Jesus.[43] It will come as no surprise when here too they allow their chief priests and elders to influence their judgement and persuade them into siding with Barabbas rather than Jesus.

Rather curiously after the apparently unlimited choice in verse 15, Pilate restricts the choice of the crowd in verse 17 to two men: Jesus Barabbas or Jesus who is called Christ. The depoliticizing of this choice has already been noted. Barabbas is briefly described as a 'famous prisoner' whilst Jesus is offered to the Jewish crowd not as the King of the Jews but by a title with profound religious connotations – Messiah. The charge has reverted to that which was uppermost in the Jewish trial (26.63, 68). Despite the gentile governor's perceptive equation of 'King of the Jews' with 'Christ', there is no sense in which the Matthean Pilate is trying to release Jesus here by appealing to the religious sympathies of the crowd. The role of Pilate and the Jewish authorities in the passion account parallels that of Herod I in the infancy narrative. There the Jewish King received news of the birth of the King of the Jews from the gentile magi (2.2) and automatically substituted this with 'Christ' when he discussed the matter with the chief priests and scribes of the people (2.4). Yet whether the child is referred to as 'King of the Jews' or as 'Christ' does not alter Herod's alarm at his birth, nor his intention to have him killed (2.13, 16–20).[44] The prophecy of 2.6 clearly shows that the Christ was expected to be a *ruler* of Israel

[41] Individual members of the crowds accept him as Son of David at 9.27 (two blind men), 15.22 (the Canaanite woman) and 20.30–1 (two blind men).

[42] Matthew links the titles Son of David and Christ at 1.6, 20–1 and 21.5–9. Whilst Davidic descent is clearly important for this evangelist, it is transcended by Jesus' identity as the Christ, as Jesus' debate with the Pharisees underlines (22.41–5). The reader knows that the Christ is not only the Son of David but more importantly the Son of God (16.16), a fact which is perceived only by the disciples and the gentile centurion after Jesus' crucifixion (27.54).

[43] For example, 11.20–4, 23.27–39, 26.47, 55 and 27.20–5.

[44] The same verb ἀπόλλυμι is used of both Herod's intention to destroy the infant Jesus (2.13) and the advice of the Jewish leadership (27.20).

and so even someone claiming the religious title could potentially pose a threat to the ruling authorities.[45]

Pilate's question, therefore, as in Mark, is a challenge to the people and an attempt to gauge Jesus' popularity.[46] Yet unlike Mark, Matthew has little interest in the characterization or motivation of Pilate, either the historical governor or the portrayal of him within his own narrative. The psychology of Pilate pales into insignificance next to Matthew's overriding concern to present the Jewish crowd with a choice: a prisoner or the Christ? The question of whether to accept or reject Jesus as the Christ would still be a vitally important one to Matthew's Jewish–Christian readers and would have been the major area of controversy between them and the Judaism which they had left. The question then would be loaded with contemporary relevance.

Verses 19 and 20 provide a dramatic break in the action, adding suspense to the narrative.[47] The chief priests and elders in verse 20 are clearly backing Barabbas: not only do they persuade the people to ask for their candidate but they also ask them to demand the destruction of Jesus.[48] In the previous verse, however, a lone voice has spoken out for Jesus, taking the surprising form of a gentile

---

[45] Whether the *historical* Roman governor would have been aware of such expectations, or would even have equated 'King of the Jews' with 'Christ', does not matter here. Historically, it is quite probable that a Roman governor would have acquainted himself with the religious expectations of the people he governed. The Matthean Pilate obviously does make these connections and the first readers of the gospel would presumably have found Matthew's portrayal credible.

[46] The explanatory note in verse 18 echoes Mark – Pilate knew that the Jewish leaders had delivered Jesus up out of *envy*. As in the Markan source, far from convincing the Roman governor of Jesus' innocence, this knowledge would only strengthen Pilate's desire to find out exactly what kind of a following Jesus really did command. His question in verse 17 is therefore, like Mark 15.9, an attempt to establish Jesus' popularity.

[47] The majority of translations give the word 'besides' for the Greek δέ in this verse which T. H. Robinson (*Gospel*, p. 227), commenting on the Moffat text, admits is 'perhaps, too strong an expression for the Greek connecting particle used here'. It may be better to see this verse going not with verses 17–18 as an addition or expansion to Pilate's offer, or even a preparation for the handwashing in verse 24, but as forming a contrast with verse 20 where the Jewish leaders persuade the crowd to ask for Barabbas (the NEB captures something of this sense when it translates the δέ in verse 19 as 'while' and that in verse 20 as 'meanwhile'). In this case, Matthew is again highlighting the dramatic parallelism between the two men – the intercessor on behalf of Jesus (Pilate's wife) is guided by God whilst those who will shout against Jesus (the Jewish people) are led by men.

[48] In Mark the chief priests stir up the people to ask only for Barabbas' release; it is the people themselves who come to the conclusion that Jesus 'the King of the Jews' must be crucified (15.11, 13).

woman – Pilate's wife. She urges Pilate to 'have nothing to do with that righteous man (τῷ δικαίῳ ἐκείνῳ), for I have suffered much over him today in a dream'.[49]

As mentioned before, dreams are an accepted method of divine communication in Matthew and other Graeco-Roman literature. One surprising aspect here, however, is that at all other times in this gospel it is the ones who are to make the important decisions who receive divine guidance through dreams. But in this particular case it is not the one in control, Pilate, who has the dream but his wife. Was Matthew simply making use of an earlier tradition involving Pilate's wife? Or, as R. E. Brown suggests, has the evangelist cast her in the common role of the noble pagan woman favourable to Judaism found, for example, in the pages of Josephus?[50] Was the portrayal of Pilate familiar to the evangelist from Mark's gospel (and possibly also Philo's *Embassy to Gaius* and negative oral Jewish appraisals) unlikely to recommend the governor as a recipient of divine communication? Perhaps the important point here is that Pilate has taken his seat as the judge (verse 19). He retains his neutrality in the affair whilst his wife (under divine guidance) pleads for Jesus and the Jewish leaders persuade the crowd to shout for Barabbas. Presumably at this point Pilate could have listened to his wife and granted the amnesty to Jesus. It was, after all, apparently entirely his own decision to offer the people a choice in verse 17. Yet he does not do so. He ignores his wife's caution and reiterates his previous question to the assembled crowd: 'Which of the two do you want me to release for you?'

The people give their choice: Barabbas. In answer to Pilate's next question: 'What shall I do with Jesus who is called Christ?' the people's judgement comes as no surprise to the reader after verse 20: 'Let him be crucified!' The dramatic tension which characterized the Markan account has disappeared: as soon as the Jewish people accept the candidate of their leaders, their desire for Jesus' death follows inevitably. Jesus' only hope of acquittal lies with Pilate who, as he sits in judgement, has already heard a divinely inspired witness to Jesus' righteousness. But the Matthean Pilate will not

---

[49] See 3.15 and the centurion's confession in Luke 23.47. Apocryphal literature named Pilate's wife as Claudia Procla or Procula. She has also, with not much likelihood, been identified as a granddaughter of Augustus. She was canonized in the orthodox church. For further information see Fascher, *Weib* and Rosadi, *Trial*, pp. 215–17.

[50] Brown, *Death*, p. 806.

jeopardize his own position for Jesus. Having established that the Jewish crowd wants Barabbas released, he continues to probe the people about Jesus. Pilate seems undecided at this point: a Messiah with no popular support could hardly undermine the authority of Rome or the Jewish aristocracy which worked so closely with the governor. He continues his line of questioning, 'Why, what evil has he done?'

At this a riot threatens to break out. The people shout out their previous judgement all the more (περισσῶς ἔκραζον). Responding to the precariousness of the situation, Pilate quickly determines on his course of action. He will send Jesus for crucifixion as the crowd requests and Roman law demands, but before he does so he will make sure that no reprisals can fall upon his head and stresses that it is the crowd itself who have condemned the one claiming to be the Messiah. In verse 24 he uses a Jewish ritual of handwashing to symbolize that it is the Jewish crowd which has demanded the death of Jesus: the crowd is responsible and not he.[51] Pilate's words also reflect OT imagery, in particular 2 Samuel 3.28 and Psalm 26.6: 'I wash my hands in innocence'. This passage and 27.4, which also focuses on the question of guilt for Jesus' death, are the only occurrences of the adjective 'innocent' (ἀθῷός) in the NT. But whilst Judas in 27.4 uses 'innocent' to describe Jesus, Pilate uses the adjective to describe himself. This is significant: Pilate is not proclaiming Jesus' innocence (though the textual variant adds this), but affirming that he is not responsible for Jesus' execution. Matthew's Pilate, then, is disassociating himself from Jesus' death by behaving in the manner of a pious Jew. The ritual in Deuteronomy 21.1–9 which absolves the people of Israel from the guilt of an unsolved murder has been turned about to reflect the innocence of a gentile governor.

Pilate continues his address to the crowd, 'See to it yourself' (ὑμεῖς ὄψεσθε). This has striking parallels with 27.4 where the chief priests and elders tell Judas to 'See to it yourself', and is part of the Matthean theme of one actor attempting to shift responsibility on to another. In verse 25 the Jewish people offer to bear the consequences should there be any repercussions for Jesus' death: 'His blood be on us and on our children'. At this, Pilate releases Barabbas and sends Jesus to be crucified.

---

[51] For evidence of handwashing as a means of protective purification in the Graeco-Roman world see Brown, ibid., p. 834.

Matthew's use of ἡγεμών

Before moving on from Pilate's characterization, one further point needs some consideration: Matthew's use throughout this scene of the title 'hēgemōn' (ἡγεμών).

Whilst Mark refers to the Roman prefect throughout this scene only by his cognomen or a personal pronoun, Matthew often replaces 'Pilate' with ἡγεμών – a general term meaning 'governor' which can loosely be used of any leading Roman.[52] The name Πιλᾶτος has been retained five times by Matthew[53] whilst the designation ἡγεμών is used of him six times.[54] The two terms appear to have been used entirely randomly throughout the narrative.

How are we to account for Matthew's usage of these two designations for the Roman prefect? At first sight the most obvious explanation is that he is using the terms for literary effect, to provide variation within the narrative. Matthew has heightened the sense of conversation within the Roman trial and for reasons of clarity needs frequently to reiterate who the speaker is. Rather than writing Πιλᾶτος every time the prefect is referred to (as Mark does eight times) Matthew may have interchanged Πιλᾶτος with ἡγεμών to relieve the monotony. One problem for this explanation, however, is verse 11a. This phrase is Matthean, repeating verse 2 and setting the scene for the Roman trial after the description of Judas' suicide in verses 3–10: 'Jesus stood before the governor'. If Matthew's use of ἡγεμών was merely to avoid repetitive use of Πιλᾶτος, it would be reasonable to expect the designation 'Pilate' here since he has not been mentioned for the last eight verses. Yet Matthew's Roman trial opens with Jesus standing before a ἡγεμών and it is only in verse 13 that the governor is named. The title stresses the official, Roman side of the hearing and suggests that Matthew's interest was not so much in the *historical prefect of Judaea* who sent Jesus to crucifixion but in his identity as *a Roman governor*.

Perhaps Pilate in Matthew's presentation is to be seen as a 'type'

[52] For example, 1 Pet. 2.14, Luke 2.2
[53] Corresponding to Mark's first, third, fifth and eighth usage of the name (i.e. Mark 15.1, 3, 9, 15, and the washing of hands, Matt. 27.24).
[54] Replacing Mark's second and fourth usage (i.e. Mark 15.2 and 4, supplementing Mark 15.1 and Mark's indefinite statement in 15.6 and two other statements without Markan parallels, Matt. 27.11a and 21).

of Roman governor with whom his readers may well be familiar. He is not interested in religious questions but the upholding of Roman law. His primary concern is to avoid riots amongst the people; a man who works closely with and allows himself to be influenced by the priestly authorities and influential men of Judaea.

Conclusion

The Matthean Pilate plays a much less significant role within the Roman trial scene than the Markan Pilate. His characterization is secondary to Matthew's major concern to show the Jewish people persuaded by their leaders into rejecting the Messiah and their acceptance of the consequences which this involved. The governor attempts to show his innocence by publicly washing his hands and telling the Jewish crowd to see to Jesus' execution themselves. Yet, like the chief priests in 27.4 who say the same words to Judas, Pilate is already too deeply implicated and cannot abdicate his responsibilities. Pilate and the Jewish authorities, together constituting the rulers of Judaea, mirror Herod I in the infancy narrative. All these leaders feel threatened by the messiahship of Jesus and wish to have him eliminated.

To a large extent this can be seen as a development from Mark's account. There Pilate skilfully manipulated the crowd by his challenging use of the title 'King of the Jews' into shouting for Jesus' crucifixion. The Roman prefect could then send Jesus to his execution knowing that the people had acquiesced to it (even demanded it) and that reprisals could not fall upon his own head. Similar themes are at work in Matthew's presentation but with one important alteration: the Jewish crowd no longer require a manipulative Roman governor to influence them. All hints of political pressure have been removed, both from Pilate's questions regarding Jesus and Matthew's description of Barabbas. The Jewish people are simply asked to choose between the Messiah and another prisoner. This they do, asking for the release of Barabbas and passing the death sentence on Jesus. As in the Markan source, the people demand crucifixion and take responsibility for it, but this motif has been significantly highlighted by Matthew and all hints of external pressure from Pilate have been removed, giving at times a rather colourless picture of the governor.

Finally, it is clear that Matthew's chief concern is with the breakdown of relations between his own Christian readers and

Judaism. Primary guilt for the death of Jesus, according to Matthew, lies with the Jewish authorities but the Roman governor is not entirely exonerated. This would fit in well with a community which found itself facing the growing intrusion of pharisaic authority in its region, particularly in Galilee and Coele-Syria where the emerging rabbinic movement was centred.[55] This location might also fit in well with Matthew's portrayal of Pilate. Whilst not so harsh and calculating as in Mark, the Matthean Pilate is none the less indifferent towards Jesus and willing to let the Jewish authorities have their way as long as he does not have to take the onus of responsibility. This would tie in with Rome's gradually emerging acceptance of the court decisions in religious law of the sages at Yavneh, an acceptance which could be threatening to the Christian communities there.[56] It would not be surprising if their attitude towards Rome was uncertain, one in which governors could be menacing or indifferent, and Roman leaders were led in their decisions by Jewish authorities.

[55] Schürer, *History*, vol. 1, pp. 525–8; Safrai, *CRINT*, pp. 406–9; White, 'Crisis', pp. 238–42; Segal, 'Jewish', p. 36.

[56] Evidence for an *official* act on the part of the Roman administration authorizing the revival of jurisdiction by the Jewish courts is not strong. However, the sages at Yavneh did in effect begin to take on the role of the Jerusalem Sanhedrin as the supreme law-court of Israel, a role which was at least tolerated by Rome. A tradition recorded in pSanh 1.2 (19b) (also pSanh 1.4 {19c and d}) refers to certain questions put to R. Johanan b. Zakkai (the first leader of Yavneh, c. 70s – 80s) by an unnamed 'hēgemōn'. Whoever this governor might have been, the 'tradition may be best viewed in the context of others concerning R. Johanan's contacts with the Roman authorities with a view to their sanctioning the foundation of the school at Yavneh, as indicating that R. Johanan's concerns included matters of civil law' (Jackson, 'Roman Influence', p. 162; see generally pp. 161–5). Several rabbinic texts relating to the mid- to late 90s when Gamaliel II took over the leadership suggest a certain amount of interaction between the sages and Rome – see Safrai, *CRINT*, pp. 406–9 for references. See also Saldarini, *Pharisees*, who regards the Pharisees as a client group of Rome, and Clark-Wire, 'Gender', p. 111.

6

PILATE IN LUKE-ACTS

From the Jewish Christian world of Matthew, we move to the much more gentile outlook of the two-volume work known as Luke-Acts. The gentile character of this work, however, should not be over-stressed. The Jewish atmosphere which pervades the gospel suggests that many of the recipients of Luke's work did not convert from paganism but were previously sympathetic towards Judaism. Luke's interest in table-fellowship and the Law indicates that his audience included many people who had been Jews and God fearers before their conversion to Christianity.[1]

Like the other gospel writers, Luke probably had a specific community in mind.[2] Exactly where this community was located is unknown. Perhaps the most that can be said with certainty is that it was in a large city of the Roman Empire.[3] Although various cities have been suggested – for example, Caesarea,[4] Rome[5] or Philippi – tradition associates Luke-Acts with Antioch.[6] This would make good sense of the prominence in Acts of that city (11.19–13.3).

[1] Esler, *Community*, pp. 31–45 and Maddox, *Purpose*, pp. 31–56.

[2] Esler (*Community*, p. 26), commenting on Luke's use of 'little flock' in Luke 12.32, suggests 'that they were members of a small Christian community beset by difficulties from within and without'; see also Acts 20.17–35. Other scholars assume Luke has a much larger readership in mind, for instance, L. T. Johnson, 'Luke-Acts', p. 405.

[3] Luke often adds the word πόλις to his Markan source. The focus of teaching is nearly always in cities and his immersion in Hellenistic culture also probably indicates an urban setting; see Cadbury, *Making*, pp. 245–9 and Esler, *Community*, p. 29.

[4] Suggested by Klein, 'Zur Frage', pp. 467–77.

[5] Conzelmann ('Luke's Place' p. 302), suggested that the author grew up in the Aegean region but actually wrote his two works in Rome. Rome is also favoured by Creed, *Gospel*, p. lvi.

[6] Eusebius *EH* 3.4.6, 24; Jerome *De viris illustribus* vii. The second-century Gnostic Basilides and Marcion's teacher, Cerdo, were both Antiochenes and both used only Luke's gospel (Leaney, *Commentary*, p. 4). The Western text of Acts 11.28, if not original, is an early second-century testimony to Luke's relationship with Antioch; see Ellis, *Gospel*, p. 54.

Furthermore, if the numerous references to Roman officials and soldiers throughout Luke-Acts reflect Luke's own community,[7] the headquarters of the Syrian legate would be a likely place to find such people.[8]

The dating of Luke-Acts is similarly uncertain. Arguing that Luke does not know the outcome of Paul's trial in Rome, several scholars suggest that the whole two-volume work is to be dated to the early 60s.[9] Probably the majority of commentators today, however, assume that Luke used Mark in the composition of his gospel and that Luke 21.20–4 presupposes the fall of Jerusalem, both of which would indicate a later date. Since Luke does not seem to know any of Paul's letters (some of which were collected and circulated c. 95 CE[10]), and as he says in Luke 1.1 that many had written before him, Luke-Acts is probably to be dated sometime in the 80s.[11]

Pontius Pilate is referred to five times in Luke's gospel. Three of these occur before the trial, 3.1–2a, 13.1 and 20.20c. The Roman hearing itself is described in 23.1–25 and Pilate is briefly referred to again in 23.52 when Joseph of Arimathaea asks for Jesus' dead body. Pilate is again mentioned in Acts at 3.13, 4.27 and 13.28 (all in connection with Jesus' execution).

This chapter will briefly look at Luke's sources and major themes within the passion narrative before turning to consider the characterization of Pilate within Luke's gospel. Finally it should be

[7] Esler, *Community*, p. 210.
[8] Scholars favouring Antioch include Ellis, *Gospel*, p. 54; Strobel, 'Lukas', pp. 131–4; Fitzmyer, *Gospel*, p. 53; Esler, *Community*, p. 231, note 36; C. F. Evans, *Luke*, p. 15.
[9] For example, Robinson, *Redating* and L. Morris, *Luke*, p. 26.
[10] Finegan, 'Original Form', pp. 85–103.
[11] Marshall (*Luke*, p. 35) suggests not long after 70 CE, as does Ellis (*Luke*, pp. 55–8). Fitzmyer (*Gospel*, pp. 53–7) puts it slightly later at 80–5 and Creed (*Gospel*, p. lvi) at 80–90. Esler suggests mid- to late 80s to early 90s, *Community*, p. 29. An exceptionally late date was argued by O'Neill (*Theology*, chapter 1), who dated Luke-Acts to 115–30.
Tradition ascribes the writing of Luke-Acts to Luke the physician, a companion of Paul referred to in Col. 4.14, 2 Tim. 4.11 and Phlm. 24 (Irenaeus, *Adv. Haer*. iii.1, and the anti-Marcionite prologue). Cadbury (*Style*), however, has shown that Luke may have had no more medical knowledge that the average educated layperson. Whoever the author was, he was most likely a gentile Christian; see Fitzmyer, *Gospel*, pp. 35–53. For a summary of those scholars who suggest that the author was a Jewish Christian see Ellis, *Luke*, p. 52.

possible to see how this portrayal of the governor fits in with the references to him throughout Acts.

Luke's sources

As already indicated, the majority of scholars assume that Luke relied heavily upon Mark in the composition of his gospel. Into this he has added material common to Matthew (often referred to as a single written source, Q) and his own traditions, which may have come down to him in either written or oral form, or both (often referred to as L). Although he generally follows Mark closely,[12] within the passion account Luke moves away from this source, often to a considerable degree, leading several scholars to suggest he may be following a new source at this point.[13] The results of recent studies on this question by scholars such as M. L. Soards and F. J. Matera, however, have shown that there is no evidence that Luke made use of another written passion narrative. The additions and alterations which he makes to Mark can all be explained by his use of L material and his own particular theological interests.[14]

Lukan themes influencing the portrayal of Pilate

As was the case with Mark and Matthew, certain prominent themes within Luke's narrative have shaped the way in which Pilate has been portrayed. Five themes in particular deserve attention.

(1)   Throughout his gospel and Acts, Luke shows a marked tendency to link significant Christian events with imperial history. For example, Jesus' birth at Bethlehem came about because of a decree of Caesar Augustus, a decree which was followed unquestioningly by Joseph (Luke 2.1–7). In this way, Luke has shown the politics of Rome working hand in hand with God's divine purpose for salvation. Similarly in Acts, Agabus' prophecy of the world famine, which Luke tells us

---

[12] L. T. Johnson, 'Luke-Acts', p. 406.

[13] For example, Taylor, *Passion Narrative*; Sloyan, *Jesus*; Bailey, *Traditions*; Marshall, *Gospel*, p. 852; Grundmann, *Evangelium*, p. 421.

[14] See Soards, *Passion*, which concentrates on chapter 22 and especially Matera, 'Luke 22.66–71', and 'Luke 23.1–25'. This view is also held by Fitzmyer – for a full discussion see *Gospel*, pp. 1365–8; also C. F. Evans, *Luke*, p. 859 and Creed, *Gospel*, p. lxiii.

occurred in the time of Claudius, was the impetus for sending Paul and Barnabas to Jerusalem with relief aid (11.28). Claudius' expulsion of Jews from Rome allowed Paul to meet and stay with Priscilla and Aquila in Corinth (18.2), whilst the decision of Gallio, the proconsul of Achaia, allowed Paul to continue his work in Corinth 'many days longer' (18.12–16). For Luke, the decrees of Roman Emperors and governors and events during their reigns, even though not always positive in themselves, have allowed Christianity to flourish.[15] This strongly suggests that Luke's readers had a particular interest in the relationship between Christianity and the Roman Empire.

This is borne out further by the fact that in Luke's gospel the Jewish trial has the air of a preliminary hearing (22.66–71) whilst the Roman proceedings are much longer and form the only real trial of Jesus.[16] In this gospel the Jewish court does not reach a verdict, nor is Jesus bound as a condemned man before he meets Pilate. The only official verdict is that passed by the Roman prefect in 23.24. How Jesus fared in a Roman court was obviously of great significance for Luke's audience.

(2)   Linked to Luke's interest in the position of Christianity vis-à-vis Rome is his positive evaluation of the majority of Roman administrative or military personnel with whom the early Christians came into contact. Even those who were not converted are described favourably: for example, the centurion of Luke 7.1–10,[17] Julius in Acts 27.3 or the centurion in 27.42–3. Quite a number of them accept Christianity: for example, the soldiers of Luke 3.14, Cornelius in Acts 10.1–11.18 and Sergius Paulus in Acts 13.6–12. Luke repeatedly emphasizes that the hero of Acts, Paul, is himself a Roman citizen (16.37–40, 22.24–9, 25.10–12).

---

[15] Walaskay, *And So*, p. 26 and Esler, *Community*, pp. 201–2.

[16] Whilst Mark devotes only fifteen verses to the hearing before Pilate, Luke devotes twenty verses to it (and five to the hearing before Herod which, coming in the middle of the Roman trial, gives the impression that Jesus is in Roman hands even longer. Conversely, Mark's Jewish trial occupies twelve verses (Mark 14.53, 55–65) whilst Luke's is narrated in only six. In effect, Luke presents his audience with one trial comprising of four scenes which is why there is no Jewish condemnation in 22.66–71; see Matera, 'Luke 23.1–25', p. 551.

[17] Even if the centurion is historically unlikely to have been a Roman citizen, he still upholds Roman interests in the province and it is as such an upholder of the Roman regime that Luke portrays him. See Sherwin-White, *Roman*, p. 124 and Walaskay, *And So*, p. 33.

There is, however, one group of Roman officials in Luke-Acts who do not receive such positive descriptions: these are the governors before whom Christians are put on trial. Whilst they may serve an invaluable role in publicly declaring the political innocence of Christianity before Rome (so Pilate and Festus) or enabling the spread of the gospel (so Gallio), their characters are questionable in the extreme.

Taking Gallio first, although his ruling was beneficial for Paul and the spread of his message, the governor dismissed the case without even a preliminary hearing and completely ignored a public disturbance involving Sosthenes, the ruler of the synagogue, right in front of his tribunal (Acts 18.12–17). The overriding impression of Gallio is that he did not want to get involved with the case. In Acts 24 Felix allowed Paul to speak in his own defence against his Jewish accusers but showed a reluctance to come to any decision, putting the case off in verse 22 until Lysias arrived. In fact, the case was put off for two years (verse 27), during which time Felix was said to have visited Paul often. His motive, however, was not an interest in what Paul had to say but, according to verse 26, because he hoped that Paul would offer him a bribe in return for his release. At no time did he give an opinion as to Paul's guilt and seemed completely disinterested in justice. Succeeded by Porcius Festus, he left Paul in prison – Luke points out that this was not because he thought Paul was guilty but because he wanted to do the Jews a favour (v. 27). A similar motive is extended to Festus in 25.9 who, instead of trying Paul in Caesarea, suggested that he stand trial in Jerusalem. Paul says that the governor knows that he has done no wrong against the Jews (v. 10) and seems to be accusing Festus of giving him up to them (v. 11). Paul's only hope of a fair trial is to appeal directly to Caesar (v. 11).[18]

In Luke-Acts, therefore, there is always a distinction between these governors as the *representatives of Roman law* (which consistently finds Jesus and his followers innocent of any political crime) and their *weak, self-seeking characters* (which occasionally hinder the proper implementation of that law, especially when the Jewish authorities have had a hand in

---

[18] See also the magistrates of Acts 16.35–9.

the proceedings[19]). It will not be surprising, therefore, if Pilate also conforms to this pattern.

(3) Luke's attitude towards the Jewish nation at times seems quite ambiguous.[20] In general, the Jewish leadership are antagonistic towards Jesus and plot his death (e.g. 5.17, 21, 6.7), though at times the Pharisees are friendly towards him (e.g. 13.31). The crowds respond positively towards Jesus to the extent that they hinder the attempts of their leaders to do away with him (e.g. 19.47–8, 20.19, 21.38, 22.2, 6, 53). During the trial before Pilate, however, a dramatic change takes place in the people. Having been summoned by the governor in 23.13 along with their chief priests and rulers to hear Pilate's assessment of the charges, they spontaneously cry for crucifixion.[21] Although he does not hide Pilate's verdict on the case, Luke clearly shows that this was in accordance with Jewish wishes: 'So Pilate gave sentence that *their demand* should be granted' (v. 24). Luke's presentation even goes so far as to give the impression that Jesus was crucified by Jews – grammatically the subjects of the verbs in 23.26, 32 and 33 are still the chief priests, rulers and the people of verse 13.[22] Acts 2.22–3, 3.12–13, 4.27 and 13.27–9 similarly put responsibility for the death of Jesus on the inhabitants of Jerusalem and their leaders.[23] Yet later, at the cross, the Jewish leaders

---

[19] Esler (*Community*, pp. 203–5) makes a similar point as does Walaskay (*And So*, pp. 23–4). Acts records no instance of Roman intervention without previous Jewish or pagan agitation; see Conzelmann, *Theology*, p. 140.

[20] This ambiguity has led to various interpretations. At one extreme J. T. Sanders (*Jews*) regards the whole of Luke-Acts as anti-Semitic. Others claim that Luke deliberately diminishes the role of the Jewish people in the death of Jesus, for instance, L. T. Johnson, 'Luke-Acts', pp. 414–15.

[21] The urgency of the crowd's demand has been intensified by Luke: Mark's aorist imperative Σταύρωσον αὐτόν (v. 13) has been converted to a more emotional present imperative and doubled for emphasis, Σταύρου σταύρου αὐτόν (v. 21). There is no need for the chief priests to stir up the crowd in Luke's presentation (as in Mark 15.11).

[22] Assuming that the soldiers referred to in verse 36 are *Roman* soldiers, the majority of commentators maintain that Luke cannot avoid the historical reality that Jesus died at Roman hands, but only wants to give the impression that he was executed by Jews, for example, C. F. Evans, *Luke*, p. 859. J. T. Sanders (*Jews*) however, argues that the soldiers are Jewish and that Luke has consciously described a *Jewish* crucifixion, see also Walaskay, 'Trial', p. 92. In Luke, three of Jesus' four passion predictions give the impression that his death will be at Jewish hands (9.22, 44–5, 17.25). Only in 18.32–3 are gentiles mentioned and their role appears to be a passive one.

[23] In Luke 24.20 two of Jesus' Jewish disciples lay the blame on the chief priests

ridicule Jesus whilst the people first watch (23.35) and then
return home beating their breasts (23.48). The spectacle has
led them to repentance and remorse. Despite rejecting the
Messiah, Israel has not been totally rejected in Luke's
presentation.

Perhaps the reason for Luke's ambiguous description of the
Jewish people and their sudden unexpected demand for Jesus'
death before Pilate is summed up by C. A. Evans:

> Luke emphasizes Jewish responsibility for Jesus' death, not
> because of anti-semitic hatred, but because of his desire to
> place the Messiah's death firmly within the framework of
> biblical (i.e. Israelite) history. Jesus' rejection and death are
> prophesied in the Scriptures and are in keeping with
> Israel's 'historic' (biblical) habit of persecuting the
> prophets'.[24]

(4) In connection with this portrayal of the Jewish people is
Luke's presentation of Jesus as a rejected prophet[25] and
innocent martyr who goes unjustly to his death.[26] The theme
of Jesus' innocence is given special prominence during the trial
and crucifixion narrative. Pilate publicly declares Jesus innocent three times (23.4, 14, 22); Herod too is said to have found
no crime in him (23.15). Even one of the criminals crucified
with Jesus corroborates Pilate's verdict (23.41), and a centurion standing by the cross utters 'the last word and true
verdict of Jesus' life and death'[27] – 'Certainly this man was
innocent' (23.47). Luke shows his readers that even though
Jesus' innocence was recognized by Roman and Herodian

and rulers whilst in 4.10, 5.30 and 7.52 members of the Jewish council are accused of
causing Jesus' death themselves.
[24] C. A. Evans, 'Luke's View', p. 55. Jervell argued that Luke presented the
Jewish people as divided in their attitude towards Jesus. 'Israel' is an important term
throughout Acts referring to 'repentant' (i.e. Christian) Jews and emphasizes the
continuity between the promises to Israel and Christianity; cf. *Luke*, pp. 41–74.
[25] For example, 4.24, 7.16, 39, 13.31–3, 23.27–31, 24.19–20, Acts 3.22–3. For a
fuller discussion see Carroll, 'Luke's Crucifixion', pp. 113–14.
[26] The equation of Luke's Jesus with a martyr has been customary since Dibelius,
Tradition, p. 201; see also Carroll, 'Luke's Crucifixion', pp. 118–21 and Talbert,
Reading, pp. 212–13. Rather than a martyrdom, Green ('Death', pp. 21–8) suggests
that Luke presents Jesus' death as the Isaianic servant, whilst Karris suggests that
Luke wants to show Jesus as the innocently suffering righteous one ('Luke 23.47',
pp. 77–8).
[27] Carroll, 'Luke's Crucifixion', p. 118.

rulers, he unjustly went to his death because of *Jewish* machinations.

If Pilate's declarations of Jesus' innocence were to have any real value, however, they had to be made with respect to specific charges.[28] In 23.2, instead of the unspecified accusations found in his Markan source,[29] Luke supplies the charges brought by the Jewish hierarchy. It is one general charge and two specific examples: Jesus is said to have perverted their nation, forbidden the payment of tribute to Caesar and claimed to be Christ, a king.[30] All three accusations have been carefully prepared for by Luke in his preceding narrative; a portrayal which has shown the falsity of all three claims.

The first and most general charge – that of perverting the nation – which, in the context seems to imply political incitement against Roman authority,[31] has been prepared for in 9.41 where Jesus describes the nation as already perverse, indicating that its perversity is not a result of Jesus' teaching.[32] The second accusation – Jesus' specific command not to pay tribute – has already been dealt with at 20.20–5. There the Jewish leaders attempted to force Jesus to take a stand on a politically delicate yet burning contemporary issue:[33] should

[28] C. F. Evans, *Luke*, p. 845.

[29] Mark 15.2. Although Mark does not specifically say so, the reader must assume that Jesus was accused of claiming some kind of kingship, otherwise Pilate's question makes little sense.

[30] Similar charges will be levelled against Paul in Acts 24.5–6, 12, 25.8 and also against Jason and others in Acts 17.6–9.

[31] The verb διαστρέφω can be used in a religious sense meaning 'to turn away from the true faith' as in 1 Kings 18.17–18, Acts 13.8, 10, 20.30. This is the sense in which Marcion interpreted the charge, adding καὶ καταλύοντα τὸν νόμον καὶ τοὺς προφήτας (and abolishing the Law and the prophets) after ἡμῶν (Epiphanius, *Adv. Haer.* 1.3.316, 317, 346). But in view of the two clearly political charges which follow, the apparently synonymous use of the more politically sounding verb ἀνασείω in verse 5, and the Jewish use of τὸ ἔθνος ἡμῦν before the Roman governor to denote their 'nation' rather than their faith or laws, it seems best to understand the charge in a political sense: Jesus is accused of inciting his fellow countrymen to sedition; see C. F. Evans, *Luke*, p. 845. J.T. Sanders notes that similar charges were levelled against Moses by Pharaoh (Exod. 5.4) and against Elijah by Ahab (1 Kings 18.17). In fact, Moses, Elijah and Jesus are carrying out God's will; it is only evil rulers who consider their activity seditious: cf. *Jews*, p. 7.

[32] For a contrary view see Cassidy who argues that the charge does carry some weight in that Jesus has freely criticized the existing orders of society and those supporting them and called for radically different social patterns: cf. *Jesus*, p. 65.

[33] It is possible that Jewish Christians in Luke's community may have had to pay the *fiscus Judaicus* introduced by Vespasian and payable by all Jews throughout the Empire, in addition to the other provincial taxes.

one pay tribute to the Emperor or not? Jesus' answer was clever. His reply set up two spheres, that of Caesar and that of God, in which each can make legitimate demands. Paying taxes to Caesar was permissible as long as it did not interfere with one's duty to God.[34] The charge put by the Jewish authorities to Pilate is clearly a distortion of Jesus' answer at 20.25. The third charge is more difficult. Although Luke's readers do believe that Jesus is the Christ,[35] a king of the Davidic line,[36] and at certain points in the preceding narrative he seems to accept this designation,[37] Jesus has never referred to himself as a king, certainly not in the political sense in which the Jewish leadership has presented the matter to Pilate. Jesus' messiahship, for Luke, is better expressed by his identity as teacher, prophet and martyr. The charge is a deliberate distortion of Jesus' messiahship in terms which would be almost sure to attract the interest of a Roman governor. The reader knows that all these charges are false distortions and realizes that Jesus is innocent of all the Jewish accusations.

An interesting feature of Luke's trial before Pilate is that, except for the exchange in 23.2–3, the charge of kingship which dominated the Markan account has disappeared.[38] Although Luke's Pilate still addresses the people three times as in Mark, the politically challenging questions of Mark 15.9 and 12 have been completely reworked, omitting the references to 'King of the Jews'. Instead, in Luke's presentation the dominant charge is that of stirring up the people, a charge which appears with varying verbs three times.[39] The impression is that Jesus stands trial because of his teaching rather than on account of politically dubious messianic claims.

[34] This is the view held by the majority of commentators: cf. Creed, *Gospel*, p. 247; C. F. Evans, *Luke*, pp. 708–9; Derrett, 'Luke's Perspective', pp. 42–3. See, however, Cassidy, *Jesus*, p. 58.

[35] 2.26, 4.41, 9.20.

[36] For example, 1.32–3, 2.4, 3.31, 18.37, Acts 17.7.

[37] Jesus is hailed as 'the *king* [absent in Mark and Ps. 118.26] who comes in the name of the Lord' at his entry into Jerusalem in 19.38 and does not reject the title. Later in the gospel, after the resurrection, the Lukan Jesus speaks of himself as Christ, 24.26, 46.

[38] A similar feature was found in Matthew's presentation, see p. 128 above. In Luke, the titles 'King of the Jews' and 'Christ' reappear at the crucifixion – 23.37, 38 and 23.35, 39.

[39] 23.2 (διατρέφω – distort/pervert), 23.5 (ἀνασείω – stir up), and 23.14 (ἀποστρέφω – pervert/incite to revolt).

Conversely, Barabbas' insurrectionary activity has been highlighted. Whilst Mark does not specifically say that Barabbas was involved in the uprising and murder,[40] Luke leaves the reader in no doubt as to his complicity. Furthermore, the insurrection is located 'in the city' and would presumably be well known to the assembled crowd (v. 19). The contrast between Barabbas and Jesus is starkly underlined in the final verse of the trial narrative: Pilate 'released the man who had been thrown into prison for insurrection and murder, whom they asked for; but Jesus he delivered up to their will' (v. 25). The choice of the Jewish crowd, Luke shows, was not an innocent teacher and prophet but an insurrectionary and murderer, a political rebel against Rome.[41]

The crowd's culpability is highlighted all the more by Luke's drastic reworking of the Barabbas scene. Whereas Mark began his narrative by describing the so-called *privilegium paschale* and introducing Barabbas, setting up the element of choice from the beginning, Luke has omitted any reference to the amnesty and only introduces Barabbas *after* the crowd has demanded his release.[42] The effect of this is to focus the reader's attention on the relationships between Jesus, Pilate and the Jewish people. No choice has been given to the crowd and so their spontaneous cry for a political rebel rather than Jesus is all the more blameworthy.

(5) Although Luke's community do not seem to be experiencing any form of systematic persecution themselves,[43] Jesus' martyrdom presents them with an example should their faith be put to the test. Acts shows Christian disciples who were similarly called to suffer for their faith: Stephen and James were both executed, Paul and Peter both imprisoned. An intriguing feature about the trials in Acts are their parallels

---

[40] See pp. 111–12 above.

[41] This is emphasized again in Acts 3.14.

[42] Verse 17 – ἀνάγκην δὲ εἶχεν ἀπολύειν αὐτοῖς κατὰ ἑορτὴν ἕνα (and he was forced to release one man to them at the festival) – is omitted by many early witnesses, for instance, p[75], A and B; others have this or a variant form either here or after verse 19. The evidence suggests that the verse is a secondary gloss based on Mark 15.6 and Matt. 27.15, making the reference to Barabbas in verse 18 less abrupt.

[43] See Walaskay, *And So*, p. 11 and J. T. Sanders, *Jews*, p. 23. For an opposing view see Conzelmann, 'Luke's Place', p. 301. Compared with the other gospels, references to endurance in the face of trouble or hardship in Luke are few – 8.15, 9.23–7, 18.1–8, 21.12.

with the trials of Jesus found either in Luke or in his Markan source.

Acts 6.9–7.60, for example, describes the trial of Stephen before a Jewish council and his subsequent death. A remarkable feature of this account is that many of the details associated with the Jewish trial of Jesus, which Luke has omitted from his Markan source, have found a place here: the false witnesses (6.13, Mark 14.56); the accusation of speaking against the Temple (6.13–14, Mark 14.58); the charge of blasphemy (6.11, Mark 14.64) and the anger of the council (7.54, Mark 14.63–4). Luke seems to have deliberately modelled Stephen's trial around material which in his source belonged to that of Jesus before the Jewish council. Even more striking are the parallels between Paul's trials and those of Jesus. Paul is also brought before a Jewish council (Acts 22.30–23.10), before the Roman governor Felix at which time accusations are brought by the Jewish high priest, elders and spokesmen (24.1–23); before Festus (25.6–12); and before both the Herodian King Agrippa and Festus (25.23–26.32). In exactly the same way that Jesus' innocence was stressed by the Roman and Herodian rulers, so is Paul's lack of guilt: 23.29, 25.25, 26.31–2. Are these parallels simply coincidental, or has one set of trials been influenced by the other?

This question has particular significance regarding Jesus' trial before Antipas (23.7–12). No other gospel even alludes to this trial;[44] the section contains a greater number of characteristically Lukan words than can be found in the rest of the passion narrative[45] and the questions of judicial procedure which it raises are considerable. These features led M. Dibelius to conclude that this section is a Lukan invention based on Christian reflection on Psalm 2.1–2, cited explicitly in Acts 4.26–8 – 'for truly were gathered together . . . . both Herod and Pontius Pilate' (v. 27).[46] Yet the proceedings do not describe a conspiracy of the two men against Jesus and it is just as plausible that Luke inserted the trial for some other

---

[44] The only other reference to it in the NT is at Acts 4.26–8. Not even John, who has other points of similarity with Luke, refers to this event. Luke seems particularly interested in Antipas, for statistics see Brown, *Death*, p. 764.

[45] See Hoehner, 'Why Did?', p. 84 and Brown, *Death*, p. 761.

[46] Dibelius, 'Herodes'; followed by Burkill, 'Condemnation', pp. 330–1; Creed, *Gospel*, p. 280 and Loisy, *L'Evangile*, pp. 544–5.

reason and used Psalm 2 to justify its inclusion.[47] The most convincing hypothesis regarding the trial before Antipas is that of P. W. Walaskay who suggests that Luke inserted a trial before a Herodian to parallel Paul's trial before Agrippa.[48] This suggestion has several features in its favour. First, Luke seems to have no information as to what went on during Jesus' trial before Herod; all the events are taken either from various other parts of the gospel or are discreditable elements from Mark 15.1–5 which Luke has omitted in his presentation of the trial before Pilate. Second, since Paul's trial was more recent and perhaps therefore fresher in the memories of his community, Luke may have wanted to show that all the trials experienced by the great apostle to the gentiles had already been anticipated in the trials experienced by Jesus.

The trial before Antipas, therefore, is most probably a literary composition designed to parallel Jesus' trials with those of Paul. So an analysis of the proceedings themselves and Pilate's motives for sending Jesus to Antipas belongs not to the realm of historical inquiry but to Luke's literary art and the way he wishes to portray Jesus in Roman/Herodian hands.[49]

Luke's gospel, then, shows an interest in how Jesus fared in a Roman court. Pilate will act as an official voice to Jesus' innocence, though we should not necessarily expect a particularly positive picture of him to emerge. Luke also wants to show the Jewish people rejecting their Messiah as they did the prophets of old. His account will contrast the innocence of Jesus with the insurrectionary Barabbas and highlight the parallelism between Jesus' trial and those of Paul in Acts. When we turn to the trial narrative, it will be these themes which are uppermost and which shape Luke's presentation of Pilate.

---

[47] Fitzmyer describes the relation of this story to Ps. 2.1–2 as 'tenuous indeed': cf. *Gospel*, p. 1179.

[48] Walaskay, *And So*, p. 43 and 'Trial', pp. 88–9; followed by, amongst others, Matera, 'Luke 23,1–25', p. 545.

[49] In the later gospel of Peter responsibility for Jesus' death has shifted from Pilate to Herod, GPet. 1.1–2.5.

The characterization of Pilate in Luke

References to Pilate before the Roman trial

Unlike Mark's presentation, Luke's narrative refers to Pilate three times before the trial. An important effect of this is that his readers are already familiar with the prefect to some degree before he appears as Jesus' judge. The three passages will be examined in turn.

(1)   'In the fifteenth year of the reign of Tiberius Caesar, when Pontius Pilate was governor of Judaea . . .' (3.1).

Luke opens his account of the ministry of John the Baptist with a stylized dating typical of other ancient writers in which he firmly sets the beginnings of the Christian movement within imperial history.[50] The dating adds credibility to the narrative: the fixed and specific time references suggest that Luke will be accurate in what he has to relate (backing up his declared intention in the prologue, 1.1–4). To a large extent, all the rulers mentioned in 3.1–2a represent Roman interests, from the Herodian client kings to the Jewish high priest(s) appointed by the Judaean prefect.[51] Pilate takes his place next to Tiberius as the Emperor's representative in the province, the governor of Judaea. The verse gives us no information regarding Pilate's character but simply sets the scene, locating the drama on the imperial stage and linking Pilate closely with imperial interests.

(2)   'Some people present at that time told him about the Galileans whose blood Pilate had mixed with their sacrifices' (13.1).

In its context, this reference to a contemporary event introduces a discussion and a parable on the need for repentance (13.1–9). Those who related the incident to Jesus thought that the Galileans had been especially sinful. Jesus' response shows his audience that they are just as much in danger of divine

---

[50] See Rienecker, *Linguistic*, vol. 1, p. 211. Historically, this information is not as straightforward as it may first appear; for various reconstructions see Hoehner, *Herod*, pp. 307–12 (Appendix vii).

[51] For the appointment of the high priests (which during Jesus' ministry was the responsibility of the prefect of Judaea) and the division of Herod I's kingdom between his sons see above, pp. 1–19.

judgement if they do not repent. Yet despite the verse's terse introductory nature, the reader can still put together some picture of Pilate.[52]

The description of the Galileans here is all too brief. Despite the occasional equation of Galilee with insurrectionary activity, there is no indication in Luke-Acts that the author intends to describe anything more than their geographical origin.[53] Luke's 'Galileans' then seem to be simply pilgrims from Galilee offering their sacrifices in the Jerusalem Temple (presumably at Passover).[54] Similarly, Luke gives us no clues as to Pilate's motivations for having them killed. The governor might have feared that a riot could break out, but Luke says nothing of this. Instead, his gruesome Greek expression ὧν τὸ αἷμα Πιλᾶτος ἔμιξεν μετὰ τῶν θυσιῶν αὐτῶν suggests a barbaric slaughtering in the same way that the sacrificial victims themselves have just been killed.[55] Pilate's behaviour, narrated starkly and devoid of any explanation, appears cold and insensitive.

(3)   '. . . so that they might hand him over to the power and authority of the governor' (20.20c).

This verse forms an introduction to the controversy over the payment of tribute to Caesar (20.20–6). Luke's Markan source left the precise course of action determined upon by the Jewish leaders (there the Pharisees and Herodians) rather vague; they attempted only to 'entrap him in his talk' (Mark 12.13). Luke's account, however, plainly shows that the intention of the scribes and chief priests is to force Jesus to take a stand on a political issue which will then be used in evidence against him before the Roman governor.

The reference to the governor (ἡγεμών) at this point serves an important literary function. The phrase 'so that they might hand him over' (ὥστε παραδοῦναι αὐτὸν) recalls Jesus' prediction of his passion in 18.32. In 20.20–1 the reader sees how this handing over to the gentiles will take place and connects it with the question about the payment of tribute to Caesar. These themes will reappear in 23.1–2 where Jesus is brought

---

[52] For a historical evaluation of 13.1 see below, pp. 194–6.
[53] See Luke 22.59, 23.6, Acts 1.11, 2.7, 5.37.
[54] So also Marshall, *Gospel*, p. 553 and Fitzmyer, *Gospel*, p. 1006.
[55] See Derrett, 'Galileans', p. 103 and Winter, *Trial*, p. 177, note 9.

before Pilate by the members of the Sanhedrin and charged with forbidding the payment of tribute.

Prior to the Roman trial, then, the reader has been introduced to Pilate as the Roman governor of Judaea, a man representing imperial interests in the province. He is a governor who will use violence when necessary, and before whom the Jewish leaders plan to bring Jesus.

The characterization of Pilate in the Roman trial: Luke 23.1–25

After their preliminary hearing, the members of the Jewish council bring their prisoner before Pilate in 23.1 and charge him with perverting the nation, forbidding the payment of tribute and claiming to be Christ, a king. The scene has been set for a political trial. A Roman governor could not afford to allow a suspected political agitator to go free and could be relied upon to examine the case with the utmost thoroughness.

By way of examination, Pilate picks up on the third charge against Jesus asking, as in the other gospels, 'Are you the King of the Jews?' Jesus ambiguously replies, 'You say it' (Σὺ λέγεις).[56] These words must be taken by Pilate as a denial, otherwise his following statement is incomprehensible:[57] 'I find no crime in this man' (Οὐδὲν εὑρίσκω αἴτιον ἐν τῷ ἀνθρώπῳ τούτῳ). Even so, such a statement at this point in the trial is entirely unexpected. Jesus faces serious political charges and yet Pilate has proclaimed him innocent with only the briefest of interrogations. Luke is presenting us here with quite a different scene from that found in Mark and Matthew. There, Jesus' silence in the face of the many accusations of the Jewish leaders and lack of any kind of defence meant that the Roman judge would have no choice but to find him guilty.[58] In Luke's presentation, however, Jesus is not silent in Pilate's court. He has answered the prefect's question and the case has barely begun. The charges of subverting the nation and forbidding tax payment have not even been touched upon. As P. W. Walaskay puts it: 'With a case of treason, Pilate should have proceeded

---

[56] For a more detailed discussion see above, p. 107.
[57] Grundmann, *Evangelium*, p. 422.
[58] See above, especially p. 108.

further with his case *extra ordinem*. A Roman court would not have been content with any other than its own investigation.'[59]

Luke obviously wants his readers to understand that Pilate quickly recognized Jesus' innocence despite the Jewish accusations against him and that there was no point in trying him further. In J. A. Fitzmyer's words: 'the evangelist is interested only in the conclusion reached by Pilate'.[60] Yet at another level, it is an odd portrait of a Roman governor which emerges. He appears to have dismissed serious political accusations and is surprisingly unwilling to try the case properly.[61]

In verse 5 the first charge of stirring up the people is repeated, this time with greater urgency. The precise identity of those speaking is ambiguous: either we are to assume that it is still the members of the Sanhedrin or, in the light of the preceding verse, that the multitude has also joined forces with the chief priests in accusing Jesus. The emphasis falls on Jesus' teaching, fitting in well with the frequent portrayal of Jesus as a teacher in this gospel.[62] The vast extent of Jesus' teaching is also stressed and mirrors the geographical framework of the gospel as a whole – throughout all Judaea, from Galilee to Jerusalem.[63] A political agitator who hailed from Galilee and who had brought his revolutionary teaching right up to Jerusalem could hardly be ignored by the representative of Roman rule. Surely now Pilate will have to try Jesus on a political charge.

Yet again, Pilate declines to take the case seriously. In verse 6 he picks up the earlier reference to Galilee and inquires whether Jesus is a Galilean. Clearly, in Luke's presentation, the prisoner is completely unknown to Pilate. If Jesus was any threat whatsoever to the state, the governor must have received reports about him already. Finding that Jesus belonged to Herod's jurisdiction, Pilate determines to send the prisoner to him (v. 7). Luke gives no motives

---

[59] Walaskay, 'Trial', p. 85.

[60] Fitzmyer, *Gospel*, p. 1474.

[61] Black ('Arrest', p. 23) notes 'Pilate shows an obvious reluctance to deal with the case'.

[62] For example, 8.49, 9.37, 10.25, 12.13, 18.18, 19.39, 20.21, 28, 39, 21.7; see Matera, 'Luke 23.1–25', pp. 540–1.

[63] 'Judaea' probably refers to the whole of Palestine (rather than the Roman province) since Luke seems to want it to incorporate Galilee. Hoehner ('Why Did?', p. 85) regards it as equivalent to the whole 'land of the Jews' (as in Acts 10.37, 39); see also Goulder, *Luke*, p. 757.

for Pilate's actions at this point;[64] earlier at 13.1 he was apparently quite ready to deal with troublesome Galileans himself. The overriding impression here is that the governor seizes a convenient opportunity to rid himself of an irritating case in which he is being pressurized by the Jewish leaders to try a man whom he considers harmless.[65] The reference to Galilee gives a way out of the stalemate between Pilate and the chief priests: by handing the whole case over to Herod, Pilate need have nothing further to do with it.[66]

The Roman prefect is too weak to insist on releasing the prisoner he has proclaimed innocent. Instead, he passes the case on to someone else, relinquishing Roman control over an allegedly political revolutionary and handing him over to the jurisdiction of a native prince. This is hardly a favourable picture of the Roman judge.

The trial before Herod Antipas, verses 8–11

Although a thorough consideration of the proceedings before Antipas is not within the scope of the present study, some features within it need to be highlighted.

Superficially, Luke's readers might expect the pro-Roman Herodian tetrach automatically to endorse Pilate's judgement.[67] But

---

[64] Several motives have, however, been suggested by modern scholars. Assuming the historicity of the proceedings before Herod, Mommsen, *Römisches*, pp. 356–7, suggested that in the early principate a trial was conducted in the home province of the accused (*forum domicilii*), but this law was later changed so that the accused was tried in the province in which his crime was committed (*forum delicti*). Sherwin-White, however, successfully challenged this, suggesting instead that at the time of Jesus trials occurred in the province in which the crime took place (*forum delicti*): cf. *Roman*, pp. 28–31. This fits in with Felix trying Paul for misdeeds in Jerusalem, even though his home province was Cilicia (Acts 23.34–24.26). In this case, even if the scene were historical, Pilate would not be compelled to hand Jesus over to Antipas.

[65] Although commenting on Pilate's *historical* reasons for sending Jesus to Antipas, Hoehner reaches a similar conclusion, 'Why Did?'.

[66] Several scholars suggest that Pilate wished to obtain Herod's opinion, rather than to transfer the case to him: for instance, Marshall, *Gospel*, p. 854; Verrall, 'Christ', pp. 332–3; Manson, *Gospel*, p. 256; Brown, *Death*, p. 765. If the trial before Herod were historical, then this might have been the case. However, it is not the impression which Luke's narrative conveys. Verse 23.15 clearly suggests that Herod could have dealt with Jesus in an appropriate way had he found him guilty; he seems to have been under no obligation to return the prisoner. See Schürer, *History*, vol.1, p. 349.

[67] He was, after all, dependent upon Roman support for his position; see p. 3 above.

Luke has incorporated several references to Herod throughout his gospel which add tension to this encounter. He imprisoned John the Baptist because he reproached him for his marriage to Herodias and for 'all the evil things which he had done' (3.19–20) and finally beheaded him (9.7–9). He was perplexed by Jesus and wanted to see him (9.7–9) and by 13.31 even the Pharisees are warning Jesus to 'get away from here, for Herod wants to kill you'.[68] Jesus sends back the message that he intends to go to Jerusalem, 'for it cannot be that a prophet should perish away from Jerusalem' (13.32–3). In 23.8–11 this long-awaited meeting takes place and the reader cannot help but fear that Jesus will suffer the same fate as John the Baptist.

Verse 23.8 recalls 9.9, stating that Herod wanted to see Jesus because of his reputation and hoped to see him perform a sign.[69] Jesus, however, makes no answer to the tetrarch's repeated questions (v. 9). In verse 10, the chief priests and scribes who have followed Jesus vigorously accuse him, though the content of these charges is not specified. Disappointed or perhaps annoyed by Jesus' silence,[70] Herod proceeds to treat Jesus contemptuously with the aid of his soldiers.[71] The only mockery in Luke's account is at Jewish hands: by the leaders at 22.63–5, Jewish leaders and soldiers at 23.35–7 and here at the Herodian court.[72] Clearly, in Herod's view, any claims Jesus may have made are utterly worthless and contemptible; so much so that he gives Jesus a gorgeous robe, a magnanimous gesture indicating that he is no threat to the tetrarch.[73] Jesus is then sent back to Pilate.

[68] Verrall ('Christ', p. 329) seems to be ignoring the plain meaning of the words when he claims that 'it was not in the design of this author to prepare us for enmity on the part of Herod against Christ'. Contrast Brown who writes that Luke's statements give 'the impression of an unstable character capable of homicidal violence': cf. *Death*, p. 769.

[69] For Luke's use of signs see ibid., p. 770.

[70] Grundmann, *Evangelium*, p. 425.

[71] The textually uncertain και in verse 11, if original, may stress the tetrarch's involvement – 'even Herod' or 'also Herod'; see Metzger, *Textual*, p. 179. Verrall rightly notes that Herod's behaviour mocks the Jewish accusers as much as Jesus: cf. 'Christ', p. 342.

[72] There is no humiliation at the hands of Roman soldiers in Luke (as in Mark 15.16–20). Luke shows that Jesus was respected by Roman authorities: cf. Goulder, *Luke*, p. 756. A further reason for moving the mockery up to this point is that it allows Pilate to hand Jesus over directly to the Jewish crowd for crucifixion in 23.25, thereby enhancing the impression that they actually crucify Jesus.

[73] Many commentators take this robe as further mockery of Jesus' messianic claims. Since some Latin MSS describe the robe as *albus*, Danker suggests that Luke has in mind the white toga worn by political aspirants in Polybius' *History* 10.5.1: cf.

In verse 12 Luke adds a curious note explaining that Herod and Pilate became friends from that day on. The reason for their former enmity is not obvious from Luke's account: it may have arisen from Pilate's slaughter of the Galileans in 13.1, but this is far from clear.[74] What is important within Luke's narrative is that the trials of Jesus have brought two very different rulers together; both play their part in the events leading up to Jesus' execution, as Acts 4.27 will make explicit.

Pilate's summing up, verses 13–15a

The case has been returned to Pilate. The previously unwilling judge is now forced to take some kind of action. In Luke's presentation, there is no Passover amnesty to which Pilate can resort, either to assess Jesus' popularity or to release him. At first Pilate appears to act with a certain amount of decisiveness. He takes the initiative and summons the chief priests, rulers and the people together.[75] Although there is evidence that Roman law did take the clamour of the people (*furor populi*) seriously, even to the point of determining the prisoner's punishment,[76] this does not seem to be what Luke intends at this point. Pilate appears to have summoned the people together specifically to tell them *his* judgement on the case, not to ask for *theirs*.

After reiterating the main charge – that of perverting the people – Pilate presents his findings to the assembled crowd. He claims to have examined Jesus and to have found him innocent. Ἀνακρίνειν ('to judge') is a technical term corresponding to the Latin *cognitio* referring to an examination by a magistrate.[77] But Pilate has engaged in only the briefest possible examination of the prisoner;

Commentary, p. 465. Fitzmyer, however, asserts that there is no suggestion that the robe had anything to do with Jesus' alleged kingship but, 'it is chosen to mock his guiltlessness': cf. *Gospel*, p. 1482.

[74] Taking 23.12 and the trial before Herod as historical, this is Blinzler's suggestion ('Niedermetzelung', pp. 24–49). Hoehner (*Herod*, pp. 175–6) and Goulder (*Luke*, p. 759) suggested that the enmity was caused by the incident concerning the gilded shields narrated by Philo, *Embassy* 299–305 (see chapter 2 above).

[75] The same verb συγκαλέω is used in Acts 5.21 and 28.17 of calling together a council; see Matera, 'Luke 23. 1–25', p. 548. 'Rulers' here probably refers to the lay nobility as at 19.47, possibly also the scribes; see Grundmann, *Evangelium*, p. 425.

[76] See Haacker, 'Wer war schuld', p. 34 and Bauman, *Impietas*, pp. 189–90.

[77] It is used at Acts 4.9, 12.19, 24.8 and 28.18.

he has refused to become involved in the proceedings and passed Jesus on to Herod. The readers may suspect that he is once again trying to avoid dealing with the case. The important point here, however, is the Roman governor's second declaration of Jesus' innocence. To this, he adds that Herod too reached the same conclusion since he returned Jesus.[78] Clearly the Lukan readers are to assume that Herod would have put Jesus to death had he found him guilty of any of the charges (as presumably in 13.31). Luke has now provided the two witnesses required by Deuteronomy 19.15 to Jesus' innocence.[79] Both are influential people whose opinion would not be dismissed lightly, one a Roman governor, the other a Jewish tetrarch.

Conflicting verdicts, verses 15b–23

Pilate says that Herod has returned Jesus 'to us' (πρὸς ἡμᾶς).[80] Luke's readers would presumably find nothing strange in the prefect's use of the plural here for other Romans could say 'us' while meaning 'me'.[81] Yet, on a different level, the plural may have significance. This seems to be the first indication that the people are going to have a say in the fate of Jesus. The judge of Jesus will no longer be Pilate alone but the chief priests, rulers and the Jewish crowd.

The Roman judge dramatically gives his verdict on the case and proceeds to tell the assembled gathering what he intends to do with the prisoner. The sentence, however, does not follow from his previous verdict: if Jesus is not guilty of any of the Jewish charges and does not deserve death, why then does Pilate say 'therefore' I will chastise him? He seems to be suggesting that he give Jesus not the *flagellatio* administered before crucifixion in Mark 15.16–20[82]

[78] οὐδέ may have the sense of 'not even Herod'; if so, Pilate may mean that Herod, as a Jew, might be more easily expected to see what crime had upset the Jewish leaders in Jerusalem.

[79] In the same way that two witnesses attest that Jesus is the promised Messiah at the beginning of the gospel (Simeon and Anna in 2.22–38), so now Luke has provided two witnesses at the end of Jesus' life to emphasize that Jesus is no political threat: cf. Grundmann, *Evangelium*, p. 424.

[80] Despite the textual variant here ('for I sent you to him', supported by A, B, D, ℵ and others), this is the most likely reading; see Metzger, *Textual*, p. 179.

[81] See, for instance, Cicero *De oratore* 3, 168 and Josephus *Ant.* 20.157.

[82] On the basis of *Dig.* 28.19.7, Sherwin-White (*Roman*, p. 27) suggests that there were three grades of beatings in the Empire: *fustes*, *flagella* and *verbera*. Although the precise differences between them are uncertain, παιδεύειν (meaning 'to bring up',

but a milder disciplinary beating. This lighter beating was often associated with a warning when the governor decided that the situation did not require a formal *cognitio*, for example, when dealing with juvenile gangs or acts of negligence.[83] Again Pilate seems to be trying to avoid a formal trial. Yet the very fact that he has declared Jesus innocent but is willing to give him a mild beating to placate the crowd shows that he is already beginning to bow to Jewish pressure.

The chief priests, rulers and crowd do not accept Pilate's verdict and shout back their own – 'Away with this man!' (Αἶρε τοῦτον) – a cry which is echoed later in connection with Paul in Acts 21.36, 22.22 (and Isa. 53.8). Instead of Jesus, they demand the release of Barabbas, one who was certainly guilty of perverting the nation by his insurrectionary activity.

The scene continues with two more sets of parallel verdicts: each time Pilate tries to release Jesus and each time the crowd shouts against him. Whilst Pilate's verdict has remained virtually the same on all three occasions, that of the crowd becomes more intense: 'Away with this man (and release to us Barabbas)', 'Crucify, crucify him!', 'But they were urgent, demanding with loud cries that he should be crucified'. The demands of the people reach a crescendo until in 23b Luke dramatically records that their voices prevailed. The verbs used express the forcefulness of the crowd: ἐπίκειμαι ('to be urgent') and κατισχύω ('to overpower').

The sentence, verses 24–5

Luke's is the only gospel to admit that Pilate passed sentence, but he makes it plain that it reflects the crowd's verdict, not the Roman governor's: 'so Pilate gave sentence that their demand should be granted'.[84] It is not so much a condemnation of Jesus as a decision that what the priests, leaders and people want should be done.[85] The final verse is almost pitiful. Pilate meekly hands over an

'educate', instruct' or 'correct') seems to correspond to the lightest of these, the *fustigatio*, or disciplinary beating; see C. F. Evans, *Luke*, p. 854 and Grundmann, *Evangelium*, p. 426. Fitzmyer not very convincingly suggests that Pilate is using an euphemism for *flagellatio* here, 'probably to salve his own conscience': cf. *Gospel*, p. 1484.

[83] See Sherwin-White, *Roman*, pp. 27–8 for references.

[84] ἐπέκρινεν in verse 24 has the technical nuance of issuing an official sentence; see also 2 Macc. 4.47, 3 Macc. 4.2.

[85] Matera, 'Luke 23.1–25', p. 549 and Walaskay, *And So*, p. 44.

insurrectionary and murderer, a political rebel against Rome, in response to the demand of the people he is supposed to govern. It must be remembered that there has been no armistice or *privilegium paschale* in Luke. The fate of Barabbas has nothing whatsoever to do with that of Jesus in Luke's presentation; Pilate does not have to release either prisoner. The effect of this is that Pilate's actions are all the more reprehensible: not only does he allow a man to be crucified whom both he and Herod have found innocent, but he releases a political prisoner simply because the crowd asks for it. In the governor's court injustice has triumphed over justice.

Conclusion

In a drastic revision of his Markan source, Luke's major apologetic purpose in 23.1–25 is to use Pilate as the official witness to Jesus' innocence and to lay the blame for Jesus' crucifixion first on the intrigues of the chief priests (vv. 1–12) and then on representatives of the whole Jewish nation (vv. 13–25). This theme continues throughout Acts where Roman involvement nearly always follows Jewish plots.[86] But once Pilate has three times declared Jesus innocent, Luke does not seem intent upon painting a glowing picture of Roman administration. In fact, quite the reverse seems to be the case. As C. H. Talbert notes, 'Pilate appears more as an advocate who pleads Jesus' case than as a judge presiding over an official hearing'.[87] He refuses to become involved with the charges and simply declares Jesus innocent. He does not want to bother with the case and seizes the opportunity to pass Jesus on to Herod. But Herod, who does question Jesus at length, albeit for self-interested motives, sees Jesus as no threat and returns him to the governor. Pilate seems in control as he summons Jewish representatives to his tribunal but soon shows signs of weakness. Eventually he convicts a man whom he has declared innocent and releases a rebel and murderer because of the demand of the people. Bowing to Jewish pressure he undermines not only his own judgement but also that of Herod. In the end, Jewish mob pressure has triumphed over Roman justice. The weak Pilate has let down first himself and Herod, second the Roman administration he represents.

This presentation of Pilate is consistent with the references to

---

[86] Incidents where Roman involvement follows *pagan* agitation can be found at 16.19–24 and 19.23–41.

[87] Talbert, *Reading*, p. 217.

him in Acts. Acts 13.28 simply states that the people of Jerusalem and their leaders asked Pilate to have Jesus killed though they could charge him with nothing deserving death. Verse 3.13 charges a Jewish audience with delivering Jesus up and denying him in the presence of Pilate who had decided to release him. Both these passages lay the blame for Jesus' crucifixion on the Jewish people, their leaders or both. Acts 4.25–8, however, does not contain such extreme anti-Jewish bias and, after quoting Psalm 2.1–2, reads:

> for truly in this city there were gathered together against thy holy servant Jesus, whom thou didst anoint, both Herod and Pontius Pilate, with the gentiles and the peoples of Israel, to do whatever thy hand and thy plan had predestined to take place.   (4.27–8, RSV)

Obviously, Luke would not have included the psalm and the subsequent commentary on it if he felt it was completely at variance with his presentation of the Roman trial. Although he clearly wants to lay the bulk of the blame on the Jewish chief priests, Pilate's lack of interest and weakness inevitably lead him to a place in this evil alliance. The Roman governor has not been whitewashed.

In this way, Pilate's characterization conforms to that of other Roman judges in Luke-Acts. Luke consistently draws a distinction between Roman law which sees no harm in Christianity and its weak or even corrupt governors through whose incompetence Jewish opponents of the new movement could claim some victories.

Finally, what does this portrayal of Pilate tell us about the perception of Rome held by Luke's community? For over two-and-a-half centuries the widely held scholarly consensus has been that Luke composed his two-volume work as an apology for Christianity addressed to a Roman magistrate, Theophilus.[88] Yet this theory is not without serious flaws. First, there is no suggestion in the two volumes of widespread persecution or injustice at Roman hands which would necessitate such a work. Second, Luke's narrative is dotted with several references which would not be likely to commend Christianity to Rome: for example, he openly refers to

---

[88] This view was first put forward by Heumann in 1721 (cf. Esler, *Community*, p. 205, note 10); for a similar interpretation see Cadbury, *Making*, pp. 5–7. For a history of research into Luke's political apologetic see Walaskay, *And So*, pp. 1–14. This view is still held by some: for instance, Fitzmyer, *Gospel*, p. 10 and C.F. Evans, *Luke*, pp. 108–11.

Simon as a zealot (Luke 6.15, Acts 1.13); he makes no attempt to cover up Jesus' command to buy swords (Luke 22.35–8); nor does he attempt to hide the kingly aspect of Jesus' messiahship (Luke 19.38). This would be extremely curious if Luke were writing for a non-Christian Roman audience.[89]

More recently, P. W. Walaskay has turned the traditional theory around, arguing that Luke-Acts is not an apology for the church but an apology for Rome directed at Luke's own community. Some people perhaps tended to deprecate the imperial government; some may have 'anxiously awaited the coming of the Lord and saw little value in developing a dialogue with the enduring state'; all would have been attempting to work out their new social relationship with the Empire without the prop of Judaism.[90] Again, this theory is not without its drawbacks. Most importantly, whilst it is clear from Luke-Acts that the relationship between Luke's community and Judaism was a crucial issue, there is no evidence for either the deprecation of Rome or an expectation of an imminent parousia within the two writings. Furthermore, if it were Luke's purpose to portray Rome in a positive way, why has he included inconsequential details which only serve to show the representatives of Rome in a poor light: for example, Felix hoping for a bribe (Acts 24.26) or Pilate's slaughter of the Galileans (Luke 13.1)? Luke's readers would hardly be impressed by the picture of Pilate which the evangelist presents. Pilate's most important function is to provide an official Roman proclamation of Jesus' innocence; why would this be needed in such a community?

Another more likely solution to this problem has come from P. F. Esler. Like Walaskay, he assumes that Luke is writing to address internal problems within his community rather than the non-Christian Roman world at large. According to Esler,

> among the members of Luke's community were a number of Romans serving the Empire in a military or administrative capacity ... part of Luke's task was to present

---

[89] Other such passages can be found at 1.52, 4.18–19, 12.49, 51, Acts 5.29, 42, 21.38, 28.31. For a fuller discussion see Walaskay, *And So*, pp. 15–22. See also Cassidy (*Jesus*) who argues on the basis of these and other references that Luke has no political apologetic directed towards Rome.

[90] Walaskay, *And So*, pp. 64–7. A similar view was put forward by Maddox who suggested that Luke was trying to cultivate a sober, inoffensive style of life and attitude towards the Roman government such as that advocated in Rom. 13.1–7 and 1 Pet. 2.11–17; the evangelist was anxious to avoid both Christian self-assertiveness towards Rome and voluntary martyrdoms: cf. *Purpose*, pp. 96–7.

Christian history in such a way as to demonstrate that
faith in Jesus Christ and allegiance to Rome were not
mutually inconsistent'.[91]

Luke's narrative shows that the state was on Jesus' side and that to
confess yourself a Christian was no crime against Roman law.[92]

This would account for Luke's interest in Rome generally and
also why the Roman trial occupies such an important position in
his narrative. Such a readership would also account for the negative
portrayal of Roman governors: if Roman judges found Jesus and
Paul innocent (as Luke stresses), then their deaths need to be
accounted for by other means; for Luke, God's purposes are
effected by a combination of Jewish machinations and the weak or
depraved characters of the Roman governors before whom Jesus
and Paul were brought. Christian Romans would presumably not
feel offended by these portrayals as the pages of Luke and Acts are
full of positive pictures of Romans with whom they could identify,
including Paul himself. For such a community Luke's presentation
of Pilate served an invaluable role. He officially proclaimed Jesus'
innocence but at the same time through his weak, malleable and
ineffectual character, provided the means by which Jesus' Jewish
opponents were able to have him executed.

[91] Esler, *Community*, p. 210. He also suggests that Luke wanted to appeal to
Roman Christians by stressing the ancestral nature of Christianity in a similar way
to Josephus' concern to emphasize the ancestral nature of Judaism in his *Antiquities*:
cf. ibid., pp. 212–15.
[92] See Goulder, *Luke*, p. 761 and Conzelmann, *Theology*, p. 140.

7

PILATE IN JOHN'S GOSPEL

Virtually all scholars are in agreement that John's gospel was written for a Christian community which had recently and traumatically broken away, or been expelled, from the Jewish synagogue.[1] There are points of similarity here with Matthew's gospel in that, despite the Jewishness of many parts of the gospel,[2] the author is vehemently hostile towards his Jewish neighbours. The work seems to presuppose the fall of the Temple in 70 CE[3] but, since the discovery of the Rylands papyrus, cannot be later than about 100–10.[4] Most scholars are agreed that a date of roughly 85–95,

[1] John 9.22, 12.42 and 16.2 all refer to this expulsion. See in particular Martyn, *History*; Brown, *Community*; Meeks, 'Breaking'; Segovia, 'Love'; Kysar, 'John'; Hengel, *Johannine* and commentaries by Schnackenburg (*Gospel*), Barrett (*Gospel*) and Lindars (*Gospel*).

[2] For example, the allusions to Gen. 1.1 in the prologue, the references to the Passover (2.13, 6.4, 11.55 and 13.1) and the frequent use of OT images (10.11, 15.1–4, 6.51). For a fuller discussion of both the Jewish and Hellenistic background to John's gospel see Barrett, *John and Judaism*; Brown, *Gospel*, vol. 1, pp. lii–lxvi; Schnackenburg, *Gospel*, pp. 119–49.

The author of the gospel has traditionally been seen as either John the son of Zebedee, John the Elder of 2 and 3 John or the Beloved Disciple (who may be either of the first two). Many scholars are content to accept that we do not know the author's identity (e.g. Kysar, 'John', p. 920 and Lindars, *Gospel*, pp. 28–34). Hengel (*Johannine*, pp. 102–8) maintains that the author was John the Elder; Barrett, Brown and Schnackenburg suggest a disciple of John son of Zebedee (Brown tentatively suggests that this may have been John the Elder). For a fuller discussion see Barrett, *Gospel*, pp. 100–27, Brown, *Gospel*, pp. lxxxvii–cii and Schnackenburg, *Gospel*, pp. 75–104.

[3] This is suggested by the fact that the Sadducees and the scribes familiar to us from the synoptics are no longer present, reflecting conditions after 70. Also 2.13–22 may be an attempt to present Jesus as the replacement of the destroyed Temple: cf. Kysar, 'John', p. 919. J. A. T. Robinson, however, dates the gospel to before the fall of Jerusalem: cf. *Redating*, pp. 244–311.

[4] The Rylands Papyrus 457 (p^{52}) was found in Egypt and is probably to be dated at about 125–50. Since it is unlikely to have been the original, some time must have elapsed for the gospel to be known and copied.

that is, the reign of Domitian, would fit well with the circumstances to which the gospel is addressed.[5]

Locating this community is not an easy task. Suggestions have ranged from Alexandria, Antioch (or elsewhere in Syria)[6] to Batanaea or lower Galilee.[7] Ephesus, however, is the traditional place of authorship[8] and this city has several points in its favour. First, though few would hold that the author of John's gospel also wrote Revelation, the two works may have come from the same general location and Revelation explicitly mentions Ephesus (1.11, 2.1). There was also a strong and influential Jewish community in Ephesus[9] which seems to have been engaged in bitter disputes with the Christian community (Rev. 2.9). Furthermore, Ephesus was the capital of the Roman province of Asia and this dominant Roman regime would explain John's interest in Jesus' Roman trial. Though none of these points is conclusive and certainty is impossible, the

---

[5] Some scholars (e.g. Martyn, *History*), have tied the conflict in John to the promulgation of the *birkath ha minim*, an amendment to the 12th of the 18 Benedictions at the time of Gamaliel II (80–115) in Jamnia which (Martyn claims) excluded Christians and heretics from the synagogue. Unfortunately, we do not know the exact date, the precise wording or the intention of this prayer. Besides, the conflict in John seems to stem from local synagogues and their leaders rather than from a central decision from Jamnia. Historically, it is likely that local Jewish–Christian disputes eventually led to the formulation of the *birkath ha minim*. It is probably at this earlier stage that the Jewish–Christian conflict described in John's gospel (and also in Matthew's) is to be located. See Hengel, *Johannine*, pp. 114–15 and Meeks, 'Breaking', p. 102, who refers to the *birkath ha minim* as 'a red herring in Johannine research'.

Lindars (*Gospel*, p. 42) suggests a date of 85–95; Barrett (*Gospel*, p. 128) suggests c. 100; Brown puts it at 90–100. The latter is probably correct in his assertion that the gospel underwent several revisions (he suggests five) before it reached its final form (ibid., pp. lxxx–lxxxvi; see also Hengel, *Johannine*, pp. 102–8).

[6] Dodd (*Johannine*, pp. xxxviii–xlvii), highlighted the parallels between 1 John and Matthew, suggesting that John's gospel, like Matthew's, originated at Antioch. However, this depends upon Matthew having been written in Antioch, which is far from certain (see above, pp. 121–2).

[7] For instance, Wengst, *Bedrängte*, suggested the Southern part of Agrippa II's kingdom. Due to the importance of 'Galileans' and 'Samaritans' in John's gospel and the lack of any explicit reference to the dominant pagan society, Meeks suggests the gospel was composed in a Greek city of lower Galilee: cf. 'Breaking', pp. 94–104. Lindars (*Gospel*, pp. 43–4) and Hengel (*Johannine*, p. 115) doubt a Palestinian origin. Furthermore, Bassler ('Galileans') has shown that the terms 'Galileans', 'Samaritans' and 'Jews' can be read as symbolic designations relating not to origin but faith.

[8] Irenaeus, *Adv. Haer.* 2.22.5 and 3.3.4 (quoted by Eusebius *EH* 3.23.3–4 and 4.14.3–8).

[9] Acts 18.19, 24–28, 19.8–20. For the prominence and influence of Jews in the cities of Asia Minor see Hengel, *Johannine*, p. 116.

following discussion will take Ephesus as the general area of composition.[10]

Apart from the chiliarch and the soldiers at Jesus' arrest (18.3), Pilate is the only Roman with whom Jesus comes into contact. As in the synoptic gospels, the governor plays his part in the passion narrative as the judge of Jesus at 18.28–19.16a. In 19.19–22 John has added another story describing a dispute between Pilate and 'the Jews' regarding the title on the cross. Finally Pilate makes a brief third appearance at 19.38 when, as in the synoptic gospels, Joseph of Arimathea asks for Jesus' dead body.

This chapter will look at the sources behind John's passion account and important Johannine themes which have shaped his portrayal of the Roman trial narrative before turning to evaluate the characterization of Pilate in this gospel. After this we shall have looked at the description of Pilate in all four gospels and chapter 8 will go on to examine the historical background to the gospel accounts of Pilate.

John's sources

Whether we can assume that John and his readers were familiar with the synoptic passion accounts is uncertain. At one extreme, several scholars assert that John knew and used Mark, Luke or all of the synoptics.[11] At the opposite end of the scale, others think that John did not make use of any synoptic gospel or synoptic sources and was dependent instead on an independent passion source.[12] A more moderate view, and one which will be assumed throughout this chapter, is that John was acquainted with some of the sources or traditions behind Mark (and possibly Luke), or ones

---

[10] Although he admits the case is 'not strong', Ephesus is favoured by Barrett, *Gospel*, p. 131; Lindars (*Gospel*, p. 44) is uncertain between Ephesus and Syria. Brown (*Gospel*, vol. 1 pp. ciii–iv), Lightfoot (*St John's*, p. 2) and Hengel (*Johannine*, pp. 109–24) all favour Ephesus. Schnackenburg seems to want to have the best of all possibilities when he suggests that the Johannine tradition originated in Palestine and was subjected to Syrian influences before it was written down in Ephesus: cf. *Gospel*, p. 152.

[11] For instance, Barrett, *Gospel*, pp. 34–5; Lee, 'St Mark' (dependence on Mark); Bailey, *Traditions*, p. 121 (dependence on Luke); Sabbe, 'Trial' and Neirynck, 'John' (both argue John was dependent on the synoptics).

[12] Exponents of this view include Gardner-Smith, *St John*; Bultmann, *Gospel*, pp. 653–4; Dodd, *Historical*, part 1a; Meeks, *Prophet*, p. 18, note 4 and Brown, *Gospel*, vol. 1 p. xlvi.

similar to them, but not necessarily with any of the synoptics in their final form.[13] The major reason for accepting Johannine knowledge of at least the traditions behind Mark is that the characterization of Pilate which emerges from John's gospel has several points of similarity with that in Mark, as will become clear in the following discussion.

Johannine themes culminating in the trial before Pilate

As with the other gospels, certain motifs and theological themes may have influenced the evangelist's portrayal of the governor. When assessing the Johannine Pilate, therefore, it is worth considering the following notable points.

(1) John's gospel is unique in that Roman involvement in this narrative comes not just with the handing over to Pilate but also at the arrest of Jesus. Whilst this is a purely Jewish affair in the synoptics,[14] Judas is accompanied in the Fourth Gospel by both representatives of 'the Jews' and by soldiers (18.3). If there was any doubt that John is referring to *Roman* troops here, it is dispelled by the reference to the χιλίαρχος in verse 18 who is clearly the leader of the σπεῖρα, or cohort. Furthermore, John cannot be using Roman military terms anachronistically to refer to non-Roman troops, as occurs in the LXX,[15] since he goes on to refer to Jewish officers. So in the Fourth Gospel, Jesus is clearly arrested by Roman troops. Whether John found this detail in a reliable historical tradition or whether he inserted it himself is not important for the flow of the narrative. What is important is that Roman involvement in Jesus' death, according to John, begins right from his arrest.

Nor is this involvement only minimal. John states that a whole σπεῖρα was present. The exact number of men denoted by this term is not entirely clear. Σπεῖρα translates the Latin *cohors*, the tenth part of a legion, or about 600 men. This is

[13] This view is held by Buse, 'St John/Markan', pp. 215–19 and 'St John/Matthew/Luke', pp. 65–70. Borgen ('John', pp. 246–59), holds a view somewhere between the last two alternatives.
[14] Mark has Judas accompanied by ὄχλος μετὰ μαχαιρῶν καὶ ξύλων παρὰ τῶν ἀρχιέρων καὶ τῶν γραμματέων καὶ τῶν πρεσβυτέρων (14.43); Matthew describes the crowd as πολὺς and omits the reference to scribes (26.47); in Luke it is the ἀρχιερεῖς καὶ στρατηγοὺς τοῦ ἱεροῦ καὶ πρεσβυτέρους themselves who have come to arrest Jesus (22.52).
[15] Brown, *Gospel*, p. 808 makes this point.

consistent with the reference to the χιλίαρχος in verse 18 which was often used to translate the Latin *tribunus militum* or commander of a cohort. Even if σπεῖρα is taken to refer only to a maniple of 200 men, John's account suggests that a substantial number of troops was involved.[16] These came out to arrest Jesus with weapons in 18.3, obviously expecting resistance from either him or his followers.[17]

Leaving aside the historicity of this scene, what John portrays on a dramatic-literary level is a fairly large military operation involved in the arrest of Jesus. John's readers would surely know that these Roman troops could only have been placed at the disposal of the Jewish leadership by the prefect himself. Although John has not actually recorded that 'the Jews' have enlisted the help of the Roman prefect, his readers could infer it both from the account of the arrest and from the Jewish plot in chapter 11 where the chief priests and Pharisees express their fear that the Romans will take severe measures against Jesus' increasing popularity (11.48). John's account, then, suggests that Pilate had already become involved in the plot against Jesus *prior* to his arrest.

(2) John's description of this scene illustrates another point which will be highlighted later in the trial: the Johannine Jesus is perfectly in control of the situation and goes willingly to his fate. This has been prepared for in the Good Shepherd discourse in chapter 10, a chapter which is of great importance for understanding the Roman trial narrative and one which will be returned to at many points in the following discussion. In 10.11 Jesus says 'the good shepherd lays down his life for the sheep'; in verse 14 he says that he *is* the good shepherd and continues: 'I lay down my life, that I may take it again. No one takes it from me, but I lay it down of my own accord. I have power to lay it down, and I have power to take it again' (vv. 7–8). Faced with Jesus' revelation of himself in the words 'I am he' (Ἐγώ εἰμι), the group sent to arrest Jesus draw back

---

[16] Historically, Winter, who thinks that Roman troops were involved in Jesus' arrest, suggests that these figures would be far too high and thinks it more likely that Jesus was arrested by a *decurio* and ten men: cf. *Trial,* p. 29. If there is any accuracy to the report in Acts 23.23, however, the Romans may have occasionally used disproportionately large numbers of men. See p. 197 below.

[17] Those who arrest Jesus in the synoptics are similarly armed: cf. Mark 14.43, Matt. 26.47, Luke 22.52.

and fall to the ground (18.6). Those acting with the authority of 'the world' have no power over him.

(3) John's description of the Roman trial itself is much longer than any of those found in the synoptics. Its importance within the narrative is emphasized further by the lack of any formal *Jewish* trial in this gospel. The reader has never been in any doubt that 'the Jews' want to arrest Jesus[18] or even to kill him[19] – in 11.47–53 the Sanhedrin meet and, apparently in Jesus' absence, condemn him to death. Yet John records no formal Jewish trial of Jesus before he is handed over to Pilate. Jesus is taken to Annas (18.13) who questions him 'about his disciples and his teaching' (v. 19) and then sends him to Caiaphas (v. 24). The reason for this appearance before Annas is not entirely obvious. Certainly he does not pass any formal sentence and John twice makes it clear that Annas is not the High Priest (18.13, 24). If there is to be any formal Jewish conviction of Jesus it should be before Caiaphas in his official capacity as High Priest. Yet of any proceedings which may have occurred before Caiaphas, John is completely silent. Some of the features belonging to the synoptic account of the Jewish trial have been scattered throughout the gospel, especially in chapter 10 where 'the Jews' ask Jesus if he is the Christ and then accuse him of blasphemy (vv. 22–39). But here, at the point where we would expect to find the Jewish charges against Jesus, the scene changes to recount the story of Peter's final two denials and the subsequent cock-crow thus masking the fact that John has said nothing about the meeting between Caiaphas and Jesus. In the Fourth Gospel, then, Jesus' only trial after his arrest is at the hands of the Roman prefect, Pontius Pilate.

(4) Even a cursory reading of John 18.28–19.16a reveals a carefully formulated structure, arranged not so much on content as the location of the individual scenes.[20] Although R. Bultmann divided this section into six scenes (taking 19.1–8 as one unit)[21] and W. A. Meeks adds 19.17–22 to the trial narrative,[22] the overwhelming consensus amongst scholars is that the verses

---

[18] 7.30, 32, 44 (here it is 'the people'), 45–6, 10.39, 11.57.
[19] Whilst Mark states this explicitly only once, John mentions it frequently: 5.16–18, 7.1, 19, 25, 8.6, 37, 40, 44, 59, 10.31, 11.8, 50, 53.
[20] On chiastic structures in general see Leon-Dufour 'Trois Chiasmes', pp. 249–55 and Lund 'Influence', pp. 27–48, 405–33.
[21] Bultmann, *Gospel,* p. 648.   [22] Meeks, *Prophet,* p. 62.

are to be divided into seven divisions, a particularly significant number within John's gospel.[23] These are: 18.28–32, 33–8a, 38b-40, 19.1–3, 4–8, 9–11, 12–16. This structural division is emphasized primarily by the movements of Pilate between 'the Jews' who remain *outside* the praetorium and Jesus who, for most of the action, remains *inside* the praetorium. The action is arranged into two symmetrical groupings, each with three scenes and centring on the scourging in 19.1–3. In each of the groups, Pilate is outside the praetorium with 'the Jews' (and later Jesus) throughout the first and third scenes and inside with Jesus in the second scene.

This structure, which forces Pilate to move constantly between Jesus and his Jewish accusers, has often been used as a basis upon which to build John's characterization of Pilate. It is common amongst commentators to see Pilate's movement inside and outside as evidence of a vacillating and indecisive personality, or as reflecting his desperation to avoid making a decision.[24] Yet this approach has not paid sufficient attention to ancient literary (particularly biblical) methods. As R. Alter puts it:

> The fixed practice of biblical narrative, with only a few rather marginal exceptions, limits scenes to two characters at a time – or sometimes, to the exchange between one character and a group speaking in a single voice as a collective interlocutor.[25]

John is clearly following this convention. In order to highlight the exchanges between Pilate/'the Jews' and Pilate/Jesus, he locates the dialogues in different settings, only in the fifth and seventh scenes allowing all the characters to come together as in the synoptic accounts. The fact that Pilate moves inside and outside the praetorium therefore is most probably due to John's literary style rather than an attempt to make Pilate appear indecisive.

(5) An important motif throughout the Johannine trial narrative is the emphasis on Jesus' kingship. Whilst John often refers to Jesus as 'Christ',[26] the specific title 'king' is used only three

---

[23] For instance, Jesus performs seven signs, gives seven discourses and, in 4.52, heals the official's son 'at the seventh hour'. For an alternative structure see Giblin, 'John's', pp. 221–4.

[24] Thus Stibbe, *Storyteller*, p. 106.   [25] Alter, *Art*, p. 72.

[26] 1.41, 4.25–6, 27, 7.26–7, 31, 40–1, 10.24, 11.27, 12.34, 20.31.

times outside the trial narrative: 1.49, 6.15 and 12.13–15. The first occurs relatively privately when Nathanael describes Jesus as 'King of Israel' (βασιλεὺς τοῦ Ἰσραήλ) in front of a small group of disciples. 'Israel' was the preferred Jewish self-definition and this title seems to have been the Jewish messianic version of 'the King of the Jews'.[27] After the feeding of the five thousand, the people declared Jesus to be the prophet who is to come into the world (6.14). In the next verse, John states that Jesus withdrew from the crowds because he perceived that they were about to make him king (βασιλεὺς) by force. This verse gives us two important insights into John's view of kingship. First, the evangelist clearly shows that Jesus is rejecting a political kingly role. Second, he shows his readers that popular support for Jesus was such that the crowds wanted to make him their king, although the use of the term 'prophet', which in Johannine thought is an inadequate description for Jesus, shows that the crowd had not understood his mission. Again at Jesus' entry into Jerusalem (12.13–15), he is hailed by the people as 'the King of Israel'.

Less specifically, Jesus refers to himself in 10.1–30 as the 'good shepherd'. In the OT, the king or the ruler of Israel is often portrayed as a shepherd with his sheep.[28] The messianic prophecy of Ezekiel 34.23 says: 'I will set up over them one shepherd, my servant David, and he shall feed them: he shall feed them and be their shepherd'. Numbers 27.17 calls for one to be as a shepherd to Israel: the one who is appointed is Joshua whose Greek name, as C. K. Barrett points out,[29] was Ἰησοῦς. God himself could also be described using shepherd imagery.[30] The image was in use in the Graeco-Roman world as well. The Emperor Tiberius is reported by Dio Cassius as describing his Egyptian subjects as his 'sheep' and

[27] R. Mayer, 'Israel', especially pp. 310–11. The term 'King of Israel' is also applied to Yahweh in Isa. 41.21 and 44.6. In Mark 15.32 the chief priests mock Jesus as ὁ Χριστὸς ὁ βασιλεὺς Ἰσραήλ, even though the gentile title on the cross reads ὁ βασιλεὺς τῶν Ἰουδαίων (followed by Matt. 27.42). In Luke 23.37 the gentile soldiers describe Jesus as 'the King of the Jews'.

[28] For instance, Zech. 11 or the wicked rulers of Jer. 23.1–4, 2.32–8, Isa. 56.9–12, Ezek. 34. David is a shepherd-king, Ps. 78.70–2.

[29] Barrett, *Gospel*, p. 369.

[30] Pss. 80.1, 23.1, Isa. 40.11. In the NT, too, shepherd imagery is used of the sovereign: Rev. 2.27; Matt. 2.6 (quoting Micah 5.2) sees a shepherd as the messianic ruler.

Suetonius describes his advice to the Egyptian prefect on how to be a 'good shepherd'.[31]

Within the Roman trial narrative the issue of Jesus' kingship suddenly becomes prominent; the word 'king' occurs seven times. The impression is that John wants to focus on the title and to describe exactly in what sense Jesus really was a king.

(6)   Much more meaningful than kingship for John, however, is the title 'Son of God'. The gospel was written with the intention 'that you may believe that Jesus is the Christ, the Son of God' (20.31). It is possible that 'Son of God' was a messianic title based on the OT enthronement formula where Yahweh calls the Messiah his 'son'.[32] But for John's readers the title has a much deeper significance.[33] The title primarily shows the unique relationship between Jesus and the Father, a relationship based on mutual love and filial obedience.[34] Jesus shares the functions of the Father in that he too is the judge of all people and the bringer of eternal life (5.17–30). In fact, Jesus reflects the character of the Father so completely that 'to see the Son is to see the Father' (14.9). 'Both moral likeness and essential unity are included'.[35]

In 19.7 'the Jews' will charge Jesus with 'making himself' the Son of God (ὅτι υἱὸν θεοῦ ἑαυτὸν ἐποίησεν). For John's readers this accusation is completely untrue. Jesus did not *make himself* the Son of God, nor did he *become* God's Son through adoption, as was the case with the Israelite kings, but right from the beginning of time he has existed in this unique relationship with the Father.[36] In R. E. Brown's words, 'he is not a man who makes himself God, he is the Word of God who has become man'.[37]

(7)   The hostility between John's community and the synagogue expresses itself most forcibly in the author's presentation of 'the Jews'. Although on occasion this term may be used

---

[31] Dio Cassius 57.10.5; Suetonius, *Tib.* 32.2.

[32] See Dodd, *Interpretation*, p. 253; Brown, *Gospel*, p. 88; 2 Sam. 7.14, Pss. 89.27, 2.6–7. This seems to be the way in which it is used in Mark 14.61 and Matt. 16.16: cf. Dodd, p. 253.

[33] As Brown notes, Thomas' confession in 20.28 of Jesus as 'God' makes it unlikely that the gospel was written simply to show that Jesus was the Messiah: cf. *Gospel*, p. 1060.

[34] 4.34, 5.19, 8.28, 17.21.   [35] Barrett, *Gospel*, p. 72.

[36] 1.1, 18, 8.58, 17.5.   [37] Brown, *Gospel*, p. 408.

neutrally,[38] it is much more frequently used pejoratively of Jesus' opponents who are hostile to him and his message.[39] They murmur at Jesus' words (6.41), are unbelieving (9.18), want to put believers out of the synagogue (9.22) and seek to kill Jesus.[40] In 8.44 Jesus tells 'the Jews' that they are of their father the devil and that their will is to do his desires. This extreme hostility derives from one of the most striking literary features of John's gospel, its existential dualism. 'The Jews' are not simply the Jewish inhabitants of Judaea but those who reject Jesus in contrast to those who believe in him. John has a wide range of dualistic symbols which he uses to contrast those who believe with those who do not. Continually throughout the gospel Jesus or the evangelist posit two alternatives: for example, those who receive the light/those who do not (1.11–12); those who are born of the Spirit/those who are born of the flesh (3.6), he who does what is evil/he who does what is true (3.20–1); he who is of God/ he who is not (8.47). In a person's response to Jesus there is no room in Johannine thought for a third category of neutrality; one must decide either to accept the revelation or not.

Those who do not accept Jesus' revelation are 'of the world', part of the evil realm in opposition to Jesus.[41] The world hates believers (7.7, 15.8), rejoices in Jesus' suffering (16.20) and is ruled by Satan (12.31, 14.30). Jesus and believers, however, are 'not of the world' (8.23, 15.19, 17.14); they are 'from above' (3.3, 7).

One of these dualistic ideas which has a particular bearing on the portrayal of Pilate is the concept of 'truth'. The importance of the term 'truth' within the thought of the fourth evangelist is clearly recognizable from the occurrence of the noun ἀλήθεια and its two related adjectives ἀληθής (implying 'true despite appearances') and ἀληθινός (implying 'the only real') throughout Johannine literature.[42] At times John's use of these words seems to denote simply that which is in accordance

---

[38] Cf. 8.31, 10.19 and 11.19.

[39] For a full discussion of John's use of 'the Jews' see von Wahlde, 'Johannine', pp. 33–60. In common with the majority of other scholars, he believes that 'the Jews' virtually always refer to the religious authorities (pp. 45–6).

[40] See p. 164, note 5 above.

[41] Like 'the Jews', the κόσμος can very occasionally be used neutrally (e.g. 1.9 and 16.21).

[42] Out of the 163 uses of these terms in the NT, eighty-five are found in John's

with the facts; that is, the opposite to falsehood or deceit.[43] In other places, however, ἀλήθεια and its related adjectives seem to contain a deeper meaning. God himself can be described as 'true' or 'truth'.[44] The evangelist means not so much that God is faithful and steadfast but that he represents the ultimate, divine reality.[45] Since Jesus and God are one in Johannine thought, Jesus not only bears witness to 'the truth' (i.e. God), and is the means by which grace and truth are conveyed to mankind (1.17), but he *is* that truth, expressed most powerfully by the phrase 'I am the way, the truth and the life' (14.6).

Ἀλήθεια characterizes the heavenly realm above, in opposition to what is 'from below' or 'of the flesh'. Jesus can claim to be the true food or true drink in that he provides *real* food and *real* drink which lead to eternal life, whilst other forms of food and drink cannot. This involves both the idea of truth as revelation and truth as that which is opposed to what is false.

John's gospel shares with Hellenistic philosophy the conviction that divine reality, represented by God's ἀλήθεια, is in opposition to the κόσμος which lies in the power of the devil (12.31, 1 John 5.19), a murderer who knows nothing of the truth because there is no truth in him (8.44–6). But he differs radically in that God sends his only son, who is himself the ἀλήθεια, in order to save the κόσμος by his revelation of himself and the Father (3.16–21).[46] Those who accept this revelation are 'of the truth'.

John's gospel, then, assigns the Roman trial a particularly prominent place in the narrative. Roman involvement in Jesus' case begins right from his arrest. The lack of a Jewish trial in this gospel means that everything rests on the Roman proceedings. In a carefully structured presentation, John explores the charges against

gospel or the epistles. For more detailed figures see Brown, *Gospel,* pp. 499–501; the definitions of the adjectives are also taken from Brown.

[43] For instance, 4.18, 37, 10.41, 16.7. This is also the case with phrases connected with witness or testimony within the gospel (e.g. 5.31–2) and the authorial asides in 19.35 and 21.24 – 'his witness is true'.

[44] 3.33, 7.28, 8.26, 17.3 and 1 John 5.20.

[45] For the background to the term 'truth' in John see Dodd, *Interpretation,* pp. 170–80; de la Potterie, 'L'arrière-fond' and particularly Thistleton 'Truth', pp. 874–902.

[46] The important connection between ἀλήθεια and κόσμος can be inferred from the fact that two-thirds of the references to ἀλήθεια in the Johannine writings occur within passages which also deal with the κόσμος.

Jesus, both the King of the Jews and Son of God. In a gospel which accepts no middle ground, the Johannine Pilate must make a choice either for or against Jesus.

The characterization of Pilate

The general consensus amongst commentators is that John's Pilate is a weak, vacillating figure, running between Jesus and 'the Jews' in a vain attempt to release Jesus and finally capitulating before the threats of the people he is supposed to govern. Three times he proclaims Jesus' innocence and yet he does not have the strength of character to oppose the will of 'the Jews'. R. E. Brown sees Pilate as 'typical . . . of the many honest, well-disposed men who would try to adopt a middle position in a struggle that is total'; his behaviour 'illustrates how a person who refuses decisions is led to tragedy'.[47] R. A. Culpepper, too, in his literary investigation of John's gospel, writes: 'As in the other gospels, Pilate is coerced into authorising Jesus' death'.[48]

Yet even commentators who hold this view have to admit several difficulties. C. K. Barrett, for example, sees Pilate's repeated ironic references to Jesus as 'the King of the Jews' as more calculated to embitter 'the Jews' than to secure Jesus' release.[49] No reasons are given for Pilate's scourging of Jesus in the middle of the trial and R. E. Brown is forced to conclude that 'while his intentions are good, Pilate's sense of justice becomes more and more warped'.[50] In the final scene, not only does Pilate's goading lead 'the Jews' to reject their nationalist hopes, but they unconditionally accept the kingship of Caesar. Pilate has therefore, in a worldly sense, emerged as the victor.

A recent study by D. Rensberger has challenged this usual 'weak' picture of Pilate, suggesting that the Johannine Pilate is to be read instead as a 'strong' character: 'the kingship of Caesar has a cruel advocate in Pilate, who spurns both the sovereignty of Israel and the royal witness to truth'.[51] Rensberger's study of Pilate, however, is short (only four pages), and in the following discussion I hope to show that his conclusions are basically on the right lines. Pilate in John's gospel is not an impotent, well-disposed governor but, like

---

[47] Brown, *Gospel*, p. 864. Similar views are expressed by Barrett, Lindars and Morris in their commentaries.

[48] Culpepper, *Anatomy*, p. 142.

[49] Barrett, *Gospel*, p. 539. Culpepper (*Anatomy*, p. 142) also notes that this reference 'only baits their (i.e. "the Jews" ') hostility'.

[50] Brown, *Gospel*, p. 889.   [51] Rensberger, *Overcoming*, p. 98.

'the Jews', he is a representative of the hostile world which rejects Jesus. He serves an important apologetic purpose in his threefold declaration of Jesus' innocence; yet even these declarations stem from his assumption of the utter ridiculousness of Jesus' messianic claims. Although he once feels a certain amount of superstitious fear, the dominant attitude of the Johannine Pilate throughout the trial narrative is one of mockery, directed at 'the Jews', their nationalistic hopes and the prisoner himself.

Due to the length of John's trial narrative, let us divide our discussion into its seven constituent scenes (following Brown's structure).

The Roman trial

Scene 1 (18.28–32)

Without having narrated anything of the proceedings before Caiaphas, John writes that Jesus is led, presumably by 'the Jews', to the πραιτώριον, the Jerusalem residence of the governor during the feast. 'The Jews' did not enter the praetorium 'so that they might not be defiled, but might eat the Passover'.[52] On a literary-dramatic level, the evangelist has provided a reason why 'the Jews' must remain outside. The action will take place on two stages: 'the Jews' are outside whilst Jesus has been led inside. Pilate is to be the link between the two.

Pilate appears abruptly with no introduction; presumably he was familiar to John's readers from tradition.[53] After the involvement of Roman troops at the arrest, he was probably expecting the delegation.[54] In verse 29 he shows a great deal of tact and courtesy towards 'the Jews'; respecting their religious sensibilities he comes out of the praetorium to speak to them. John gives the proceedings an air of formality and so begins with the judge asking the accusers for the charge:[55] 'What accusation do you bring against this man?' Perhaps he expected a more precise formulation of the charges

[52] The historicity of this phrase and exactly what kind of impurity John means have been frequently discussed by scholars. See the discussions in the commentaries, especially Barrett, *Gospel*, pp. 531–3 and Brown, *Gospel*, pp. 845–6.

[53] Barabbas is similarly brought into the story in 18.39 with no introduction, though an explanatory note is inserted in verse 40. John assumes that his audience is familiar with the main characters in the drama.

[54] This possibility is also raised by Brown, *Gospel*, p. 866.

[55] Sherwin-White, *Roman*, p. 17.

against the prisoner after the preliminary hearings before the Jewish leaders.

'The Jews' appear to be taken aback by Pilate's question and it is difficult not to hear a tone of insolence in their reply: 'If this man were not an evildoer we would not have handed him over'.[56] Brown suggests that this impudence would not be too surprising if 'the Jews' had acted with Pilate's backing in the arrest of Jesus and naturally enough expected the governor to try their prisoner.[57] Pilate's response and the subsequent Jewish reply are difficult to interpret. Pilate says: 'Take him yourselves and judge him by your own Law'. 'The Jews' reply: 'It is not lawful for us to put any man to death'.[58] The question really revolves around whether Pilate is being serious here or cynical. If he is understood seriously, it could be argued that Pilate does not know the precise charge at this point. Annoyed at the insolence of 'the Jews', Pilate tells them to see to Jesus' trial themselves, not realizing that he is charged with a capital crime. The reply of 'the Jews' then is a round-about way of indicating that they want him executed, which (in John's narrative) they are powerless to do. This would make sense if it were not for Roman involvement in Jesus' arrest: surely Pilate would realize that 'the Jews' had only appealed for Roman aid because they wanted Jesus executed. Besides, John's readers would not expect a provincial governor to allow a disturber of the peace to pass so easily out of his hands, especially at Passover time.[59]

It may be better then to interpret the words of the Johannine Pilate cynically. He has sent Roman soldiers out against Jesus, gone outside the praetorium to meet the Jewish delegation and attempted to instigate formal procedures against the defendant, only to be met with insolence. His words may thus be a way of reminding 'the Jews' that he is the judge and without him they are not in any position to condemn Jesus. Pilate knows that 'the Jews' have no power to execute but wants to humiliate them by making them admit it. They cannot condemn anyone by their own Law and

[56] Brown, *Gospel*, p. 866. Barrett (*Gospel*, p. 533) describes it as 'extraordinary and almost incredible impudence'.

[57] Brown, *Gospel*, p. 866.

[58] For the lack of evidence regarding the right of Jewish courts to execute criminals see pp. 15–16 above. Millar suggests that this is to be understood not as an allusion to a *Roman* ban on Jews carrying out executions but as a *Jewish* law not allowing a capital trial the day before a Sabbath or festival: cf. 'Reflections', p. 375. See also m.Sanh 4.1 which, though later, may reflect the same ban.

[59] Barrett, *Gospel*, p. 533.

so their answer is a grudging reflection of this. Pilate is therefore mocking Jewish impotence regarding capital jurisdiction and also asserting his position as the only one able to judge Jesus. This theme of judicial authority will reappear in scene 6 when Jesus tells Pilate that the authority which he thinks is his is ultimately derived from God (19.11).

Scene 2 (18.33–8a)

Pilate goes inside the praetorium and summons Jesus, asking, 'Are you the King of the Jews?'[60] Presumably this was the charge with which 'the Jews' brought Jesus to Pilate's attention before the arrest. To Pilate's straightforward question, Jesus answers: 'Do you say this of your own accord, or did others say it to you?' Jesus seems to be meaning 'Have you, as a representative of Roman law and order, seen me engaging in seditious activity and brought this charge against me, or have others suggested it to you?'

Pilate's reply clearly indicates that the charge has been formed by Jesus' own ἔθνος (so stressing Jewish responsibility) and οἱ ἀρχιερεῖς. This is the first opportunity Pilate has had to try the prisoner and he is acting on a charge suggested to him by 'the Jews'. Pilate's subsequent rejoinder, 'Am I a Jew?', emphasizes that the charge is *Jewish* and at the same time distances Pilate from 'the Jews' and their allegations in that μήτι expects a negative answer. Ethnically, Pilate is certainly not a Jew, and is only acting on information given to him by others. His sharp reply may also betray an undertone of Roman contempt for the Jews.[61] The Roman governor in John's narrative has no prior knowledge of Jesus' activity other than what 'the Jews' have told him and so goes on to ask: 'What have you done?' (v. 35).

Jesus completely ignores this last question and launches into a description of his kingdom, using typically Johannine terms.[62] His words stress that his kingdom is not a worldly, political one, as the

---

[60] This charge is exactly the same in all the gospels and appears to have been derived from tradition (or at least inferred from the title on the cross): Mark 15.2, Matt. 27.11 (where it is again introduced abruptly), Luke 23.3 (in response to the Jewish accusations). On the title 'king', see pp. 106–7 above.

[61] Brown, *Gospel*, p. 852.

[62] See 8.23, 17.11, 14, 16. Unlike the synoptic accounts, references to the 'kingdom' are very rare in John. Previously βασιλεία τοῦ Θεοῦ has been referred to in 3.3 and 5. Here it is not God's kingdom but Jesus', although 17.10 shows that what is God's is also Jesus'.

lack of military activity by his followers suggests. The tense of the verb for 'fight' here – ἠγωνίζοντο – is imperfect continuous; the sense is that his followers would be fighting *now*, not just at the arrest.[63] As C. K. Barrett puts it, 'Kings of this world naturally fight for supremacy; that Jesus and his followers do not do so shows that his kingdom is of a different order'.[64]

Pilate refuses to enter into a discussion on the exact definition of Jesus' kingdom and steers the conversation back to the central theme of Jesus' kingship with the words: 'So you are a King?'.[65] The governor wants a definite statement from Jesus: is he a king or is he not? It may be significant that Pilate has dropped the reference to 'the Jews', possibly since Jesus' words in verse 36 show them to be his enemies. Again, Jesus refuses to give a concrete answer and replies: 'You say that I am'. He then goes on to explain that his central role is not one of kingship but, phrased in typical Johannine language, to bear witness to the truth (v. 37).[66] Everyone who is 'of the truth', Jesus states, hears his voice (v. 37). In reply, Pilate utters his famous question: 'What is truth?'

How did the author of the Fourth Gospel expect his readers/ hearers to understand this? Is he simply using his frequent motif of misunderstanding here? Throughout the gospel hostile, neutral and friendly characters show themselves unable to understand Jesus' words. A particularly clear example of this is Nicodemus in 3.4, who does not understand the significance of being born from above (ἄνωθεν) and interprets Jesus' words literally as physical birth.[67] In the same way, Pilate may be clutching at terms which he under- stands without comprehending the sense in which Jesus is using them. Earlier he seized on Jesus' use of 'kingdom' and asked if he were a king; here he may be seizing on the word 'truth' without any understanding of what it involves. Yet the importance of the term 'truth' in Johannine thought suggests that Pilate's words reveal more than simple misunderstanding.

---

[63] Morris, *Gospel*, p. 769; Dodd, *History,* p. 112.

[64] Barrett, *Gospel*, p. 537.

[65] Barrett (ibid.) notes that the argumentative particle οὐκοῦν seeks a definite answer and translates: 'Very well, so you are a King?'.

[66] See 3.21, 14.17, 15.26, 16.13, 17.17, 19.

[67] The Samaritan woman similarly does not understand the significance of 'living water' (4.11). In 12.34 the crowd does not understand who the 'son of man' is and in 14.5 Thomas takes Jesus' words too literally. Other examples can be found at 7.35, 8.22, 10.6, 11.12–13, 12.16, 13.7, 14.8, 16.17–18 (the failure of Mary and the disciples to recognize Jesus after the resurrection may also be part of this general motif, 20.14, 21.4).

That this is not a serious philosophical speculation is made apparent by the very next phrase: 'After he had said this, he went out to the Jews again'. The Roman governor does not wait for an answer. Nor is it primarily an expression of irritation at a prisoner who persists in countering the governor's straightforward questions with references to other-worldliness and truth, though there may be something of this on a purely literary level.[68] Instead, in exactly the same way in which Jesus' Jewish opponents in 10.20 showed that they did not belong to Jesus' sheep by the question 'Why hear him?', Pilate shows that he is not 'of the truth' by his question Τί ἐστιν ἀλήθεια; By his inability to hear Jesus with understanding and belief and his failure to recognize the truth, Pilate is not of God (8.47) and so, like 'the Jews', he is part of the unbelieving world which rejects Jesus. Furthermore, even the question is wrongly put: ἀλήθεια takes on a personal character in John, denoting the divine reality of the Father and the Son. So the appropriate question is not simply '*What* is truth?' but '*Who* is truth?' The Roman governor cannot see that 'the truth' is personified in the prisoner before him.

In verse 18.37 Jesus issued a challenge to the representative of the Roman Empire: will he respond to the truth? By his question he showed that he would not accept Jesus, and so not only Pilate but also the Empire which he represents are, in Johannine thought, part of the unbelieving 'world'. Pilate has now answered his first question, 'Am I a Jew?' The answer is 'yes'; he has joined the unbelieving world – symbolized most starkly in Johannine thought by 'the Jews' – in rejecting Jesus.[69]

[68] Stibbe, *Storyteller*, p. 107.

[69] Bultmann is surely wrong when he regards Pilate as the representative of the 'state' abstracted from 'the world'. He writes: 'the state is able to adopt the point of view that the question about ἀλήθεια has nothing to do with it'. Instead of refusal or recognition of the truth, Bultmann asserts that in this scene 'the state' chooses neutrality. It remains on the outside: it is not of the truth, but nor is it in the same category as 'the Jews', signifying 'the world: cf. *Gospel*, pp. 652–7. There are two strong arguments against this line of approach. First, as pointed out above, Johannine dualism leaves no room for neutrality. Second, the earliest Christians did not have the luxury of being able to regard 'the state' as an abstract concept, divorced from 'the world'. For them the state took on very real and concrete proportions – it was the Roman Empire, representatives of which governed their lives and actions and, on occasion, had persecuted them (Tacitus, *Ann.* 15.44; in John 16.2b and 15.20 it may be the Romans who are actually doing the persecuting). Thus, 'the state' was not an abstract concept which could respond to Jesus' revelation with neutrality but a very real part of the first-century world.

Scene 3 (18.38b–40)

This short scene is extremely difficult to make sense of. Pilate goes outside again to where 'the Jews' are waiting and declares that he finds no guilt in the prisoner; but instead of simply offering to release Jesus there and then, he alludes to a Jewish custom by which he should release one prisoner at Passover. He then asks 'the Jews' if they want him to release 'the King of the Jews' to them, to which they reply that they want Barabbas released instead.

Two problems dominate the interpretation of this scene. First, if the Johannine Pilate has genuinely found no guilt in Jesus, why does he not simply bring Jesus out to the waiting Jews and set him free? Why mention an amnesty, an offer which could potentially, and in fact does, have disastrous results in that 'the Jews' take the opportunity to demand the release of another prisoner? Second, why does Pilate refer to Jesus as the 'King of the Jews' – a title which, certainly in the final scene of the trial narrative, seems to be deliberately mocking Jewish nationalistic hopes?

The simplest solution, of course, is that John found both these elements in the tradition upon which he was dependent. Yet the evangelist does not elsewhere seem to go out of his way to add details simply because they are traditional. If he has incorporated the reference to the amnesty and the designation 'King of the Jews' here, then, it is reasonable to suppose that both make sense within the context of the narrative.

The general view of this scene is that it shows Pilate's weakness. He tells the waiting Jews that he finds no crime in Jesus, but does not have the strength of character to act on his convictions and release the prisoner. Instead, he attempts to release Jesus as part of an amnesty, referring to him as the 'King of the Jews' in order to stir the nationalistic sympathies of his audience. The Jews, however, outwit him and seize the opportunity to demand the release of another prisoner, Barabbas. The defeated prefect retreats into the praetorium and prepares his next vain attempt to release Jesus – this time by having him flogged and brought out before his enemies.

This characterization of Pilate, however, will not fit the governor encountered so far within John's trial narrative. In this gospel, Pilate is addressing exactly the same Jews – the chief priests and the officers – who handed Jesus over in 18.28–9. Whereas in Mark's narrative a crowd has gathered (15.8) and Pilate's words make sense as an attempt to gauge popular support for the messianic claimant brought to him previously by the members of the Sanhedrin (15.1), in John there is no neutral crowd. The Johannine Pilate is speaking to exactly the same people who in 18.31b admitted that they had brought Jesus to Pilate for execution. Surely he cannot now expect these same opponents quietly to acquiesce to Jesus' release? Besides, by putting the offer of release within the context of the amnesty, Pilate's actions appear even more naive and miscalculating. Not only do the chief priests, naturally enough, not want their prisoner released, but they use the opportunity to secure the release of a political activist, a ληστής (18.40). Does the fourth evangelist really want to portray his Roman prefect as completely miscalculating and ineffectual? How realistic would such a governor be to John's readers, themselves living under the authority of Rome?

Perhaps it would be useful for a moment to understand this scene in a different way; that is, *not* seeing Pilate's actions as a serious attempt to release Jesus. Certainly John does not say that Pilate wishes to release the prisoner, as he does in 19.12. The Johannine governor says to 'the Jews', 'I find no crime in him'. The ἐγώ here may be emphatic, or at least it highlights the contrast between Pilate's failure to find any political guilt in Jesus with the political allegations of 'the Jews' who handed him over. He continues: 'But you have a custom that I should release one man for you at the *Passover*; will you have me release for you the King of the Jews?' As noted before, 'King of the Jews' was the gentile form of 'King of Israel', a term associated with the awaited Messiah. John's readers would recognize the significance of the reference to Passover here, a celebration of freedom from slavery and oppression in Egypt and a feast at which messianic expectation might be at its height.[70] In fact, John's readers would presumably realize that it was because of potential messianic fervour and rioting generally in the crowded city that the Roman prefect was in Jerusalem and not at his normal residence in Caesarea.[71] It is therefore deeply ironic that the Johannine Pilate, as the representative of a pagan administration, is in a position to release the Jewish 'King' at Passover.

Pilate's words, thus, sound more like mockery of Jewish nationalistic hopes and an assertion of his power over 'the Jews' than a

---

[70] John is the only evangelist to link the custom specifically with the Passover.
[71] See pp. 7–8 above.

serious offer to release Jesus. The prefect knows that 'the Jews' want Jesus executed but takes the opportunity to mock their messianic aspirations and, indirectly, the prisoner himself. Precisely this same attitude will reappear in the final scene of the trial. 'The King of the Jews', then, was not just lifted from tradition but used specifically to mock Jewish nationalism.

The evangelist also uses this scene to incriminate Jesus' Jewish opponents further: in the context of the Passover, they utterly reject their Messiah. Instead, they expose their nationalist sympathies and ask for Barabbas. The fact that John refers to this prisoner as a λῃστής may indicate that he regards such political activists not so much as 'freedom fighters' but as 'brigands' or 'robbers' in the same sense in which Josephus uses the term.[72] Jesus' opponents have therefore rejected the true 'King of the Jews' in favour of a common criminal.[73]

Scene 4 (19.1–3)

Taken literally, the active verb ἐμαστίγωσεν implies that Pilate scourged Jesus himself. The presence of soldiers who mock Jesus in verses 2–3, however, indicates that it was they, and not the Roman governor, who carried out the scourging. Yet John's use of the active verb in verse 1 clearly shows that Pilate is responsible. John uses the same device again in 19.22 when Pilate says of the title on the cross: 'What I have written I have written'. John's readers would surely not assume that the Roman governor had set to work and written the *titulus* himself, but the active verb shows that Pilate takes responsibility for the actions of those under his command.

The word used by John to describe this beating is μαστιγόω, the usual Greek word for 'flogging' – a severe and degrading

---

[72] See Hengel, *Zealots*, pp. 41–6. Josephus 'speaks of λῃσταί especially whenever he intends to express his moral condemnation of the opponent' (p. 43) and he uses 'the word λῃσταί in order to brand the Zealots as lawless rebels and criminals in the Roman sense and as men who in the end received the punishment they deserved' (p. 45). See also the contrast between thieves and robbers (λῃσταί) and the good shepherd at 10.1.

[73] Each of the synoptic gospels explicitly notes that Pilate released Barabbas but John does not. Possibly this is because the whole narrative is reported briefly and the evangelist is not interested in recording the fate of Barabbas. The major point is that 'the Jews' reject Jesus and, by demanding the release of Barabbas, expose their nationalist sympathies.

punishment.[74] Some have seen parallels between Pilate's action here and the offer of the Lukan Pilate to discipline Jesus and then to release him (Luke 23.16, 22).[75] But Luke's verb παιδεύω implies a milder beating, intended to 'teach the prisoner a lesson'. John's audience would surely be aware of the distinctions between the different types of Roman beatings. That the flagellation was mistakenly supposed by John and his audience to be a cautionary beating, therefore, seems unlikely.

Scourging was the usual preliminary to crucifixion.[76] But so far in the Johannine narrative, Jesus has not been sentenced; crucifixion is not even mentioned until the next scene, so the flogging cannot be a preliminary to execution.[77] So why does the Johannine Pilate administer such a severe punishment to the prisoner at this stage in the proceedings? The evangelist himself gives no reasons for the prefect's harsh treatment of Jesus and a fuller inquiry will have to wait until Pilate's next appearance in scene 6.

Subsequent to the flogging, Jesus is mocked by the Roman soldiers.[78] It is possible that in John's presentation the soldiers are not just mocking Jesus as a Hellenistic king generally, but as the *Emperor*. In the Greek-speaking world the Emperor was often referred to as βασιλεύς.[79] In Acts 17.7 Jason and some others are accused of 'acting against the decrees of Caesar, saying that there is *another King*, Jesus'. Besides, as far as the gentile soldiers were concerned, 'the King of the Jews' was none other than Caesar, as even the chief priests are forced to acknowledge in 19.15. The presence of the purple garment, the crown, which may represent the

---

[74] Barrett, *Gospel*, p. 539. Mark 15.15, followed by Matt. 27.26, uses the Latinized form of the verb φραγελλόω (see Josephus, *JW* 5.449). John's word μαστιγόω and the word for 'slapped' in verse 3, ῥαπίζω, may have been drawn from Isa. 50.6, though the evangelist does not emphasize this connection.

[75] For instance, Westcott, *Gospel*, pp. 267–8.

[76] See p. 116 above.

[77] Matthew and Mark give the impression that the scourging and mockery take place after the proceedings involving Pilate are completed. The soldiers engage in their malicious jokes apparently without the presence of Pilate (Mark 15.16–20, Matt. 27.27–31). Luke has no mockery at the hands of the Roman soldiers but does record a similar incident at Herod's court (23.11).

[78] As usual, John gives no unnecessary details. He does not say how many were involved (Mark 15.16 and Matt. 27.27 mention a whole cohort) nor where the incident took place, though from verse 5 it appears to be inside the praetorium. The slapping of Jesus by the soldiers underlines the element of mockery in the proceedings (against Meeks, *Prophet*, p. 69 who denies that the soldiers are mocking Jesus). The mockery here is very similar to that in Mark, see p. 102 above.

[79] Barrett, *Gospel*, p. 543; Brown, *Gospel*, p. 880.

imperial laurel wreath, and the greeting of the soldiers all suggest that Jesus is ridiculed here as a mock-Emperor.

Scene 5 (19.4–8)

Presumably Pilate has remained inside throughout the scourging and mockery; in verse 4 he goes out to 'the Jews' again. Most commentators regard this as Pilate's second attempt to release Jesus, the first attempt with the amnesty having backfired. Thus the prefect has Jesus scourged and brings him out, still royally bedecked, in a vain attempt to appeal to either the sympathies or nationalistic hopes of the waiting Jews.[80] Accordingly, ὁ ἄνθρωπος is said to express Pilate's pity for the defendant and is translated 'Here is the poor creature!' or 'See the poor fellow!'.[81] Or, as W. A. Meeks suggests, 'Man' may have been an eschatological title in Hellenistic Judaism and Pilate is alluding to this.[82]

Yet again there are problems with a benevolent Pilate wishing to release Jesus. The prefect subjects Jesus to an extremely severe flogging, brings him out in mock kingly regalia before the same Jews who have brought him for execution, and expects them now to feel sympathetic towards the prisoner'! The Johannine Pilate in this reconstruction lacks any political astuteness or psychological awareness whatsoever. As B. Lindars notes: 'To bring him out now, already arrayed as a laughing-stock, could only invite a ribald and hostile response, the very opposite of the conditions required for a considered judgement of the case' and 'The motive given, "that you may know that I find no crime in him" . . . is extremely lame and scarcely plausible'.[83] The chief priests and officers, of course, do not feel sympathy for the prisoner; nor does the sight of the scourged man in the royal robes arouse their nationalistic sympathies. Their cry is instantaneous (ὅτε οὖν εἶδον αὐτὸν): 'Crucify him, crucify him'.

As with the Barabbas episode, it may be better not to try to twist this scene into an attempt by Pilate to release Jesus but simply to take the text at its face value. Pilate says that he is bringing Jesus

---

[80] Cf. Brown, ibid., pp. 886–9; Westcott, *Gospel*, pp. 267–8; Lightfoot *St John's*, p. 312; Morris (with reservations), *Gospel*, p. 790.

[81] Views put forward by Morris, ibid., p. 793 and Stibbe, *Storyteller*, p. 108.

[82] Meeks, *Prophet*, p. 70–1. The basis for this is Zech. 6.12. Brown is also sympathetic towards this interpretation: cf. *Gospel*, pp. 875–6.

[83] Lindars, *Gospel*, p. 565.

out to show that he finds no guilt in him; that is, political guilt –
any kingship which Jesus may claim to possess is no threat to the
Roman state. Jesus then comes out, scourged and arrayed as the
'King of the Jews'. The point is that Jesus is no threat to Roman
law and order because, the Johannine Pilate implies, he is so
completely humiliated and despised. 'Behold the man!' on Pilate's
lips therefore is contemptuous. The scourged prisoner is a parody
of Jewish messianic hopes which, 'the Jews' have already shown in
scene 3, centre on λῃσταί and political activists and can only be an
embarrassment to 'the Jews'. The Johannine Pilate is mocking not
only the Jews and their nationalistic hopes but also the prisoner
before him.

But the use of ἄνθρωπος here may go further. If Jesus was
mocked as a pseudo-Emperor, or any other 'divine' Hellenistic
king, then Pilate's contemptuous use of ἄνθρωπος may be to
contrast him further with these rulers. Historically, Tiberius was
the Emperor during Pilate's prefecture and he, like Augustus, was
only deified after his death. However, the majority of scholars agree
that the Fourth Gospel was shaped largely during the reign of
Domitian (81–96), and this Emperor did assume, at least unoffi-
cially, divine honours *during* his lifetime.[84]

To John's readers, probably living in a large Hellenistic city and
well acquainted with the divine claims of their Emperor, Pilate's
contempt and emphasis that Jesus was only mortal, would stress
just how ridiculous the prefect found Jesus' kingly pretensions. The
'King of the Jews' for the Johannine Pilate is the divine Emperor;
the scourged and mocked 'man' in front of him is only a creature of
ridicule. 'The Jews' for their part want nothing to do with this man
who parodies their messianic hopes and they cry for crucifixion.

Although Jesus has been scourged, John makes no references to
physical injuries or indignities. Throughout the entire trial narrative
John's perceptive readers can see that the true kingly qualities of

---

[84] See Suetonius, *Domitian* 13.2, who writes that the Emperor insisted on being
referred to as *'dominus et deus noster'*. Dio Cassius refers to the same ruler as master
and god (δεσπότης, θεός) in 67.4.7 and 67.13.4. It may also be significant that in
20.28 Thomas addresses Jesus as ὁ κύριός μου καὶ ὁ θεός μου. This combination
occurs in pagan literature (Barrett, *Gospel*, pp. 572–3) and in the LXX as a
translation of YHWH elohim, though, as Brown (*Gospel*, p. 1047) points out, never
in precisely this form. The usual formula is κύριε, ὁ θεός μου and the closest to John
20.28 is Ps. 35.23, 'my God and my Lord'. Rev. 4.11 addresses God who, in
Johannine thought, is one with Jesus, as ὁ κύριος καὶ ὁ θεὸς ἡμῶν. It is possible that
in 20.28 John is contrasting Jesus with the Roman Emperor: it is Jesus and not
Domitian who can truly claim this title.

Jesus transcend Pilate's mockery and the insistent demands of 'the Jews' for crucifixion. They may also see a deeper meaning in the contemptuous words of the Johannine prefect. By using 'man', John may be making Pilate unconsciously refer to the 'Son of Man' who is lifted up on the cross and yet by that very act is exalted in glory.[85] Paradoxically, the hour of the Son of Man's glorification (12.23, 13.31) is when he is most mocked and humiliated by 'the world'.

The Johannine Pilate within the narrative, however, knows nothing of these things. The chief priests and officers cry for crucifixion and Pilate replies: 'Take him yourselves and crucify him'. H. Schlier took this as a serious suggestion, indicating that Pilate's control was so far gone that he was willing to allow 'the Jews' to crucify a man whom he had found innocent.[86] But two features indicate that this offer is not to be taken seriously. First, although there is some evidence to suggest that the Jews *may* have used crucifixion as a standard punitive measure at certain times throughout their history,[87] John has 'the Jews' inform Pilate (and the readers) in 18.31 that they do not have the right to inflict the death penalty themselves. Second, 'the Jews' in verse 7 do not take the prefect's words seriously. In fact, quite the reverse; they remount the attack with a religious charge. R. E. Brown sees the governor's words as 'an expression of Pilate's exasperation'[88] whilst L. Morris suggests that they are 'the sudden wild statement of a man who is goaded into speaking unreasonably'.[89] But since Pilate's tone has previously been one of mockery, it may be better to interpret this verse too in the same light.

The Roman prefect is reminding 'the Jews' that they have no right to pass a capital sentence upon the prisoner, whether by

---

[85] See 3.14–15, 8.28, 12.23, 34, 13.31. The Aramaic *bar nasa*, which is literally translated 'son of man', can mean simply 'man'. See Barrett, *Gospel*, p. 541 and Lindars, *Gospel*, p. 566. Bultmann suggests that the term stresses the incarnation: 'the declaration ὁ λόγος σὰρξ ἐγένετο has become visible in its extremest consequences': cf.*Gospel*, p. 659.

[86] Schlier, 'Jesus', pp. 56–74.

[87] In a reconstruction of col. xxiv of the Temple Scroll, which comments on Deut. 21.18–21 and the execution of eight hundred Jews by Alexander Jannaeus, Yadin suggests this document recognizes that crucifixion could be used as a Jewish form of execution for specific political crimes: cf. 'Pesher Nahum', pp. 1–12. See also Ford, 'Crucify Him', pp. 275–8; Bammel, 'Crucifixion', pp. 162–5 and Fitzmyer, 'Crucifixion', pp. 493–513. Against Yadin is Baumgarten ('Temple Scroll', pp. 472–81) who thinks that the scroll refers to hanging.

[88] Brown, *Gospel*, p. 877.   [89] Morris, *Gospel*, p. 795.

crucifixion or any other means. As in Scene I, he is mocking their status as occupied people and asserting his own authority over them.[90] His subsequent 'For I find no crime in him' again shows that Pilate sees Jesus more as a creature to be despised and mocked than any serious threat to Rome.

In the face of this mockery, Jesus' opponents within the Johannine narrative change their tactics, now bringing a religious charge: 'We have a law, and by that law he deserves to die, because he has made himself the Son of God' (19.7).[91] The effect of this charge on Pilate is considerable. In verse 8 the evangelist tells us that he was/ became μᾶλλον ἐφοβήθη. Some have taken this as meaning 'more afraid' and have therefore been forced to assume that John is abbreviating a longer account or have looked for indications of fear in Pilate's previous behaviour.[92] It is more likely though that μᾶλλον indicates a change in Pilate's attitude.[93] In contrast to the scathing, mocking prefect, who was previously so sure of his position and authority over 'the Jews', Pilate now becomes afraid. No reasons are given to explain this sudden fear. It is reasonable to suppose, however, that it is based on superstition. Greek and Roman mythology contains numerous examples of gods taking on human form or begetting children: Homer refers to the sons of Zeus or other gods as the/a 'son of god';[94] Heracles could refer to Zeus as 'father'.[95] Compare also the experiences of Paul and Barnabas in Lystra (Acts 14.8–18). To a Hellenistic mind, the allegation could suggest that Jesus was 'a divine man with magical powers of occult origin'.[96] Also, since 'the Jews' have already exposed their nationalistic hopes in Scene 3 and shown that their political allegations against Jesus have no substance, the Johannine Pilate may conclude that the accusation of 'making himself the Son of God' is the real Jewish charge against Jesus and is not to be taken lightly.

[90] So Cassidy, *John's*, p. 46.

[91] This charge was also prominent at 10.22–39, the nearest parallel in John to the synoptic Jewish trial. Now that Jesus' 'hour' has arrived, the Jewish charge reappears.

[92] Thus Bultmann, *Gospel*, p. 511.

[93] See Matt. 25.9 for a similar use of the word.

[94] *Iliad* 5.683, *Odyssey* 11.568.

[95] See Epictetus, *Dissertationes* 2.16.44, 3.24.14–15.

[96] Brown, *Gospel*, p. 877–8.

Scene 6 (19.9–11)

Accordingly, Pilate enters the praetorium again (presumably taking Jesus inside too) and asks the prisoner, 'Where are you from?', a question which might follow on naturally from the charge that he was making himself the Son of God.[97] The reader knows that Jesus is from the Father, or from above,[98] but if Nicodemus did not understand this then the Roman governor is even less likely to. Jesus, therefore, remains silent. This silence seems to exasperate Pilate who asks: 'Do you not know that I have power to release you, and power to crucify you?' (v. 10). The theme of the governor's authority, which seems to have been present implicitly in the previous narrative reappears explicitly in this scene. Here Pilate is using ἐξουσία, with the possibility of release or crucifixion which it involves, to force Jesus to answer his previous question. Instead, Jesus turns on the governor's use of ἐξουσία, stating that his ἐξουσία comes not from the Emperor, as Pilate believes, but from above (ἄνωθεν).[99] The governor would have no power whatsoever (the οὐδεμίαν is emphatic) if it had not come from God.[100] Pilate's double use of ἐξουσία is reminiscent of 10.17–18. There Jesus says that he has the power to lay down his life and the power to take it up again, a charge which he has received from the Father. It is clear that it is not the Roman governor who has the power/authority to execute Jesus but Jesus himself who lays down his own life. Pilate's authority ultimately derives from God. Thus 'the crucifixion does not contravene the authority of God but lies within its purpose'.[101]

Jesus goes on to say: 'Therefore he who delivered me to you has the greater sin'. To whom is John referring here? Owing to the surprisingly frequent use of παραδίδωμι to describe the handing over or betrayal of Jesus by Judas in the Fourth Gospel and the use of the singular participle, Barrett thinks that Judas is again referred

[97] A similar question is addressed to Jesus in Luke 23.6 where the Lukan Pilate inquires to which province Jesus belongs before sending him to Herod.
[98] 3.8, 7.27–8, 8.14, 9.29.
[99] A similar idea is expressed in Rom. 13.3–4.
[100] The same idea is expressed by John the Baptist in 3.27 when he says that no one can receive anything except what is given him from heaven. As Barrett points out, 19.11 is the Johannine literary device of misunderstanding in reverse. Usually a theological word is taken in a literal sense by Jesus' hearers; here, Pilate's use of the word ἐξουσία in a secular sense is transformed by Jesus into the absolute ἐξουσία of God (*Gospel*, p. 542).
[101] Ibid., p. 543.

to here.[102] But it is 'the Jews' who hand Jesus over to Pilate and παραδίδωμι is twice used of their actions (18.30, 35). Indeed, it is difficult to see why Jesus should launch into an attack on Judas at this point. It seems more likely that the singular participle is to be taken as generic, meaning that the one who betrays the Messiah is more guilty than the one who judges him. In this case, it probably refers to 'the Jews', or at least to the chief priests and others who have actually handed Jesus over.[103] Primary guilt for Jesus' execution, therefore, according to John, rests with 'the Jews', but this is no exoneration of Pilate. The Jewish sin may be *greater*, but Pilate is nevertheless involved in a sinful action. Although he condemns Jesus with the ἐξουσία given to him from above, he is nevertheless part of the hostile 'world'.

Scene 7 (19.12–16a)

At this, Pilate sought to release Jesus (v. 12). The phrase ἐκ τούτου can be taken temporally or causally but in either case it appears to mean that as a result of his brief interview with Jesus Pilate now wants to release him. This is the first time that the governor has attempted to free the prisoner, though precisely what has brought about this change of attitude is not stated. It is possible that, like the soldiers in Gethsemane, John wants to show that the pagan governor could not remain entirely unaffected by the prisoner before him, especially when the religious charge was to the fore. The imperfect use of ἐζήτει ἀπολῦσαι suggests a series of attempts, though John says nothing further.

'The Jews' within the Johannine narrative seem to realize that their introduction of the religious charge has produced entirely the wrong reaction in the governor, and so they revert to the political charge: 'If you release this man, you are not Caesar's friend; every one who makes himself a king sets himself against Caesar'. The term 'Friend of Caesar' (φίλος τοῦ Καίσαρος) may well have been used in a semi-technical sense of provincial governors at this

---

[102] See 6.64, 71, 12.4, 13.2, 11, 21, 18.2, 5, 21.20. Barrett, *Gospel*, p. 543.

[103] Brown similarly sees it as a reference to Caiaphas, or more generally to 'the Jews': cf. *Gospel*, pp. 568–9; Lindars sees it as a reference to the Jewish people as a whole. Dodd (*Interpretation*, p. 427) is probably correct to suggest that verses 10 and 11 here reflect early Christian discussion concerning the responsibility for Jesus' death. If so, guilt is primarily attached to 'the Jews' but 'lesser guilt' also rests with Pilate. Even though his ἐξουσία to take part in Jesus' hour has come from God, he is not exonerated.

time.[104] But irrespective of whether the historical Pilate actually used it, the meaning is clear: if the prefect were to release a messianic pretender he would not be protecting the interests of the Emperor. This argument seems to have had the desired effect on Pilate – he brings Jesus outside and sits down on the judgement seat (βῆμα).[105]

[104] In Hellenistic times the 'Friends of the King' were a special group honoured by the King for loyalty (1 Macc. 2.18, 3.38, 10.65; 3 Macc. 6.23; Josephus, *Ant.* 12.298). The 'Friends of Augustus' were a well-known society in the early Empire. Coins of Herod Agrippa I frequently read 'Philokaisar', a designation which Philo also gives him (*In Flaccum* 40). Bammel suggests that the title *amicus Caesaris* was old enough to be used at least in a semi-technical sense in this conversation: cf. 'Philos', pp. 205–10. Sherwin-White (*Roman*, p. 47) suggests that the term 'friend' is often used for official representatives of the Emperor at this time. There is, however, no other evidence to link the title with Pilate.

[105] Josephus, *JW* 2.301, describes Florus' βῆμα which stood in the forecourt of the governor's residence with steps leading up to it. The most eminent people of the city presented themselves before the tribunal.

Several scholars have suggested that the verb ἐκάθισεν here is used transitively (e.g. de la Potterie, 'Jésus', pp. 217–47 and Giblin 'John's', pp. 221–39), in which case it would mean that Pilate sat *Jesus* upon the judgement seat. As Barrett (*Gospel*, p. 544) notes, it would lend further dramatic parallelism to the sequence of events in 19.2, 3 and 5 where Jesus is dressed and crowned as a king (v. 2), hailed by the soldiers (v. 3) and brought out to his subjects, 'the Jews' (v. 5); now in verse 13 he would be enthroned. Pilate's words in verse 14, 'Behold your King!', would also achieve a greater dramatic intensity if Jesus was actually enthroned. On a more theological level, it would fit in with the Johannine concept of Jesus as the real judge (5.30, 8.16, 12.31, 47, 16.11; see Brown, *Gospel*, p. 880). Some traditional support for this interpretation can also be found in GPet. 7 and Justin's *Apology* 50.35.6 where the Jewish people sit Jesus on the judgement seat and mock him. Persuasive as these arguments may appear, however, the weightier ones seem to point in favour of an intransitive reading (see Blinzler, 'Entscheid', pp. 175–82). The only other use of καθίζω in John is intransitive (12.14, so too is 8.2) as it is commonly in the rest of the NT (Barrett, *Gospel*, p. 544). If the verb was used transitively, we should expect it to be followed by a pronominal object, which it is not. Furthermore, ἐκάθισεν ἐπὶ βήματος is a natural expression for a judge sitting upon the judgement seat; Josephus uses it of Pilate in *JW* 2.172. Finally, the Johannine narrative would lose all credibility if the Roman governor is seen to have placed a prisoner on the judgement seat. But it is not impossible that John deliberately intends a double meaning here. Brown (*Gospel*, p. 881) alleges that previous instances of Johannine double meaning have not been based on syntactical obscurities, but we have already noted two instances in which John's use of active verbs suggests that Pilate has carried out something which, in all probability, was done by his soldiers (19.1, 22). This deliberate ambiguity will be met again at the end of the trial narrative (19.16–18) where the subjects of the verbs παρέλαβον and ἐσταύρωσαν are not stated and should logically and grammatically still be the ἀρχιερεῖς of verse 15. The ambiguity shows that although the Roman soldiers actually carry out the crucifixion (19.23), the moral responsibility lies with 'the Jews'. In the present scene too John may want to be deliberately ambivalent: on the level of the narrative, Pilate sat on the judgement seat, but for those who can see behind the human scene, the son of man is seated on his throne (Barrett, *Gospel*, p. 544).

He is about to pass sentence.[106] The suspense of the narrative, however, is momentarily broken by a description of where the βῆμα was located and a note that it was the sixth hour – the time at which the slaughter of the Passover lambs began.[107] The Passover setting has dominated John's account more than any of the others. The approach of the feast has guided the actions of Jesus' antagonists who, in 11.55–7, plot to arrest him if he comes to Jerusalem for the festival and here, in the Roman trial scene, are forced to remain outside the gentile governor's praetorium to avoid ritual uncleanliness. Now John brings the Passover into prominence again, dramatically paralleling Jesus' condemnation and execution with the paschal sacrifice.[108]

Pilate says to 'the Jews' 'Behold your King!' (Ἴδε ὁ βασιλεὺς ὑμῶν) which R. E. Brown regards as 'a final gesture of defiance and perhaps still with a half-hearted hope he can obtain clemency'.[109] But it is difficult to see how Pilate's words could hope to achieve Jesus' release. The prefect knows beyond any doubt that 'the Jews' have utterly rejected Jesus, and to describe the scourged prisoner, still dressed in mock-kingly regalia, as *your* king could only humiliate 'the Jews' further. After a brief attempt to release Jesus at the mention of the religious charge, Pilate seems to have reverted to his former position: that of mockery. As Barrett remarks, 'the helpless prisoner of Rome is the only king they are likely to have'.[110]

The reaction of 'the Jews' is the same as in verse 6 when Pilate said 'Behold the man!'. This time they shout, 'Away with him, away with him, crucify him!' (Ἆρον ἆρον, σταύρωσον αὐτόν).[111] Pilate pushes them further, as in Mark: 'Shall I crucify your King?' Again the prefect stresses that the prisoner is *your* king. This time the chief priests alone answer (the ὑπηρέται of verse 6 are not mentioned): 'We have no king but Caesar'. In the OT, God alone is the only true king of Israel (Judg. 8.23, 1 Sam. 8.7); this kingship

[106] Matt. 27.19 seems to envisage the governor seated on the βῆμα throughout the whole trial, as do the accounts of Paul before Festus in Acts 25.6, 17. However, it may have been necessary to sit here only when passing sentence.

[107] Exod. 12.6 states that the lamb was to be kept alive until 14 Nisan, then slaughtered in the evening. This took place between the ninth and the eleventh hour (i.e. approximately 4–6 pm); see Josephus, *JW* 6.423. For a description of the celebration of the feast see E. P. Sanders, *Judaism*, pp. 132–8.

[108] See Millar ('Reflections') for the prominence of Passover in John's account, especially pp. 377–9.

[109] Brown, *Gospel*, p. 894.   [110] Barrett, *Gospel*, pp. 545–6.

[111] Compare Luke 23.18 and Acts 21.36.

would be made visible in the rule of the Davidic king (2 Sam. 1.11, 16). By claiming that the Emperor is their only king, 'the Jews' finally reject the sovereignty of God and his Messiah. In John, this rejection takes place just as preparations for the feast celebrating God's deliverance of his people were about to begin and forms a stark contrast to the words of the Passover haggadah which praised the kingly reign of God.[112] At this, almost as if he had been waiting for it (τότε οὖν), Pilate handed Jesus over 'to them' for crucifixion.

The title on the cross (19.19–22)

Again Pilate and 'the Jews' clash over the question of Jesus' kingship. Pilate has a sign written in Aramaic, Latin and Greek affixed to the cross reading: 'Jesus of Nazareth, the King of the Jews' (Ἰησοῦς ὁ Ναζωραῖος ὁ βασιλεὺς τῶν Ἰοθδαίων). The mockery here is obvious. Crucifixion was the most humiliating of Roman punishments, generally reserved for slaves or political agitators, usually from the lower classes.[113] Furthermore, 'a hanged man is accursed by God' according to Deuteronomy 21.23. The figure of Jesus and the title clearly served to ridicule Jewish messianic hopes. Not surprisingly, 'the Jews' take offence and ask Pilate to alter it. Pilate, however, stands firm in his mockery and replies 'What I have written, I have written' (Ὃ γέγραφα, γέγραφα).

Conclusion

The Johannine Pilate is far from a weak and vacillating governor. He takes the case seriously and examines Jesus but quickly realizes that he is no political threat to Rome. He seizes on the opportunity, however, not only to mock the prisoner but also to ridicule 'the Jews' and their messianic aspirations. Only once does he try to release Jesus and that is after the religious charge has been brought against him, a charge which the superstitious pagan finds alarming. Brought back to reality by the political threats of 'the Jews', Pilate resumes his mockery. But this time he is on the judgement seat and he is guiding 'the Jews' in a certain direction. Although he finds Jesus' messianic claims ridiculous, he reasons that the prisoner *is*

---

[112] See Meeks, *Prophet*, p. 77 and E. P. Sanders, *Judaism*, p. 135.
[113] Josephus describes it in *JW* 7.203. See Hengel, *Crucifixion*, pp. 1–10.

claiming some kind of kingship and could be dangerous in the crowded city at Passover time. By the final scene, Jesus is to be put to death. But Pilate will exact a high price from 'the Jews'. If they want Jesus executed, they must not only renounce their messianic hopes but unconditionally accept the sovereignty of Caesar. Only after this does Pilate hand Jesus over for crucifixion. The Johannine Pilate, particularly in Scene 6, is reminiscent of the Roman governor in Mark's account. In both the prefect is harsh and manipulative, mocking the people and goading them into rejecting their messianic beliefs.

Pilate's failure to respond to Jesus means that he has allied himself with the hostile 'world' represented in Johannine thought by 'the Jews'.[114] In the Fourth Gospel, both 'the Jews' and Pilate are hostile towards Jesus.[115] Neither hear the word of Jesus and so are not of his 'sheep'. Although on one level the Roman trial represents the judgement of Jesus, on a deeper, more significant level it is Pilate and 'the Jews' who are judged. The trial represents the first part of Jesus' saying in 12.31: 'Now is the judgement of this world, now shall the ruler of this world be cast out'. 'The ruler of this world' in Johannine thought is Satan, but he has his representatives in earthly rulers – 'the Jews' as religious, social leaders and Pilate representing the authority of Rome.[116] In the proceedings before Pilate, all earthly authority is judged and found wanting by its response to Jesus.

The contrast between the true, dignified, other-worldly kingship of Jesus and that of Caesar implies that each member of John's community, constantly coming up against the might of imperial Rome, 'will always have to decide vis-à-vis the Empire whether Jesus is his king or whether Caesar is'.[117]

---

[114] Meeks, *Prophet*, p. 67.

[115] A similar tradition can be found in Acts 4.25–7 (which also includes Herod).

[116] 1 Cor. 2.8 expresses a similar idea.

[117] Meeks, *Prophet*, p. 64. Cassidy (*John's*, pp. 84–8) suggests that John's gospel was written not only to strengthen people experiencing persecution but also to counter the claims of the imperial cult.

8

HISTORICAL EVENTS BEHIND THE
GOSPEL NARRATIVES

The gospel narratives refer to two incidents involving Pilate – the slaughter of the Galileans in Luke 13.1 and the trial of Jesus of Nazareth in all four. The possible historical events behind these narratives will be discussed in this chapter.

Historical events behind Luke 13.1

Nothing further is known of this incident, either from biblical or non-biblical sources, and the reference to it here in Luke is extremely brief. We are told only that Pilate has mingled the blood of some Galileans with their sacrifices. Since there is no trace of this in the works of Josephus who, as a former commander of Galilee, might be expected to have a particular interest in the fate of Galileans, several scholars have suggested that Luke has misreported another event from first-century Palestine. Virtually all known events from Pilate's term of office have been proposed.

C. H. Kraeling thought that Luke was actually referring to the time when Pilate brought military standards into Jerusalem (*JW* 2.169–74, *Ant.* 18.55–9).[1] But, as we saw earlier, that incident led to a relatively peaceful protest in Caesarea which ended without bloodshed. A. T. Olmstead linked Luke 13.1 with the aqueduct protest (*JW* 2.175–7, *Ant.* 18.60–2).[2] There is, however, no indication in Josephus that those caught up in the protest were Galileans; the natural assumption is that they were Judaean subjects of Pilate. J. Wellhausen suggested that the incident should be linked to the Samaritan uprising (*Ant.* 18.86–7).[3] Again, those

---

[1] Kraeling, 'Episode', pp. 286–8. See above, pp. 79–85, for discussion of this incident.
[2] Olmstead, *Jesus*, pp. 147–9. This was also raised as a possibility by Smallwood, *Jews*, p. 163 and Schwartz, 'Pilate', p. 398.
[3] Wellhausen, *Evangelium*, p. 71.

involved are not Galileans but Samaritans and there is no hint in Luke 13.1 that the event occurred in the vicinity of Mount Gerizim. Other suggestions are Archelaus' slaughter of 3,000 at about Passover time (*JW* 2.8–13, *Ant.* 17.213–18)[4] and, with even less probability, the execution of six thousand Jews by Alexander Jannaeus (*Ant.* 13.372).[5] With the possible exception of the aqueduct episode, none of these incidents seems remotely close to what Luke describes. It appears that Luke 13.1 refers to an otherwise unknown event.

Does the gospel account itself give us any clues which might help us to reconstruct what actually happened? First of all, the context of 13.1–5 seems to imply that the number of Galileans killed was not particularly high. I. H. Marshall thinks that it may have been no more than a couple whilst J. A. Fitzmyer suggests less than the eighteen killed by the tower at Siloam (v. 4).[6] We can also be fairly certain that the season was Passover since this was the only time when the Israelites slaughtered their own sacrifices.[7] This took place in the Temple and raises the immediate question of the precise nature of Pilate's crime. Luke's description gives the impression that the Galileans were killed in the Temple itself at the point of sacrificing. Did Pilate's men not only kill the Galileans but also desecrate the Temple?[8] Unfortunately, the account in Luke 13.1 is too brief to be able to reconstruct the events with any certainty, but P. Winter is probably correct in his assertion that the reference to mingling Galilean blood with their sacrifices is 'oriental picture language' and does not necessarily imply that Pilate's men actually entered the Temple.[9]

So far, then, a small number of Galileans have been killed at the time of the Passover. But who were these pilgrims and how did they attract Roman attention? O. Cullmann, followed by G. Vermes, suggested that 'Galileans' should be interpreted as Galilean Zealots in the line of Judas the Galilean and his sons, their sacrifices being not religious offerings but pro-Roman sympathizers whom they

---

[4] S. E. Johnson, 'Note', pp. 91–5 and Derrett, 'Galileans', p. 103.

[5] T. Zahn, cited by Fitzmyer, *Gospel,* p. 1007.

[6] Marshall, *Gospel*, p. 553 and Fitzmyer, *Gospel*, p. 1006.

[7] M.Pes v. 6, Lev. 1.5. See Jeremias, *Jerusalem*, pp. 78–9 and E. P. Sanders, *Judaism*, pp. 135–8.

[8] This seems to be implicit in the discussions of Fitzmyer, *Gospel*, p. 1006 and Smallwood, *Jews*, p. 163.

[9] Winter, *Trial*, p. 177, n. 9; see also Cullmann, *State*, p. 14 and Marshall, *Gospel,* p. 553.

had killed.[10] S. Freyne, however, highlights the relative peace in Galilee during Antipas' reign.[11] There is no evidence for any organized 'Zealot movement' whether in Galilee or elsewhere in Palestine during the 20s and 30s.[12] It is not impossible that the Galilean pilgrims were caught up in some kind of isolated anti-Roman demonstration to which Pilate put an end, but we have no way of reconstructing what form that may have taken.

Dating the incident is equally uncertain. J. Blinzler suggested that the Galileans were those who wanted to make Jesus king in John 6.15 and that the incident occurred at the Passover of 29, a Passover when Jesus was not present in Jerusalem.[13] This, however, is extremely hypothetical and the incident could have taken place at any time during Pilate's term of office.[14]

Perhaps the most that can be said about this incident is that for some unknown reason Pilate had a small group of Galileans executed whilst they visited Jerusalem for the Passover. If the event involved only a few people and there was no suggestion of any defilement of the Temple, then it is not particularly surprising that Josephus does not mention it. All the occurrences which he does describe were fairly large-scale demonstrations and we know of at least one other incident involving Pilate which he omits (*Embassy* 299–305). It is not only possible but quite likely that Pilate's governorship contained many such brief outbreaks of trouble about which we know nothing. The insurrection in which Barabbas was caught up, if historical, may well be another example (Mark 15.7, Luke 23.19).

The historical trial of Jesus

The complex set of historical questions which surrounds Jesus' trial has given rise to a vast amount of literature and cannot all be investigated here. The following discussion will look only at Pilate's involvement in the affair.

As we have seen, the evangelists' portrayals of Pilate have been shaped to a great extent by their own particular theological and

---

[10] Cullmann, *State*, p. 14 and Vermes, *Jesus*, p. 47.
[11] Freyne, 'Bandits', pp. 53–4; see also Hengel, *Zealots*, pp. 56–9.
[12] See Zeitlin, 'Zealots'; Smith, 'Zealots' and Horsley, 'Josephus' and 'Popular'. Hengel, (*Zealots*, p. 338) too, doubts that this was a Zealot uprising.
[13] Blinzler, 'Niedermetzelung', pp. 43–9.
[14] So also Winter, *Trial*, p. 176, note 9.

apologetic concerns. This accounts for, amongst other things, Pilate's threefold declaration of Jesus' innocence in Luke and John; his mockery in Mark and John; and his offer of the choice between Jesus and Barabbas in Matthew. Legendary or theological additions have also been made to the narrative, such as the story of Pilate's wife's dream or Pilate's handwashing in Matthew and the sending of Jesus to Herod in Luke. Despite extensive differences, however, there is a certain agreement amongst the evangelists regarding the basic facts, an agreement which may well go beyond literary dependency and reflect actual historical events.

All four gospels describe Jesus' arrest. The synoptics suggest that this was an entirely Jewish affair whilst John has Roman troops involved. John's account is probably more accurate in this regard since it would be unlikely that Pilate knew nothing of the prisoner before he appeared before him in his praetorium.[15] The Jewish leaders then enlisted Roman support, had Jesus arrested and kept him in their custody for a night. That Caiaphas and the chief priests were involved seems certain. Quite possibly they were also joined by the lay leaders known variously as elders, rulers and scribes in the gospel accounts.[16] Whether there was a Jewish trial and condemnation (as Mark and Matthew record) or only a preliminary hearing (as Luke and John suggest) is uncertain.[17] Whichever was the case, early the next morning the Jewish leaders brought Jesus to the Roman prefect, a fact corroborated by Josephus in the *Testimonium Flavianum*.[18] The reasons for this transferral of custody are not clear. On the basis of John 18.31 it is generally assumed that

---

[15] Strobel makes the same point: cf. *Stunde*, p. 136. Several scholars accept the historicity of John's account at this point, suggesting that the synoptics omitted the reference to soldiers here for apologetic reasons (e.g. Winter, *Trial*, pp. 44–50 and Smallwood, *Jews*, p. 168). Others find it difficult to believe that Roman troops would allow a prisoner to be held in Jewish custody (e.g. Barrett, *Gospel*, p. 518 and Bultmann, *Gospel*, p. 637). In view of the co-operation which existed between the Jewish and Roman authorities, however, it does not seem unreasonable that Pilate allowed the Jewish leaders some time to examine the prisoner first. The Captain of the Temple, mentioned in Luke, may well have headed the arresting party as McLaren (*Power*, p. 94) suggests.

[16] See Goodman, *Ruling*, p. 115 and McLaren, *Power*, p. 91.

[17] For different scholarly views compare Lietzmann (*Prozeß*) and Winter, (*Trial*) with Blinzler, (*Trial*) and Sherwin-White, (*Roman*, pp. 24–47). See Catchpole, 'Problem', pp. 47–65; E. P. Sanders, *Judaism*, pp. 486–8; and McLaren, *Power*, pp. 96–7 for bibliography.

[18] *Ant.* 18.64. This timing is given by both Mark and Matthew and accords well with what we know of the daily routine of a Roman official; see Pliny, *Ep.* 3.5.9–11, 6.16.4–5 and Sherwin-White, *Roman*, p. 45.

the Jewish leaders no longer had the right to inflict the death sentence. There is, however, no outside evidence to confirm this.[19] The few isolated examples we have of Jewish executions from this time suggest rather that the high priest's council retained some capital jurisdiction over religious matters.[20] If this was the case, Jesus was probably handed over to Pilate because of the particular charge with which he was accused. This seems to have been one of claiming to be the 'King of the Jews', that is, some kind of political aspirant or insurrectionary. All four gospels give this charge a central place during the trial and also record its presence on the *titulus* at the crucifixion. Such a charge would surely have been too embarrassing to the early Christians for them to have fabricated it.[21]

Although there is a paucity of evidence, it is probable that trials of non-citizens throughout the provinces at this period were carried out according to *cognitio extra ordinem*.[22] Although he would still follow the general rules of Roman law, this allowed the governor a greater flexibility in dealing with difficult or unusual cases and also in determining the sentence. Of the actual exchange between Pilate and Jesus we can say very little. The gospel accounts are either very scanty (so Mark and Matthew) or theologically motivated and contradict one another (so Luke and John). They are all surely correct, however, when they maintain that the interrogation centred on Jesus' claims to kingship. A trial by *cognitio* also allowed for multiple charges and so other accusations could have been brought against Jesus as the gospels suggest.[23] In the end, whether because of Jesus' lack of a defence (as Mark and Matthew suggest), or because of political expediency, Pilate sentenced Jesus to death by crucifixion.[24]

[19] The precise meaning of the verse is itself open to interpretation, see above, pp. 176–7.

[20] See pp. 15–16 above.

[21] On this charge see Harvey, *Jesus*, pp. 2–5 and *Constraints*, pp. 12–13. Bammel suggests that the wording on the *titulus* is 'in all likelihood authentic': cf. 'Titulus', p. 363.

[22] Sherwin-White, *Roman*, pp. 24–7; Schürer, *History*, vol. 1, p. 370; Brown, *Death*, pp. 710–22. For the view that trials by *quaestio* were still valid in the early imperial period see Kunkel, 'Quaestio' and Haacker, 'Schuld', pp. 32–3.

[23] Sherwin-White, *Roman*, p. 26.

[24] Strobel (*Stunde*, pp. 136–7) argues for a formal death sentence; see also Sherwin-White, *Roman*, p. 47. That Jesus was executed by Pilate is also attested by Tacitus, *Ann.*, 15.44, though it is possible that Tacitus' information was derived from Christian sources. Bammel, however, argues that Jesus was crucified by Jews rather than the Romans: cf. 'Trial', pp. 437–51.

This bare outline is probably all we can say about the trial of Jesus with any degree of certainty. One intriguing question, however, is what parts a Passover amnesty and another prisoner known to us as Barabbas might have played in the historical events. A historical inquiry into the amnesty is complicated by the lack of agreement within the gospels themselves over the precise nature of the release. Matthew and Mark both suggest that it was a custom of the Roman governor (or his predecessors) and locate it simply at 'the festival season', though clearly the Passover is implied (Mark 15.6, Matt. 27.15). John 18.39 specifically locates the amnesty at Passover but implies that it was a *Jewish* custom.[25] The amnesty then was either a custom introduced by the Romans into Judaea or taken over from the previous Jewish rulers, in which case it may have gone back to Hasmonaean or Herodian times.[26]

Scholars have searched in vain to find evidence for any kind of regular Passover amnesty in Judaea at this time. M.Pesahim 8.6a is often cited but the text seems to refer to the Passover arrangements to be made for someone whose prison sentence is due to end at the feast rather than to an amnesty.[27] Isolated amnesties are, however, occasionally referred to elsewhere in the Roman world. A papyrus from 85 CE records the release of Phibion by G. Septimus Vegetus and an Ephesian inscription from 441 records the release of another prisoner.[28] It is not impossible that the release of a prisoner at about the same time as Jesus' trial was a single act of clemency rather than an act associated with a regular custom.[29] Pilate, and possibly other governors, may have occasionally released lesser criminals as a gesture of Roman goodwill, especially during such a potentially volatile festival as the Passover. The chief priests may have played the role of negotiators in securing the release.

But was the fate of Barabbas really linked as closely with the fate of Jesus as the gospel writers suggest? A. Bajsic and A. Strobel both suggested it was. Taking Mark's account as broadly historical, they argued that Jesus was used as a political tool by Pilate. The

---

[25] The reference in Luke 23.17 (which is almost certainly secondary) is not particularly clear and suggests only that Pilate was obliged to release a prisoner.

[26] See Chaval, 'Releasing', pp. 273–8 followed by Blinzler, *Trial*, Excursus X, pp. 218–21.

[27] For a fuller discussion see Winter, *Trial*, pp. 131–3. Strobel, however, thinks that this text does refer to an amnesty which went back to pre-Roman times: cf. *Stunde*, pp. 120–4.

[28] Papyrus Florentinus 61. See Deissmann, *Light*, p. 269, note 7.

[29] Gnilka, *Evangelium*, p. 301 and Lührmann, *Markusevangelium*, p. 256.

possibility that Barabbas would be released under the amnesty, a man charged as a political rebel and murderer, was deeply worrying to the Roman governor. Recognizing that Jesus was not a serious threat to Rome, the astute prefect decided to risk annoying the Jewish leaders and offered to release their prisoner to the people instead. Pilate, however, overestimated Jesus' popular support and the plan backfired when the people asked for Barabbas.[30] Persuasive as this view is, however, it is dependent upon a regular Passover amnesty – for which there is no evidence – and the assumption that Barabbas was a dangerous political criminal – which is not the view of all the evangelists.[31] It is possible that the two men became associated in Christian tradition because their trials occurred on the same day. Barabbas was released either because the accusations against him did not stand up in court or, perhaps more likely given the gospel accounts, because of an isolated act of clemency by Pilate. Christian thought began to reflect on the injustice of Barabbas' release and Jesus' crucifixion and the two men became associated in the tradition. Or perhaps there was some uncertainty as to whether Barabbas or Jesus would benefit from the prefect's magnanimity from the start. The precise historical relationship between Barabbas and Jesus (if any) is impossible to reconstruct.[32] It is similarly difficult to determine what role (if any) a crowd may have had in the proceedings.[33]

[30] Bajsic, 'Jesus' and Strobel, *Stunde*, pp. 127–30.

[31] Barabbas is one of the most obscure characters in the entire gospel tradition. Mark 15.7 says that he was *among* the rebels in prison who had committed murder in the insurrection; Matt. 27.16 describes him as a well-known prisoner; Luke 23.19 writes that he had been thrown into prison for an insurrection started in the city and for murder; John 18.40 describes him as a robber. The reconstruction of Bajsic and Strobel is largely dependent on Mark but this evangelist does not specifically state that Barabbas was himself a dangerous insurrectionary.

Not all scholars believe Barabbas to have been an historical person. Rigg ('Barabbas') and Maccoby ('Jesus') suggested that Jesus Barabbas was another name for Jesus of Nazareth. Part of the Jewish crowd had shouted for Jesus, referring to him as 'Jesus Barabbas', but the evangelists (or their tradition) had not wanted to acknowledge any Jewish support and so turned Jesus Barabbas into another person. Loisy saw a link with the imbecile Karabas who was mocked as a king during Agrippa I's visit to Alexandria at Passover time (Philo, *In Flaccum* 36–9). He suggested that Pilate gave Jesus to the soldiers as Barabbas (= Karabas) to make fun of: cf. *Marc*, p. 454. See also S. L. Davies, 'Bar Abbas', pp. 260–2. These views, however, have not generally won any wide acceptance and the majority of commentators see him as a political criminal; see Winter, *Trial*, pp. 131–43.

[32] For an extensive bibliography divided into scholars who see the Barabbas scene as historical and those who do not, see McLaren, *Power*, p. 93, n. 2.

[33] Strobel puts great importance on this, suggesting that Pilate appealed to the *vox populi* to avoid unrest: *Stunde*, pp. 124–7.

Astronomical and calendrical calculations suggest that the trial took place at the Passover of either 30 or 33 CE.[34] Although other dates have occasionally been put forward,[35] the majority of scholars favour one of these. To a great extent the discussion has revolved around the alleged link between Pilate, Sejanus and an anti-Jewish plot. Several scholars, taking the accounts of Pilate in Josephus, Philo and the gospels fairly uncritically, have emphasized the harshness of Pilate in Jewish sources and the supposed weakness of Pilate in Christian ones. They explain this by suggesting that all the events recorded by the Jewish writers (except the incident with the Samaritans which led to Pilate's deposition) happened whilst Pilate had the backing of his powerful ally, the anti-Jewish prefect of the Praetorian Guard, Sejanus. The trial of Jesus, however, must have occurred after Sejanus' assassination in October 31, i.e. Passover 33. Thus the governor's weakness and final capitulation was a result of the changed political climate in which his own position was suddenly much more precarious.[36] This theory has two main weaknesses. First, there is no evidence for the existence of an anti-Jewish plot between Sejanus and Pilate.[37] Second, as the whole of this study has tried to show, there is no fundamental discrepancy between the Pilate of the gospels and that of Josephus and Philo.[38] Both 30 and 33, therefore, remain equal possibilities.[39]

The above reconstruction, though only in its barest outline, gives the impression of a competent governor working alongside the Jewish hierarchy in executing a suspected political agitator. D. R. Schwartz notes the parallels between Pilate's handling of Jesus and Antipas' move against John the Baptist recorded by Josephus: 'it

[34] See Fotheringham, 'Evidence', pp. 146–62 and Finegan, *Handbook*, p. 161.

[35] For example, Eisler (*Messiah*, p. 17), claimed that the Maximinian *Acta Pilati* referred to by Eusebius (*EH* 1.9) were not forgeries and proved that the date of the crucifixion was 21 CE (the dates in *Ant.* 18.135 and 139 being Christian forgeries based on Luke 3.1). For fuller discussion and evidence that Pilate came to office in 26 see p. 1 above.

[36] See the introduction and chapter 1 for a fuller account of this view. Those holding this position include Stauffer, *Jerusalem*, pp. 16–18; Bammel, 'Philos', cols. 205–10; Doyle, 'Pilate's Career'; Maier, 'Episode', pp. 4–13; and Wansbrough, 'Suffered', pp. 92–3.

[37] See p. 23 above.

[38] McGing makes the same point: cf. 'Pontius', pp. 428–38.

[39] Turner ('Chronological'), though rejecting the Sejanus link, favours 33; so too does Smallwood, *Jews*, p. 168, n. 82. Those in favour of 30 include Kraeling, 'Episode', pp. 288–9 and Finegan, *Handbook*, p. 161. For fuller discussions of the historical data see Turner, ibid., pp. 67–74 and Maier, 'Episode', pp. 4–13.

would be much better to strike first and be rid of him before his [John's] work led to an uprising, than to wait for an upheaval, get involved in a difficult situation and see his mistake'.[40] Doubtless Pilate supposed that by executing the leader the movement would quickly fade away.

[40] *Ant.* 18.118; Schwartz, 'Pontius', p. 400.

CONCLUSION

Pontius Pilate is one of the few New Testament characters about whom we have two lengthy descriptions coming from roughly contemporary non-biblical sources. The material concerning him, therefore, affords us an interesting opportunity to assess the way in which all these sources, both biblical and non-biblical, treat historical characters. How far did each writer feel bound by historical events? How far has each allowed his own particular bias to influence his portrayal of Pilate?

This study has examined all six sources in turn – Philo, Josephus and the four gospels. In each case it has become apparent that the author's portrayal of Pilate has been influenced to a great extent by his own particular theological, apologetic and/or community situation. Yet despite the strongly interpretative nature of the sources, it has been possible to piece together something of the historical Pilate.

As the prefect of Judaea from 26 to 37 CE, Pilate was charged with maintaining law and order in the imperial province, overseeing legal matters and supervising the collection of taxes. The issue of coinage also fell within his duties. Archaeological evidence shows that Pilate, unlike other governors of Judaea, minted coins containing both Jewish and Roman designs. Although the pagan designs may not have been particularly offensive, the coins do seem to reflect a tendency to want to bring Judaea into line with other Roman provinces. Despite its size, the province presented many difficulties; not least was the fact that it was composed of different ethnic groups, each with its own religious sensitivities. It was therefore particularly important that the prefect maintained good relations with the Jewish high priest Caiaphas and the aristocracy.

The episode of the standards narrated by Josephus shows a governor intent on inaugurating his government with a firm hand. He appears to be reluctant to take any nonsense from the people he is to rule. Yet at the same time he can show flexibility and an ability to stand down in the interests of preserving the peace. The construction of the aqueduct shows him working alongside the priestly authorities. It was perhaps conceived as a joint venture, Jewish and Roman authorities working together for the benefit of the people of Jerusalem. Yet even when matters got out of hand, he does not appear to have resorted to undue aggression. The early years of Pilate's governorship were made particularly difficult by the absence of the Syrian legate. The protection normally afforded by the legate's four legions was missing and so it would have been particularly important to quell uprisings before they escalated.

The execution of Jesus was in all probability a routine crucifixion of a messianic agitator. Pilate, however, executed only the ring-leader and not his followers. This may again betray a dislike of excessive violence, but also indicates prudence at the potentially volatile Passover season. Again, the governor appears to have worked closely with the Jewish hierarchy.

An event recorded only by Philo illustrates Pilate's attempt to show loyalty to his Emperor. It is significant that he seems to have gone out of his way to make sure that the shields did not contain images and had them hung in his own residence – surely the most appropriate place in Jerusalem for them.

Finally, in a passage referred to only by Josephus, we hear of how Pilate put down a Samaritan uprising. A good governor could not allow such a potentially dangerous movement to escalate; he was therefore acting well within his duties as the protector of Roman law and order. His actions were again not unnecessarily severe, for only the leaders and influential people were put to death. It was, however, because of Samaritan complaints about Pilate's handling of this affair that he was sent back to Rome. But there is no certain indication that Vitellius thought that Pilate had been too heavy-handed; the legate simply decided to refer the whole matter to Tiberius. The outcome of Pilate's trial is unknown but even if the verdict had been in Pilate's favour the fact that he had governed for ten years and the accession of a new Emperor meant that it was the obvious time to accept a new commission.

With this sketch of the historical prefect in mind, we are in a better position to see how each of the six writers has interpreted Pilate as a literary character within their narratives and to begin to suggest reasons for each particular portrayal. Philo, for example, describes Pilate's character as utterly contemptible, his government oppressive. Yet this characterization conforms to that of others in Philo's *Legatio* and *In Flaccum* who disrespect the Jewish nation and its Law and stems ultimately not so much from the historical Pilate as from both Philo's political apologetic (the aim of which is to persuade Claudius not to adopt Gaius' attitude towards the Jews) and his theology (in which the enemies of the Jews are the enemies of God).

Josephus, too, does not rate Pilate highly. However, as this study has demonstrated, even within his two works, the *Antiquities of the Jews* and the *Jewish War*, Pilate is portrayed in a slightly different manner. In the earlier work, the *Jewish War*, Pilate is shown as insensitive towards the Jewish people and their Law, yet he can be moved by a religious demonstration and dislikes excessive bloodshed. Josephus uses the two events in Pilate's governorship to strengthen the *War*'s foremost apologetic aim – the insistence that resistance against Rome is futile; only passive acceptance of imperial rule can produce harmony amongst subject peoples. The *Antiquities* on the other hand is far more negative in its assessment of Pilate's character. This work shows a much greater interest in the personal histories of characters within the story, even incidental ones. The relationship between guilt and fate, particularly with regard to the Jewish Law, is also explored. Pilate sets himself up against that Law, and it is this attitude which ultimately determines his fate and leads to his removal from the province.

Above all, I have tried to show that the gospel accounts of Pilate are not uniform. They do not all present a 'weak' Pilate as is often supposed. In fact, the whole usual demarcation between the 'harsh, aggressive Pilate' of Jewish sources and the 'weak, vacillating Pilate' of Christian ones is much too simplistic. Instead, the gospels contain a great deal of diversity in their presentations of the prefect linked, as with the Jewish writers, to the needs of the community for which they were writing.

For Mark, Pilate is far from weak and vacillating. He is a skilful politician, manipulating the crowd to avoid a difficult situation, a strong representative of imperial interests. This picture of a strong, domineering governor ties in well with the element of persecution behind Mark's gospel. In Matthew's gospel, however, Pilate plays a less significant role within the Roman trial scene. The portrayal of the prefect is secondary to Matthew's interest in showing the Jewish crowd rejecting its Messiah and accepting responsibility for this action, suggesting that for Matthew's community relations with

Judaism were more serious and urgent than relations with Rome. Yet Pilate is still not described favourably: he is indifferent towards Jesus and ready to allow the Jewish leaders to have their way as long as he does not have to take responsibility.

In Luke's presentation, Pilate plays an important role as the representative of Roman law who declares Jesus innocent. Yet, like the governors before whom Christians are made to stand trial in Acts, he is of a rather dubious character. His principal characteristic is weakness as he allows representatives of the Jewish nation to force him to condemn an innocent man. In contrast, John's Pilate is manipulative, derisive and sure of his own authority. He will go along with Jewish wishes in condemning Jesus but exacts a high price from them in their acceptance of Caesar as their only king. In John's presentation, Pilate is allied with the hostile 'world' which rejects Jesus. As Jesus prepares for his glorification on the cross, all earthly rulers – Pilate representing Rome and 'the Jews' – are judged and found wanting by their negative response to him.

Since at least three of the gospels are bound by literary dependence, the obvious inference to be drawn from their accounts of Pilate is that each evangelist altered and interpreted the historical Pilate, or the Pilate of his source, in a way which had relevance for his own community. The differences highlighted by this study suggest that social context played as great a part in the presentation of early Christian events as did tradition. Certain key points had to be adhered to, but the community situation was the fundamental factor in determining the way in which each evangelist portrayed the prefect. If this is the case with the Pilate material, it is reasonable to suppose that social context was as important as tradition in the rest of the gospel narratives.

A further point which has come out of this study is that there is no evidence of a linear progression throughout the gospels in which Pilate becomes progressively friendlier towards Christianity (as was supposed by P. Winter and others). The situation was much more complex. The evangelists' presentations of Pilate (and so of Rome) were determined not so much by date as by their own social, geographical and political situations.

In the normal course of things, Pilate, like his fellow Roman governors, would have been all but forgotten; an obscure name in the pages of Philo and Josephus. Yet a chance encounter with Jesus of Nazareth ensured that his name survived in Christian recollection. It was one historical event – the trial of Jesus – which necessitated Christian reflection and therefore gave rise to the differing Christian 'Pilates of interpretation'. Yet interpretations of Pilate and his role as the judge of Jesus of Nazareth did not end with the first century, or even apocryphal or medieval literature. As the preface to this work has shown, even twentieth-century works on Pilate are interpretations, designed both to speak to their own times and situations and influenced by them. This is the case not only when the works come out of Stalinist Russia, post-war Germany or the European Union of the late 1990s, but out of any social, political or economic situation. Even popular imagination, focusing on the Roman in search of truth, the judge washing his hands or the indecisive governor, contributes to the many different 'Pilates of interpretation' of our own time.

BIBLIOGRAPHY

Sources

Josephus *The Jewish War*, trans. H. St J. Thackeray, Loeb vols. 2 and 3, London: Heinemann, 1927–8.
Jewish Antiquities, trans. L. H Feldman, R. Marcus and R. Wikgreen, Books 1–20, Loeb vols. 4–9, London: Heinemann, 1930–65.
The Life/Against Apion, trans. H. St. J. Thackeray, Loeb vol. 1, London: Heinemann, 1926.
Philo *The Embassy to Gaius*, ed. F. H. Colson, Loeb vol. 10, London: Heinemann, Cambridge, MA: Harvard University Press, 1962.
Legatio ad Gaium Introduction, Traduction et Notes, ed. A. Pelletier, Les Oeuvres de Philon d'Alexandrie, vol. 32, R. Armaldez, C. Mondésert, J. Pouilloux, Paris: Centre National de la Recherche Scientifique and Association of Friends of the University of Lyon, 1972.
Philonis Alexandrini Legatio ad Gaium, ed. E. M. Smallwood, Leiden: E. J. Brill, 1970.
In Flaccum, ed. F. H. Colson, Loeb vol. 9, London: Heinemann, Cambridge, MA: Harvard University Press, 1960.
Pliny *Pliny's Correspondence with Trajan*, ed. E. G. Hardy, London: Macmillan & Co., 1889.
Fifty Letters of Pliny, ed. A. N. Sherwin-White, Oxford, Oxford University Press, 1969.

Secondary works

Albright, W. F. and Mann, C. S. *Matthew*, Anchor Bible Commentary, New York, Doubleday, 1971.
Alexander, P. S. '"The Parting of the Ways" from the Perspective of Rabbinic Judaism', in J. D. G. Dunn, *The Partings of the Ways: Between Christianity and Judaism and their Significance for the Character of Christianity*, London: SCM, 1991, pp. 1–25.
Alter, R. *The Art of Biblical Narrative*, New York: Basic Books, 1981.
Anderson, H. *The Gospel of Mark*, New Century Bible, London: Oliphants, 1976.
Anderson, R. T. 'Samaritans', D. Literature, *ABD*, vol. 5, pp. 945–6.
Applebaum, S. 'Judaea as a Roman Province; the Countryside as a Political and Economic Factor', *ANRW* II.8 (1977), 355–96.

Attridge, H. W. 'Josephus and his Works', in S. Safrai and M. Stern (eds.), *The Jewish People in the First Century*, CRINT, Van Gorcum & Co. B. V.-Assen, 1974, pp. 185–232.

Bailey, A. *The Traditions Common to the Gospels of Luke and John*, NovTSup 7, Leiden: E. J. Brill, 1963.

Bajsic, A. 'Pilatus, Jesus und Barabbas', *Bib* 48 (1967), 7–28.

Balch, D. L. (ed.) *Social History of the Matthean Community: Cross Disciplinary Approaches*, Minneapolis: Fortress, 1991.

Balsdon, J. P. V. D. 'The Principates of Tiberius and Gaius', *ANRW* II.2 (1975), 86–94.

Bammel, E. 'Syrian Coinage and Pilate', *JJS* 2 (1950/1), 108–10.

'Philos tou Kaisaros', *TLZ* 77 (1952), cols. 205–10.

'Pilatus, Pontius', *RGG* 5 (3rd edn, 1961), cols. 383–4.

'Crucifixion as a Punishment in Palestine', in E. Bammel (ed.), *The Trial of Jesus*, London: SCM, 1970, pp. 162–5.

'Zum Testimonium Flavianum', in O. Betz, M. Hengel and K. Haacker (eds.), *Josephus-Studien* (Festschrift for O. Michel), Göttingen: Vandenhoeck & Ruprecht, 1974.

'The Trial before Pilate', in E. Bammel and C. F. D. Moule (eds.), *Jesus and the Politics of his Day*, Cambridge: Cambridge University Press, 1984, pp. 415–51.

'The Titulus', in E. Bammel and C. F. D. Moule (eds.), *Jesus and the Politics of his Day*, Cambridge: Cambridge University Press, 1984, pp. 353–64.

Bammel, E. (ed.) *The Trial of Jesus*, London: SCM, 1970.

Bammel, E. and Moule, C. F. D. (eds.) *Jesus and the Politics of his Day*, Cambridge: Cambridge University Press, 1984.

Baras, Z. 'The Testimonium Flavianum and the Martyrdom of James', in L. H. Feldman and G. Hata (eds.), *Josephus, Judaism and Christianity*, Leiden: E. J. Brill, 1987, pp. 338–48.

Barnes, T. D. 'Legislation against the Christians', *JRS* 58 (1968), 32–50.

Barnett, P. W. 'Under Tiberius all was Quiet', *NTS* 21 (1974–5), 564–71.

Barrett, C. K. *The Gospel of John and Judaism*, London: SPCK, 1975.

The Gospel According to St John, 2nd edn, London: SPCK, 1978.

Bartlett, J. R. *Jews in the Hellenistic World*, Cambridge: Cambridge University Press, 1985.

Bassler, J. M. 'The Galileans: A Neglected Factor in Johannine Community Research', *CBQ* 43 (1981), 243–57.

Bauman, R. A. *Impietas in Principem: A Study of Treason against the Roman Emperor with Special Reference to the First Century AD*, Munich: C. H. Beck, 1974.

Baum-Bodenbender, R. *Hoheit in Niedrigkeit: Johannische Christologie im Prozess Jesu vor Pilatus (Joh 18,28 – 19,16a)*, FB 49, Würzburg, 1984.

Baumgarten, J. M. 'Does TLH in the Temple Scroll Refer to Crucifixion?', *JBL* 91 (1972), 472–81.

Beare, F. W. *The Gospel According to Matthew*, Oxford: Blackwell, 1981.

Belo, F. *A Materialist Reading of the Gospel of Mark*, New York: Orbis Books, 1981.

Benoit, P. *The Passion and Resurrection of Jesus Christ*, London: Darton, Longman & Todd, 1969.

'Note sur les Fragments Grecs de la Grotte 7 de Qumran', *RB* 79 (1972), 321–4.

Bernard, J. H. *A Critical and Exegetical Commentary on the Gospel According to St John, Edinburgh: T. & T. Clark, 1928.*

Best, E. *The Temptation and the Passion: The Markan Soteriology*, SNTSMS, Cambridge: Cambridge University Press, 1965.

Mark: The Gospel as Story, Edinburgh: T. & T. Clark, 1983.

'The Date and Character of Mark', in E. Bammel and C. F. D. Moule (eds.), *Jesus and the Politics of his Day*, Cambridge: Cambridge University Press, 1984, pp. 69–89.

Betz, O. 'Probleme des Prozesses Jesu', *ANRW* II. 25,1 (1982), 565–647.

Bilde, Per *Flavius Josephus between Jerusalem and Rome: His Life, his Works and their Importance*, JSPSup 2, Sheffield: Sheffield Academic Press, 1988.

Black, M. 'The Arrest and Trial of Jesus and the Date of the Last Supper', in A. J. B. Higgins (ed.), *New Testament Essays: Studies in Memory of Thomas Walter Manson 1893–1958*, Manchester: Manchester University Press, 1959, pp. 19–33.

Blank, J. 'Die Verhandlung vor Pilatus: Joh 18,28–19,26 im Lichte der Joh. Theologie', *BZ* 3 (1959), 60–81.

Blinzler, J. 'Der Entscheid des Pilatus – Executionsbefehl oder Todesurteil?', *MTZ* 5 (1954), 171–84.

'Herodes und der Tod Jesȳ, *Klerusblatt* 37 (1957), 118–21.

'Die Niedermetzelung von Galiläern durch Pilatus', *NovT* 2 (1958), 24–49.

The Trial of Jesus, Cork: Mercier, 1959 (German edn 1951).

'Pilatus, Pontius', *LTK* 8 (1963), cols. 504–5.

Blunt, A. W. F. *Saint Mark*, The Clarendon Bible, Oxford: Clarendon Press, 1929.

Boddington, A. 'Sejanus, Whose Conspiracy?', *American Journal of Philology* 84 (1963), 1–16.

Bond, H. K. 'The Coins of Pontius Pilate: Part of an Attempt to Provoke the People or to Integrate them into the Empire?', *JSJ* 27 (1996), 241–62.

Borgen, P. 'John and the Synoptics in the Passion Narrative', *NTS* 5 (1958–9), 246–59.

'Philo', in S. Safrai and M. Stern (eds.), *The Jewish People in the First Century*, CRINT, Van Gorcum & Co. B.V.-Assen, 1974, vol. II.2, pp. 233–82.

Philo, John and Paul: New Perspectives on Judaism and Early Christianity, Brown Judaic Studies 131, Atlanta: Scholars Press, 1987.

Bornkamm, G. 'σειω σεισμός', *TDNT*, vol. 7, pp. 196–200.

Bowman, J. 'Pilgrimage to Mount Gerizim', *Eretz Israel* 7 (1964), 17–28.

'Early Samaritan Eschatology', *JJS* 6 (1955), 63–72.

Brandon, S. G. F. *The Fall of Jerusalem and the Christian Church*, 2nd edn, London: SPCK, 1957.

Jesus and the Zealots, Manchester: Manchester University Press, 1967.

The Trial of Jesus of Nazareth, London: B. T. Batsford, 1968.

'Pontius Pilate in History and Legend', *History Today* 18 (1968), 523–30.

Branscomb, B. H. *The Gospel of Mark*, Moffatt NT Commentary, London: Hodder & Stoughton, 1937.

Brown, R. E. *The Gospel According to John*, 2 vols., London: Geoffrey Chapman, 1978.

The Community of the Beloved Disciple, London: Geoffrey Chapman, 1979.

The Death of the Messiah: From Gethsemane to the Grave. A Commentary on the Passion Narratives in the Four Gospels, New York: Doubleday, 1994.

Brownlee, W. H. 'Maccabees, Books of', *ABD* (1992), vol. 3, pp. 201–15.

Broydé, I. 'Pilate, Pontius', *Jewish Encyclopaedia* (1905), vol. 10, pp. 34–5.

Bruce, F. F. 'Render to Caesar', in E. Bammel and C. F. D. Moule (eds.), *Jesus and the Politics of his Day*, Cambridge: Cambridge University Press, 1984, pp. 249–63.

Brunt, P. A. 'Charges of Maladministration under the Early Principate', *Historia* 10 (1961), 189–227.

'Procuratorial Jurisdiction', *Latomus* 25 (1966), 461–89.

Buckley, F. J. 'Pilate, Pontius', *New Catholic Encyclopaedia* (1967), vol. 11, pp. 360–1.

Bulgakov, M. *The Master and Margarita*, trans. M. Glenny, London: Collins & Harvill Press, 1967.

Bultmann, R. *History of the Synoptic Tradition*, Oxford: Blackwell, 1963.

The Gospel of John: A Commentary, Philadelphia: Westminster, 1971 (German edn 1941).

Burkill, T. A. 'St Mark's Philosophy of the Passion', *NovT* 2 (1957–8), 245–71.

Mysterious Revelation: An Examination of the Philosophy of St Mark's Gospel, New York: Cornell University Press, 1963.

'The Condemnation of Jesus: A Critique of Sherwin-White's Thesis', *NovT* 12 (1970), 321–42.

Buse, S. I. 'St John and the Markan Passion Narrative', *NTS* 4 (1957–8), 215–19.

'St John and the Passion Narratives of St Matthew and St Luke', *NTS* 7 (1960–1), 65–70.

Bussman, W. *Synoptische Studien*, 3 vols., Halle, 1925–31.

Cadbury, H. J. *The Style and Literary Method of Luke: I. The Diction of Luke and Acts*, Harvard Theological Studies VI, Cambridge, MA: Harvard University Press, 1919.

The Making of Luke–Acts, London: SPCK, 1958 (1st edn 1927).

Carroll, J. T. 'Luke's Crucifixion Scene', in D. D. Sylva (ed.), *Reimaging the Death of the Lukan Jesus*, Athenäum Monografien, Frankfurt: Anton Hain, 1990, pp. 108–24.

Cassidy, R. J. *Jesus, Politics and Society: A Study of Luke's Gospel*, New York: Orbis Books, 1978.

John's Gospel in New Perspective, New York: Orbis Books, 1992.

Cassidy, R. J. and Scharper, P. J. *Political Issues in Luke-Acts*, New York: Orbis Books, 1983.

Catchpole, D. R. 'The Problem of the Historicity of the Sanhedrin Trial', in E. Bammel (ed.), *The Trial of Jesus*, London: SCM, 1970, pp. 47–65.

The Trial of Jesus, Leiden: E. J. Brill, 1971.

Cerulli, E. 'Tiberius and Pontius Pilate in Ethiopian Tradition and Poetry', *Proceedings of the British Academy* LIX (1973), 141–58.

Chaval, C. B. 'The Releasing of a Prisoner on the Eve of Passover in Ancient Jerusalem', *JBL* 60 (1941), 273–78.

Cheeseman, G. L. *The Auxilia of the Roman Imperial Army*, Oxford: Clarendon Press, 1914.

Clark-Wire, A. 'Gender Roles in a Scribal Community', in D. L. Balch, *Social History of the Matthean Community. Cross Disciplinary Approaches*, Minneapolis: Fortress Press, 1991, pp. 87–121.

Cohen, S. J. D. *Josephus in Galilee and Rome*, Leiden: E. J. Brill, 1979.

Cohn, H. *The Trial and Death of Jesus*, London: Weidenfeld & Nicholson, 1972 (Hebrew edn 1968).

Cole, A. *Mark*, Tyndale NT Commentaries, London: Tyndale, 1961.

Collins, M. F. 'The Hidden Vessels in Samaritan Tradition', *JSJ* 3 (1972), 97–116.

Conzelmann, H. *The Theology of St Luke*, London: Faber & Faber, 1960.

'Luke's Place in the Development of Early Christianity', in L. E. Keck and J. L. Martyn (eds.), *Studies in Luke-Acts*, London: SPCK, 1968.

Acts of the Apostles, Hermeneia, Philadelphia: Fortress Press, 1987.

Cook, M. J. *Mark's Treatment of the Jewish Leaders*, Leiden: E. J. Brill, 1978.

Corbin, M. 'Jésus devant Hérode: Lecture de Luc 23,6–12', *Christus* 25 (1978), 190–7.

Cranfield, C. E. B. *St Mark*, Cambridge: Cambridge University Press, 1959.

Creed, J. M. *The Gospel According to St Luke*, London: Macmillan, 1930.

Cullmann, O. *The State in the New Testament*, London: SCM, 1957.

The Christology of the New Testament, London: SCM, 1959.

Culpepper, R. A. *Anatomy of the Fourth Gospel: A Study in Literary Design*, Philadelphia: Fortress Press, 1983.

Danker, F. W. *A Commentary on Luke's Gospel*, Philadelphia: Fortress Press, 1988.

Davies, P. S. 'The Meaning of Philo's Text about the Gilded Shields', *JTS* 37 (1986), 109–14.

Davies, S. L. 'Who is Called Bar Abbas?', *NTS* 327 (1981), 260–2.

Davies, W. D. *The Setting of the Sermon on the Mount*, Cambridge: Cambridge University Press, 1964.

Davies, W. D. and Allison, D.C. *Matthew*, 3 vols., Edinburgh: T. & T. Clark, 1991.

Deissmann, A. *Light from the Ancient East*, trans. L. R. M. Strachan, London: Hodder & Stoughton, 1927.

Derrett, J. D. M. 'Luke's Perspective on Tribute to Caesar', in R. J. Cassidy and P. J. Scharper, *Political Issues in Luke-Acts*, New York: Orbis Books, 1983, pp. 38–48.

'The Galileans and the Tower', in *New Resolutions of Old Conundrums: A Fresh Insight into Luke's Gospel*, Shipton-on-Stour: Drinkwater, 1986, pp. 100–10.

Dibelius, M. 'Herodes und Pilatus', *ZNW* 19 (1915), 113–26.

Die Formgeschichte des Evangeliums (ET *From Tradition to Gospel*), trans. B. L. Woolf and M. Sibelius, London: Ivor Nicholson & Watson, 1934.

Dobschütz, E. von 'Pilatus', in A. Hauck (ed.), *Real-Enzyclopaedie für Protestantische Theologie und Kirche*, vol. 15, cols. 397–401, Leipzig, 1904.

Dodd, C. H. *The Johannine Epistles*, London: Hodder & Stoughton, 1947.

The Interpretation of the Fourth Gospel, Cambridge: Cambridge University Press, 1953.

Historical Tradition in the Fourth Gospel, Cambridge: Cambridge University Press, 1965.

Donahue, J. R. 'A Pre-Markan Passion Narrative?', in W. H. Kelber (ed.), *The Passion in Mark*, Philadelphia: Fortress Press, 1976, pp. 1–20.

Doyle, A. D. 'Pilate's Career and the Date of the Crucifixion', *JTS* 42 (1941), 190–3.

Duke, P. *Irony in the Fourth Gospel*, Atlanta: John Knox, 1985.

Dunkerley, R. 'Was Barabbas Also Called Jesus?', *ExpTim* 74, 126–7.

Dunn, J. D. G. 'Caesar', in *DNTT*, vol. 1, pp. 269–70.

The Partings of the Ways: Between Christianity and Judaism and their Significance for the Character of Christianity, London: SCM, 1991.

Dunn, J. D. G. (ed.) *Jews and Christians*, Tübingen: J. C. B. Mohr (Paul Siebeck), 1992.

Earl, D. *The Moral and Political Tradition of Rome*, London: Thames & Hudson, 1967.

Ehrman, B. D. 'Jesus' Trial before Pilate: John 18:28–19:16', *BTB* 13 (1983), 124–31.

Eisler, R. *The Messiah Jesus and John the Baptist*, London: Methuen (ET 1931).

Ellis, E. E. *The Gospel of Luke*, Century Bible, London: Nelson, 1966.

Esler, P. F. *Community and Gospel in Luke-Acts: The Social and Political Motivations of Lucan Theology*, Cambridge: Cambridge University Press, 1987.

Evans, C. A. 'Is Luke's View of the Jewish Rejection of Jesus Anti-Semitic?', in D. D. Sylva (ed.), *Reimaging the Death of the Lukan Jesus*, Athenäum Monografien, Frankfurt, Anton Hain, 1990, pp. 29–56.

Evans, C. F. 'The Passion in John', in *Explorations in Theology*, vol. 2, London: SCM, 1977, pp. 50–66.

St Luke, London: SCM, 1990.

Everts, J. M. 'Dreams', *ABD*, vol. 2, pp. 231–2.

Eybers, I. H. 'The Roman Administration of Judaea between AD 6 and 41, with special reference to the procuratorship of Pontius Pilate', *Theologica Evangelica* (1969), 131–46.

Fascher, E. 'Pilatus, Pontius', *PW* 20 (1950), cols. 1322–3.

Das Weib des Pilatus – die Auferweckung der Heiligen, Halle: Max Niemeyer Verlag, 1951.

Feldman, L. H. 'Josephus', in *ABD*, Doubleday (1992), vol. 3, pp. 981–98.

Fenton, J. C. *Saint Matthew,* Pelican Gospel Commentaries, Harmondsworth: Penguin, 1963.

Ferguson, J. 'Roman Administration', in M. Grant and R. Kitzinger (eds.), *Civilization of the Ancient Mediterranean: Greece and Rome*, New York: Charles Scribner, 1988, vol. 1, pp. 649–65.

Finegan, J. 'The Original Form of the Pauline Collection', *HTR* 49 (1956), 85–103.

Handbook of Biblical Chronology, Princeton, Princeton University Press, 1964.

Fitzmyer, J.A. 'Anti-Semitism and the Cry of "All the People" (Mount 27:25)', *TS* 26 (1965), 667–71.

'Crucifixion in Ancient Palestine, Qumran Literature and the New Testament', *CBQ* 40 (1978), 493–513.

The Gospel According to Luke, Anchor Bible Commentary, New York: Doubleday, 1983.

Flusser, D. *The Last Days of Jesus in Jerusalem – A Current Study of the Easter Week*, Tel Aviv, 1980.

Ford, J. M. 'Crucify Him, Crucify Him and the Temple Scroll', *ExpTim* 87 (1975–6), 275–8.

Fotheringham, J. K. 'The Evidence of Astronomy and Technical Chronology for the Date of the Crucifixion', *JTS* 35 (1934), 146–62.

France, R. T. *Matthew: Evangelist and Teacher,* Exeter: Paternoster, 1989.

Divine Government, London: SPCK, 1990.

Frend, W. H. C. *Martyrdom and Persecution in the Early Church*, Oxford: Blackwell, 1965.

Freyne, S. 'Bandits in Galilee: A Contribution to the Study of Social Conditions in First-Century Palestine', in J. Neusner et al. (eds.), *The Social World of Formative Christianity and Judaism: Essays in Tribute to Howard Clark Kee*, Philadelphia: Fortress Press, 1988, pp. 53ff.

Fuks, G. 'Again on the Episode of the Gilded Roman Shields at Jerusalem', *HTR* 75 (1982), 503–7.

Gardner-Smith, P. *St John and the Synoptic Gospels*, Cambridge: Cambridge University Press, 1938.

Garnsey, P. 'The LEX IULIA Appeal under the Empire', *JRS* 56 (1966), 167–89.

'The Criminal Jurisdiction of Governors', *JRS* (1968), 51–9.

Garnsey, P. and Saller, R. *The Roman Empire: Economy, Society and Culture,* London: Duckworth, 1987.

Giblin, C. H. 'John's Narration of the Hearing Before Pilate (John 18,28 – 19,16a)', *Bib.* 67 (1986), 221–39.

Gnilka, J. *Das Evangelium nach Markus*, Evangelisch-Katholischer Kommentar zum Neuen Testaments, 2 vols., Benziger/Neukirchener, 1978–9.

Goodenough, E. R. *The Politics of Philo Judaeus*, Hildesheim: Georg Olms, 1967.

Jewish Symbols in the Graeco-Roman Period, vols. 1–13, New York: Pantheon Books, 1953.

Goodman, M. *The Ruling Class of Judaea*, Cambridge: Cambridge University Press, 1987.

Goodspeed, E. J. *Matthew: Apostle and Evangelist*, Philadelphia: John C. Winston, 1959.

Goulder, M.D. *Luke – A New Paradigm*, vol. 2, JSNTSup 20, Sheffield, JSOT, 1989.

Grant, M. *Aspects of the Principate of Tiberius*, Numismatic Notes and Monographs no. 116, New York, 1950.

Green, J. 'The Death of Jesus, God's Servant', in D. D. Sylva (ed.), *Reimaging the Death of the Lukan Jesus*, Athenäum Monografien, Frankfurt: Anton Hain, 1990, pp. 1–28.

Grundmann, W. *Das Evangelium nach Lukas*, Theologischer Handkommentar zum Neuen Testament III, Berlin: Evangelische Verlagsanstalt, 1971.

Gundry, R. H. *Matthew: A Commentary on his Literary and Theological Art*, Grand Rapids: Eerdmans, 1982.

'A Responsive Evaluation of the Social History of the Matthean Community in Roman Syria', in D. L. Balch (ed.), *Social History of the Matthean Community: Cross Disciplinary Approaches*, Minneapolis: Fortress Press, 1991, pp. 62–7.

Mark: A Commentary on his Apology for the Cross, Grand Rapids: Eerdmans, 1993.

Guterman, S. L. *Religious Persecution and Toleration in Ancient Rome*, London: Aiglon, 1951.

Gutmann, J. 'The "Second Commandment" and the Image in Judaism', *Hebrew Union College Annual* 32 (1961), 161–74.

Haacker, K. 'Samaritan', in C. Brown (ed.), *Dictionary of New Testament Theology*, Exeter: Paternoster, 1978, vol. 3, pp. 449–67.

'"Sein Blut über uns". Erwägungen zu Matthäus 27,25', *Kirche und Israel* 1 (1986), 47–50.

'Kaisertribut und Gottesdienst, Eine Auslegung von Markus 12.13–17', *TBei* 17 (1986), 285–92.

'Wer war schuld am Tode Jesu?', *TBei* 25 (1994), 23–36.

Hachlili, R. *Jewish Ornamented Ossuaries of the late Second Temple Period*, Reuben and Edith Hecht Museum, University of Haifa, 1988.

Haenchen, E. 'Jesus vor Pilatus (Joh 18,28–19,15)', *TLZ* 85 (1960), cols. 93–102.

Hare, D. R. A. *The Theme of Jewish Persecution of Christians in the Gospel According to St Matthew*, Cambridge: Cambridge University Press, 1967.

Harvey, A. E. *Jesus on Trial: A Study in the Fourth Gospel*, London: SPCK, 1976.

Jesus and the Constraints of History, London, Duckworth, 1982.

Hedley, P. L. 'Pilate's Arrival in Judaea' *JTS* 35 (1934), 56–7.

Hendrickx, H. *The Passion Narratives of the Synoptic Gospels*, London: Geoffrey Chapman, 1977.

Hengel, M. *Judaism and Hellenism*, 2 vols., Philadelphia: Fortress Press, 1974.

Crucifixion in the Ancient World and the Folly of the Cross, London: SCM, 1977.

The Zealots: An Investigation into the Jewish Freedom Movement in the Period from Herod I until 70 AD, Edinburgh: T. & T. Clark (ET 1981).

Between Jesus and Paul, London: SCM, 1983.

Studies in the Gospel of Mark, London: SCM, 1985.

The 'Hellenization' of Judaea in the First Century after Christ, London: SCM, London/Philadelphia: Trinity, 1989.

The Johannine Question, London: SCM, 1989.

'Reich Christi, Reich Gottes und Weltreich im Johannesevangelium', in M. Hengel and A. M. Schwemer (eds.), *'Königsherrschaft Gottes und himmlischer Kult' im Judentum, Urchristentum und in der hellenistischen Welt*, Wissenschaftliche Untersuchungen zum NT 55, Tübingen, J. C. B Mohr (Paul Siebeck), 1991.

Hennig, D. *L. Aelius Seianus*, Munich C. H. Beck'sche, 1975.

Herrenbrück, F. 'Wer Waren die "Zöllner"?', *ZNW* 72 (1981), 178–94.

'Zum Vorwurf der Kollaboration des Zöllners mit Rom', *ZNW* 78 (1987), 186–99.

Hilliard, A. E. and Clavier, H. 'Pilate', in J. Hastings (ed.), *Dictionary of the Bible*, Edinburgh: T. & T. Clark, 2nd edn 1963, pp. 771–2.

Hoehner, H. W. 'Why Did Pilate Hand Jesus Over to Antipas?', in E. Bammel (ed.), *Trial of Jesus: Studies in Honour of C. F. D. Moule*, London: SCM, 1970, pp. 84–90.

Herod Antipas, SNTSMS, Cambridge: Cambridge University Press, 1972.

'Pilate', *Dictionary of Jesus and the Gospels*, Downers Grove/Leicester: InterVarsity,1992.

Holzmeister, U. 'Wann war Pilatus Prokurator von Judaea?', *Bib* 13 (1932), 228–32.

Hooker, M. D. *The Gospel According to St Mark*, Black's NT Commentaries, London, A. & C. Black, 1991.

Horsley, R. A. 'Josephus and the Bandits', *JSJ* 10 (1979), 37–63.

'Popular Messianic Movements around the Time of Jesus', *CBQ* 46 (1984), 471–95.

Horsley, R. A. and Hanson, J. S. *Bandits, Prophets and Messiahs: Popular Movements at the Time of Jesus*, Minneapolis: Winston Press, 1985.

Horvath, T. 'Why Was Jesus Brought to Pilate?', *NovT* 11 (1969), 174–84.

Howell, D. B. *Matthew's Inclusive Story: a Study in the Narrative Rhetoric of the First Gospel*, JSNTSup42, Sheffield: JSOT Press, 1990.

Howgego, C. J. *Greek Imperial Countermarks: Studies in the Provincial Coinage of the Roman Empire*, London: Royal Numismatic Society, Special Publication no. 17, 1985.

Husband, R. W. 'The Pardoning of Prisoners by Pilate', *AJT* 21 (1917), 110–16.

Iersel, B. M. F. van 'The Gospel According to St Mark – Written for a Persecuted Community?', *NTT* 34 (1980), 15–36.

Reading Mark, Edinburgh: T. & T. Clark, 1989.

Isaac, B. *The Limits of Empire: The Roman Army in the East*, Oxford: Clarendon Press, revised edn 1992.

Jackson, B. S. 'On the Problem of Roman Influence on the Halakah and Normative Self-Definition in Judaism', in E. P. Sanders with A. I. Baumgarten and A. Mendelson (eds.), *Jewish and Christian Self-Definition* vol. 2: Aspects of Judaism in the Graeco-Roman Period, London: SCM, 1981, pp. 157–203.

Jeremias, J. *Jerusalem in the Time of Jesus: An Investigation into Economic and Social Conditions during the New Testament Period*, London: SCM, 1969.

Jervell, J. *Luke and the People of God: A New Look at Luke-Acts*, Minneapolis: Augsburg, 1972.

Johnson, L. T. 'Luke-Acts, Book of', *ABD*, vol. 4, pp. 403–20.

Johnson, S. E. 'A Note on Luke 13:1–5', *ATR* 17 (1935), 91–5.

A Commentary on the Gospel According to St Mark, London: A. & C. Black, 1960.

Jones, A. H. M. *Studies in Roman Government and Law*, Oxford: Blackwell, 1960.

'I Appeal to Caesar', in A. H. M. Jones (ed.), *Studies in Roman Government and Law*, Oxford: Blackwell, 1960, pp. 51–65.

'Procurators and Prefects in the Early Principate', in A. H. M. Jones (ed.), *Studies in Roman Government and Law*, Oxford: Blackwell, 1960., pp. 115–25.

Juel, D. *Messiah and Temple*, SBLDS 31, Missoula: Scholars Press, 1977.

Juster, J. *Les Juifs dans l'Empire romain. Leur condition juridique, économique et sociale*, 2 vols., Paris, 1914.

Kadman, L. 'The Development of Jewish Coinage', in *The Dating and Meaning of Ancient Jewish Coins and Symbols*, Jerusalem, Publications of the Israeli Numismatic Society, Numismatic Studies and Researches, vol. 2, 1958.

Karris, R. J. 'Luke 23. 47 and the Lucan View of Jesus' Death', in D. D. Sylva (ed.), *Reimaging the Death of the Lukan Jesus*, Athenäum Monografien, Frankfurt: Anton Hain, 1990, pp. 68–78.

Kee, H. C. *Community of the New Age*, London: SCM, 1977.

Kelber, W. H. *The Kingdom in Mark*, Philadelphia: Fortress Press, 1974.

'Conclusion: From Passion Narrative to Gospel', in W. H. Kelber (ed.), *The Passion in Mark*, Philadelphia: Fortress Press, 1976, pp. 153–80.

Kelber, W. H. (ed.) *The Passion in Mark*, Philadelphia: Fortress Press, 1976.

Kilpatrick, G. D. *The Origins of the Gospel According to St Matthew*, Oxford: Clarendon Press, 1946.

The Trial of Jesus, Oxford: Oxford University Press, 1953.

Kindler, A. 'More Dates on the Coins of the Procurators', *IEJ* 6 (1956), 54–7.

Kingsbury, J. D. *Matthew: Structure, Christology, Kingdom*, London: SPCK, 1976.

'The Title Son of David in Matthew's Gospel', *JBL* 95 (1976), 598–601.

Matthew, Proclamation Commentaries, Philadelphia: Fortress Press, 1977.

Conflict in Mark: Jesus, Authorities, Disciples, Minneapolis: Fortress Press, 1989.

'Conclusion: Analysis of a Conversation', in D. L. Balch (ed.), *Social History of the Matthean Community: Cross Disciplinary Approaches*, Minneapolis: Fortress Press, 1991, pp. 259–69.

Kinman, B. 'Jesus' "Triumphal Entry" in the Light of Pilate's', *NTS* 40 (1994), 442–8.

Klein, H. 'Zur Frage nach dem Abfassungsort der Lukasschriften', *EvT* 32 (1972), 467–77.

Knox, W. L. *The Sources of the Synoptic Gospels*, vol. 1 St Mark, Cambridge: Cambridge University Press, 1953.

Koch, K. 'Der Spruch "Sein Blut bleibe auf seinem Haupt" und die israelitische Auffassung vom vergossenen Blut', *VT* 12 (1962), 396–416.

Kraeling, C. H. 'The Episode of the Roman Standards at Jerusalem', *HTR* 35 (1942), 263–89.

Krieger, K. S. 'Pontius Pilate – ein Judenfeind? Zur Problematik einer Pilatusbiographie', *BN* 78 (1995), 63–83.

Kunkel, W. 'Quaestio', *PW* 24 (1963), 720–86.

Kysar, R. 'John, the Gospel of', *ABD*, vol. 3, pp. 912–31.

Laet, S. J. de 'Le successeur de Ponce Pilate', *L'Antiquite Classique* 8 (1939), 413–19.

Lane, W. L. *The Gospel of Mark*, The New International Commentary on the NT, Grand Rapids: Eerdmans, 1974.

Langdon, S. 'The Release of a Prisoner at the Passover', *ExpTim* 29 (1917–8), 328–30.

Leaney, A. R. C. *A Commentary on the Gospel According to St Luke*, 2nd edn, London: A. & C. Black, 1966.

Lee, E. K. 'St Mark and the Fourth Gospel', *NTS* (1956–7), 50–8.

Lémonon, J. P. *Pilate et le gouvernement de la Judée: textes et monuments*, Études bibliques, Paris: Gabalda, 1981.

Leon-Dufour, X. 'Trois Chiasmes johanniques', *NTS* 7 (1960–61), 249–55.

Levick, B. *Tiberius the Politician*, London: Thames & Hudson, 1976.

The Government of the Roman Empire, London: Croom Helm, 1985.

'The Politics of the Early Principate', in T. P. Wiseman (ed.), *Roman Political Life, 90 BC–AD 69*, Exeter Studies in History no. 7, University of Exeter, 1985, pp. 45–68.

Liberty, S. 'The Importance of Pontius Pilate in Creed and Gospel', *JTS* 45 (1944), 38–56.

Lietzmann H. 'Der Prozeß Jesu, *Kleine Schriften II: Studien zum Neun Testament*, Berlin, 1958, pp. 264–76.

Lightfoot, R. H. *The Gospel Message of St Mark*, Oxford: Clarendon Press, 1950.

St John's Gospel: A Commentary, Oxford: Clarendon Press, 1956.

Lindars, B. *New Testament Apologetic*, London: SCM, 1961.

The Gospel of John, Marshall, London: Morgan & Scott, 1972.

Lindner, H. *Die Geschichtsauffassung des Flavius Josephus im Bellum Judaicum*, AGAJU XII, Leiden: E. J. Brill, 1972.

Linnemann, E. *Studien zur Passionsgeschichte*, FRLANT 102, Göttingen: Vandenhoeck & Ruprecht, 1970.

Lintott, A. *Imperium Romanum: Politics and Administration*, London: Routledge, 1993.

Lohse, E. *Mark's Witness to Jesus Christ*, World Christian Books, United Society for Christian Literature, London: Lutterworth, 1955.

'Die römischen Statthalter in Jerusalem', *ZDPV* 74 (1958), 69–78.

Loisy, A. *L'Evangile selon Marc*, Paris: Nourry, 1912.

L'Evangile selon Luc, Paris: Nourry, 1924.

Lührmann, D. *Das Markusevangelium*, Tübingen: J. C. B. Mohr (Paul Siebeck), 1987.

Lund, N. W. 'The Influence of Chiasmus upon the Structure of the Gospels', *ATR* 13 (1931), 27–48, 405–33.

Luz, U. *Matthew 1–7. A Commentary*, Edinburgh: T. & T. Clark, 1990.

The Theology of the Gospel of Matthew, Cambridge: Cambridge University Press, 1995.

Maccoby, H. Z. 'Jesus and Barabbas', *NTS* 16 (1969–70), 55–60.

MacDonald, J. *The Theology of the Samaritans*, London: SCM, 1964.

Macgregor, G. H. C. *The Gospel of John*, Moffat NT Commentaries, London: Hodder & Stoughton, 1942.

Madden, F.W. *Coins of the Jews*, Hildesheim, Georg Olms, 1976 (first published London: Trübner & Co, 1881).

Maddox, R. *The Purpose of Luke-Acts*, Edinburgh: T. & T. Clark, 1982.

Maier, P. L. 'Sejanus, Pilate and the Date of the Crucifixion', *Church History* 37 (1968), 3–13.

Pontius Pilate, Garden City, NY: Doubleday & Co., 1968.

'The Episode of the Golden Roman Shields at Jerusalem'. *HTR* 62 (1969), 109–21.

Malbon, E. S. *Narrative Space and Mythic Meaning in Mark*, Sheffield: JSOT, 1991.

Maltiel-Gerstenfeld, J. *260 Years of Ancient Jewish Coins*, Tel Aviv: Kol, 1982.

New Catalogue of Ancient Jewish Coins, Tel Aviv: Minerva Associated, 1987.

Manson, T. W. *The Gospel of Luke*, Moffat NT Commentary, London: Hodder & Stoughton, 1930.

Marshall, I. H. *The Gospel of Luke*, Exeter: Paternoster, 1978.

Martin, R. P. *Mark – Evangelist and Theologian*, Exeter: Paternoster, 1972.

Martyn, J. L. *History and Theology in the Fourth Gospel*, New York: Harper & Row, 1968.

Marxsen, W. *Mark the Evangelist*, Nashville: Abingdon, 1969.

Massaux, E. *Influence de l'évangile de Saint Matthieu sur la littérature Chrétienne avant Saint Irénée*, Leuven: Leuven University Press, 1986.

Massebieau, M. L. 'Le classement des oeuvres de Philon', *Bibliotèque de l'Ecole des Hautes Études, Sciences Religieuses* 1, 1899, pp. 1–91.

Matera, F. J. *What are They Saying about Mark?*, New York/Mahwah: Paulinist, 1987.

'Luke 22. 66–71: Jesus before the ΠΡΕΣΒΥΤΕΡΙΟΝ', in F. Neirynck, *L'Évangile de Luc/The Gospel of Luke, Revised and Enlarged Edition of L'Évangile de Luc, Problèmes littéraires et théologiques*, Leuven: Leuven University Press, 1989, pp. 517–33.

'Luke 23. 1–25: Jesus before Pilate, Herod and Israel', in F. Neirynck, *L'Évangile de Luc/The Gospel of Luke, Revised and Enlarged Edition of*

L'Évangile de Luc, Problèmes littéraires et théologiques, Leuven: Leuven University Press, 1989, pp. 535–51.

Matthiae, K. and Schönert-Geiß, E. *Münzen aus der urchristlichen Umwelt*, Berlin: Evangelische Verlags-Anstalt, 1981.

Maxfield, V. A. *The Military Decorations of the Roman Army*, London: Batsford, 1981.

Mayer, G. *Index Philoneus*, Berlin/New York: Walter de Gruyter, 1974.

Mayer, R. 'Israel', in *DNTT*, vol. 2, especially pp. 308–11.

McGing, B. C. 'Pontius Pilate and the Sources' *CBQ* 53 (1991), 416–38.

McLaren, J. *Power and Politics in Palestine*, JSNTSup 63, Sheffield: Sheffield Academic Press, 1991.

Meeks. W. A. *The Prophet King: Moses Traditions and the Johannine Christology*, NovTSup 14, Leiden: E. J. Brill, 1967.

'Breaking Away: Three New Testament Pictures of Christianity's Separation from the Jewish Communities', in J. Neusner and E. Frerichs (eds.), *'To See Ourselves as Others See Us': Christians, Jews, 'Others', in Late Antiquity*, California: Scholars Press, 1985, pp. 93–115.

Meier, J. P. 'Matthew and Ignatius: A Response to William R. Schoedel', in D. L. Balch, *Social History of the Matthean Community. Cross Disciplinary Approaches*, Minneapolis: Fortress Press, 1991, pp. 178–86.

'Matthew, Gospel of', in *ABD*, vol. 4, pp. 622–41.

Merritt, R. L. 'Jesus Barabbas and the Paschal Pardon', *JBL* 104 (1985), 57–68.

Meshorer, Y. *Ancient Jewish Coinage*, vol. 2, New York: Amphora Books, 1982.

Metzger, B. M. *A Textual Commentary on the Greek New Testament*, London: UBS, 1975.

Meyer, E. *Ursprung und Anfänge des Christentums*, 3 vols., Darmstadt: Wissenschaftliche Buchgesellschaft, 1962 (1st edn 1921–3).

Meyshan, J. 'The Periods of the Jewish Coinage', in *Essays in Jewish Numismatics*, Publications of the Israel Numismatic Society, Numismatic Studies and Researches, vol. 6, pp. 45–7.

Millar, F. G. B. 'Reflections on the Trial of Jesus', in P. R. Davies and R. T. White (eds.), *A Tribute to Geza Vermes: Essays on Jewish and Christian Literature and History*, Sheffield: JSOT, 1990, pp. 355–81.

The Roman Near East: 31BC–AD 337, Cambridge, MA: Harvard University Press, 1993.

Mommsen, T. *Römisches Strafrecht*, Leipzig: Dunker & Humbolt, 1899.

Montgomery, J. A. *The Samaritans: The Earliest Jewish Sect, their History, Theology and Literature*, New York: KTAV, 1968 (first published 1907).

Morison, F. *And Pilate Said.*. London: Rich & Cowan, 1939.

Morris, L. *The Gospel According to John*, New International Commentary on the NT, Grand Rapids: Eerdmans, 1971.

The Gospel According to St Luke: An Introduction and Commentary, Grand Rapids: Eerdmans, 1974.

Moulton, J. H. and Turner, N. *A Grammar of New Testament Greek*, vol. 3, Syntax, Edinburgh: T. & T. Clark, 1963.

Moxnes, H. *The Economy of the Kingdom: Social Conflict and Economic Relations in Luke's Gospel*, Philadelphia: Fortress Press, 1988.

Müller, G. A. *Pontius Pilatus, der fünfte Prokurator von Judäa und Richter Jesu von Nazareth*, Stuttgart: Metzler, 1888.

Myers, C. *Binding the Strong Man: A Political Reading of Mark's Story of Jesus*, Maryknoll: Orbis Books, 1988.

Myllykoski, M. 'The Material Common to Luke and John: A Sketch', in P. Luomanen (ed.), *Luke-Acts: Scandinavian Perspectives*, Finnish Exegetical Society in Helsinki 54, Göttingen: Vandenhoeck & Ruprecht, 1991, pp. 115–56.

Neirynck, F. *Duality in Mark: Contributions to the Study of the Markan Redaction*, BETL 31, 2nd edn, Leuven: Leuven University Press, 1988.

'John and the Synoptics: 1975–90', Paper given at the 39th Colloquium Biblicum Lovaniense (1990), Leuven: Leuven University Press, 1992.

Neusner, J. *From Politics to Piety: the Emergence of Pharisaic Judaism*, 2nd edn: New York: KTAV, 1979.

Nevius, R. 'A Reply to Dr Dunkerley', *ExpTim* 74 (1962/3), 255.

Nicolet, C. 'Augustus, Government and the Propertied Class', in F. G. B. Millar and E. Segal (eds.), *Caesar Augustus: Seven Aspects*, Oxford: Oxford University Press, 1984, pp. 89–128.

Nickelsburg, G. W. E. 'The Genre and Function of the Markan Passion Narrative', *HTR* 73 (1980), 153–84.

Niederwimmer, K. 'Johannes Markus und die Frage nach dem Verfasser des zweiten Evangeliums', *ZNW* 58 (1967), 172–88.

Nineham, D. E. *The Gospel of St Mark*, Pelican Gospel Commentaries, London: A. & C. Black, 1963.

Nock, A. D. 'The Roman Army and the Roman Religious Year', *HTR* 45 (1952), 187–252.

Nolan, B. M. *The Royal Son of God*, Orbis Biblicus et Orientalis 23, Éditions universitaires Fribourg Suisse, Göttingen: Vandenhoeck & Ruprecht, 1979.

O'Callaghan, J. 'Papiros neotestamentarios en la cueva 7 de Qumran?', *Bib* 53 (1972), 91–100.

Ollivier, M. J. 'Ponce Pilate et les Pontii', *RB* 5 (1896), 247–54, 594–600.

Olmstead, A. T. *Jesus in the Light of History*, New York: Scribner's, 1942.

O'Neill, J. C. *The Theology of Acts in its Historical Setting*, London: SPCK, 1961.

Patte, D. *The Gospel According to Matthew*, Philadelphia: Fortress Press, 1987.

Pesch, R. *Das Markusevangelium*, vols. 1–2, Herders Theologischer Kommentar zum Neuen Testament, Freiburg, Herder, 1977.

Peter, H. 'Pontius Pilatus, der Römische Landpfleger in Judäa', *Neues Jahrbuch für das klassische Altertum Geschichte und deutsche Literatur* 19 (1907), 1–40.

Petersen, N. R. 'The Composition of Mk 4:1–8:26', *HTR* 73 (1980), 185–217.

Pflaum, H. G. *Les Procurateurs équestres sous le Haut-Empire Romain*, 3 vols., Paris, Adrien Maisonneuve, 1950.

Les Carrières Procuratoriennes Équestres sous le Haut-Empire Romaine, Paris: Paul Geuthner, 1960, Supplement 1982.

Piper, O. A. 'God's Good News: The Passion Story According to Mark', *Interpretation* 9 (1955), 165–82.

Potterie, I. de la 'L'arrière-fond du thème johannique de verité', *Studia Evangelica* I, Berlin, Akademie-Verlag, pp. 277–94.

'Jésus, roi et juge d'après Jn 19,13: ἐκάθισεν ἐπὶ βήματος', *Bib.* 41 (1960), 217–47.

Przybylski, B. 'The Setting of Matthean Anti-Judasim', in P. Richardson (ed.), *Anti-Judaism in Early Christianity*, vol. 1, Waterloo: Wilfred Laurier, 1986.

Purves, G. T. 'Pontius Pilate', *Hastings Dictionary of the Bible*, 1900, vol. 3, pp. 875–9.

Quinn, J. F. 'The Pilate Sequence in the Gospel of Matthew', *Dunwoodie Review* 10 (1970), 154–77.

Rajak, T. *Josephus: The Historian and his Society*, London: Duckworth, 1983.

Ramsey, W.M. *The Church in the Roman Empire Before AD 170,* London: Hodder & Stoughton, 1904.

Rau, G. 'Das Volk in der lukanischen Passionsgeschichte, eine Konjektur zu Lc 23.13', *ZNW* 56 (1965), 41–51.

Rawlinson, A. E. J. *The Gospel According to St Mark*, 3rd edn, Westminster Commentaries, London: Methuen, 1931.

Reese, T. 'The Political Theology of Luke-Acts', *Biblical Theology* 22 (1972), 62–5.

Reifenberg, A. *Ancient Jewish Coins*, 2nd edn, Jerusalem: Rubin Mass, 1947.

Rensberger, D. *Overcoming the World: Politics and Community in the Gospel of John,* London: SPCK: 1989 (1st edn *Johannine Faith and Liberating Community*, Philadelphia: Westminster, 1988).

Reventlow, H. G. 'Sein Blut komme über sein Haupt', *VT* 10 (1960), 311–27.

Rienecker, F. *A Linguistic Key to the Greek New Testament*, vol. 1: Matthew – Acts (trans. and revised by C. L. Rogers), London: Bagster, 1977.

Rigg, H. A. 'Barabbas', *JBL* 64 (1945), 417–56.

Rivkin, E. *What Crucified Jesus?*, London: SCM, 1986 (1st edn Nashville, Abingdon, 1984).

Robinson, J. A. T. *Redating the New Testament*, London: SCM, 1976.

Robinson, T. H. *The Gospel of Matthew*, Moffatt NT Commentary, London: Hodder & Stoughton, 1928.

Rosadi, G. *The Trial of Jesus*, New York: Dodd Mead, 1905.

Roth, C. 'An Ordinance against Images in Jerusalem AD 66', *HTR* 49 (1956), 169–77.

Roth, L. 'Pontius Pilate', *Encyclopaedia Judaica,* 1971, vol. 13, col. 848.

Sabbe, M. 'The Trial of Jesus before Pilate in John (18:28–19:16a) and its Relation to the Synoptists', paper given at the 39th Colloquium Biblicum Lovaniense (1990), Leuven: Leuven University Press, 1992, pp. 467–513.

Safrai, S. 'Jewish Self-government', in *CRINT*, vol. 1 pp. 337–419.

Saldarini, A. J. 'The Gospel of Matthew and Jewish-Christian Conflict', in D. L. Balch, *Social History of the Matthean Community. Cross Disciplinary Approaches*, Minneapolis: Fortress Press, 1991, pp. 38–61.

Pharisees, Scribes and Sadducees in Palestinian Society, Edinburgh: T. & T. Clark, 1989.

Saller, R. P. *Personal Patronage under the Early Empire*, Cambridge: Cambridge University Press, 1982.

'Roman Class Structures and Relations', in M. Grant and R. Kitzinger (eds.), *Civilization of the Ancient Mediterranean: Greece and Rome*, New York: Charles Scribner's Sons, 1988, vol. 1, pp. 549–73.

Sanders, E. P. *Judaism: Practice and Belief: 63 BCE – 66CE*, London: SCM, 1992.

Sanders, J. T. *The Jews in Luke-Acts*, London: SCM, 1987.

Sandmel, S. 'Pilate, Pontius', *Interpreters' Dictionary of the Bible*, 1962, vol. 3, pp. 811–13.

Sandys, J. E. *Latin Epigraphy*, Cambridge: Cambridge University Press, 1927.

Schelkle, K. H. 'Die "Selbstverfluchung" Israels nach Mount 27:23–5', in W. P. Eckert (ed.), *Antijudaismus im NT?*, Munich: Kaiser, 1967, pp. 148–56.

Schlier, H. 'Jesus und Pilatus nach dem Johannes Evangelium', in *Die Zeit der Kirche*, Freiburg: Herder, 1956, pp. 56–74.

'The State According to the New Testament', in *The Relevance of the New Testament*, New York: Herder & Herder, 1968, pp. 215–38.

Schmidt, K. L. *Der Rahmen der Geschichte Jesus*, Berlin, 1919.

Schnackenburg, R. *The Gospel According to St John*, 3 vols., London: Burns & Oates, 1980.

Schneider, G. 'The Political Charge against Jesus (Luke 23:2)', in E. Bammel and C. F. D. Moule (eds.), *Jesus and the Politics of his Day*, Cambridge: Cambridge University Press, 1984, pp. 403–14.

Schoedel, W. R. 'Ignatius and the Reception of the Gospel of Matthew in Antioch', in D. L. Balch, *Social History of the Matthean Community. Cross Disciplinary Approaches*, Minneapolis: Fortress Press, 1991, pp. 129–77.

Schürer, E. *The History of the Jewish People in the Age of Jesus Christ*, revised and ed. G. Vermes, F. Millar and M. Goodman, Edinburgh: T. & T. Clark, vols. 1–3, 1973–87.

Schwartz, D. R. 'Josephus and Philo on Pontius Pilate', *The Jerusalem Cathedra* 3 (1983), 26–45.

Agrippa I: The Last King of Judaea, Tübingen: J. C. B. Mohr (Paul Siebeck), 1990.

'Pontius Pilate's Appointment to Office and the Chronology of Antiquities, Books 18–20', in *Studies in the Jewish Background of Christianity*, Tüubingen: J. C. B. Mohr (Paul Siebeck), 1992, pp. 182–201.

'Pontius Pilate', *ABD* (1992), vol. 5, pp. 395–401.

Schweizer, E. *The Good News According to Mark*, London: SPCK, 1971.

The Good News According to Matthew, London, SPCK: London, 1975.

Segal, A. F. 'Matthew's Jewish Voice', in D. L. Balch, *Social History of the Matthean Community. Cross Disciplinary Approaches*, Minneapolis: Fortress Press, 1991, pp. 3–37.

Segovia, F. F. 'The Love and Hatred of Jesus and Johannine Sectarianism', *CBQ* 43 (1981), 258–72.

Senior, D. *The Passion Narrative According to Matthew: A Redactional Study*, Bibliotheca Ephemeridum Theologicarum Lovaniensium 39, Leuven: Leuven University Press, 1975.

Shanks, Hershel *Judaism in Stone: The Archaeology of Ancient Synagogues*, The Biblical Archaeology Society, Washington: Harper & Row/Tel Aviv: Steimatzky, 1979.

Shatzman, I. *The Armies of the Hasmonaeans and Herod: From Hellenistic to Roman Frameworks*, Tübingen: J. C. B. Mohr (Paul Siebeck), 1991.

Shaw, B. D. 'Roman Taxation', in M. Grant and R. Kitzinger (eds.), *Civilization of the Ancient Mediterranean: Greece and Rome*, New York, Charles Scribner's Sons, 1988, vol. 2, pp. 809–27.

Sherwin-White, A. N. 'Procurator Augusti', PBSR 15, NS2 (1939), 11–15.

'The Early Persecutions and Roman Law Again', *JTS* NS 3 (1952), 199–213.

Roman Society and Roman Law in the New Testament, Oxford: Clarendon Press, 1963.

'The Trial of Christ', in D. E. Nineham et al. (eds.), *Historicity and Chronology in the New Testament*, London: SPCK, 1965, pp. 97–116.

Slingerland, D. L. 'The Transjordanian Origin of Matthew's Gospel', *JSNT* 3 (1979), 18–28.

Sloyan, G. *Jesus on Trial*, Philadelphia: Fortress Press, 1973.

Smallwood, E. M. 'The Date of the Dismissal of Pontius Pilate from Judaea', *JJS* 5 (1954), 12–21.

'Some Notes on the Jews under Tiberius', *Latomus* 15 (1956), 314–29.

'High Priests and Politics in Roman Palestine', *JTS* 13 (1962), 14–34.

The Jews under Roman Rule: From Pompey to Diocletian, Leiden: E. J. Brill, 1976.

'Philo and Josephus as Historians of the Same Events', in L. H. Feldman and G. Hata (eds.), *Josephus, Judaism and Christianity*, Leiden: E. J. Brill, 1987, pp. 114–29.

Smith, M. 'Zealots and Sicarii: Their Origins and Relations', *HTR* 64 (1971), 1–19.

Soards, M. L. 'Herod Antipas' Hearing in Luke 23.8', *Biblical Theology* 37 (1986), 146–7.

The Passion According to Luke: The Special Material of Luke 22, JSOTSup 14, Sheffield: JSOT, 1987.

Souter, A. 'Pilate', in J. Hastings (ed.), *Dictionary of Christ and the Gospels*, 1908, vol. 3, pp. 363–6.

Spiedel, M. P. 'The Roman Army in Judaea under the Procurators', in *Roman Army Studies*, vol. 2, Stuttgart, Franz Steiner, 1992.

Stanton, G. N. *A Gospel for a New People: Studies in Matthew*, Edinburgh: T. & T. Clark, 1992.

Stark, R. 'Antioch as the Social Situation for Matthew's Gospel', in D. L.

Balch, *Social History of the Matthean Community. Cross Disciplinary Approaches*, Minneapolis: Fortress Press, 1991, pp. 189–210.

Stauffer, E. *Christ and the Caesars*, London: SCM, ET: 1955.

'Zur Münzprägung und Judenpolitik des Pontius Pilatus', *La Nouvelle Clio* 1–2 (1949–50), 511ff.

Jerusalem und Rom im Zeitalter Jesu Christi, Bern, Dalp-Taschenbücher 331, Franke, 1957.

Die Pilatusinschrift von Caesarea Maritima, Erlangen: Erlanger Universi-tätsreden, NF12, 1966.

Ste Croix, G. E. M. de 'Why Were the Early Christians Persecuted?', *Past and Present* 26 (1963), 6–38.

Stern, M. 'The Province of Judaea', in *CRINT*, vol. 1, pp. 308–76.

with S. Safrai (eds.), *The Jewish People in the First Century*, CRINT, Assen, Gorcum, 1974–6, especially vol. 1, pp. 308–76.

Stevenson, G. H. *CAH*, vol. 10: The Augustan Empire. 44 BC–AD 70, Cambridge: Cambridge University Press, 1966.

Stibbe, M. W. G. *John as Storyteller: Narrative Criticism and the Fourth Gospel*, SNTSMS 73, Cambridge: Cambridge University Press, 1992.

Streeter, B. H. *The Four Gospels: A Study of Origins*, London: Macmillan, 1924.

The Four Gospels: A Study of Origins, New York: Macmillan, 1929.

Strobel, A. 'Lukas der Antiochener (Bemerkungen zu Act 11,28D)', *ZNW* 49 (1958), 131–4.

Die Stunde der Wahrheit. Untersuchungen zum Strafverfahren gegen Jesus, WUNT 21, Tübingen: J. C. B. Mohr (Paul Siebeck), 1980.

Sylva, D. D. (ed.) *Reimaging the Death of the Lukan Jesus*, Athenäum Monografien, Frankfurt: Anton Hain, 1990.

Talbert, C. H. *Reading Luke: A New Commentary for Preachers*, London: SPCK, 1982.

Talmon, S. 'Wisdom in the Book of Esther', *VT* 13 (1963), 419–55.

Tannehill, R. C. *The Narrative Unity of Luke-Acts*, Philadelphia: Fortress Press 1986.

Taylor, D. B. *Mark's Gospel as Literature and History*, London: SCM, 1992.

Taylor, V. *The Formation of the Gospel Tradition*, London: Macmillan & Co., 1935.

The Gospel According to St Mark, London: Macmillan, 1963.

The Passion Narrative of St Luke: A Critical and Historical Investigation, SNTSMS 19, Cambridge: Cambridge University Press, 1972.

Thatcher, T. 'Philo on Pilate: Rhetoric or Reality?', *Restoration Quarterly* 37 (1995), 215–18.

Thistleton, A. 'Truth', *DNTT*, vol. 3, pp. 874–902.

Theissen, G. *The Shadow of the Galilean*, London: SCM, 1987.

Tilborg, S. van *The Jewish Leaders in Matthew*, Leiden: E. J. Brill, 1972.

Turner, H. E. W. 'The Chronological Framework of the Ministry', in *Historicity and Chronology in the New Testament*, D. E. Nineham et al., London: SPCK, 1965, pp. 59–74.

Twomey, J. J. 'Barabbas was a Robber', *Scripture* 8 (1956), 115–19.

Vardaman, E. J. 'A New Inscription Which Mentions Pilate as Prefect', *JBL* 81(1962), 70–1.

Vermes, G. *Jesus the Jew*, 2nd edn, London: SCM, 1983.

Verrall, A. W. 'Christ Before Herod', *JTS* 10 (1909), 321–53.

Viviano, B. T. 'Where was the Gospel According to Matthew Written?', *CBQ* 41 (1972), 182–4.

Vögtle, A. 'Die Matthäische Kindheitsgeschichte', in M. Didier (ed.), *L'Evangile selon Matthieu: Rédaction et Théologie*, BETL 29, Gembloux: Ducalot, 1972.

Wahlde, U. C. von 'The Johannine "Jews": A Critical Survey', *NTS* 28 (1982), 33–60.

Walaskay, P. W. 'The Trial and Death of Jesus in the Gospel of Luke', *JBL* 94 (1973), 81–93.

And So we Came to Rome: The Political Perspective of St Luke, Cambridge: Cambridge University Press, 1983.

Wansbrough, H. 'Suffered under Pontius Pilate', *Scripture* 18 (1966), 84–93.

Watson, G. R. *The Roman Soldier*, London: Thames & Hudson, 1969 (reprinted 1983).

Webster, G. *The Roman Imperial Army*, 3rd edn, London: A. & C. Black, 1981.

Wellhausen, J. *Das Evangelium Lucae übersetzt und erklärt*, Berlin: G. Reimer, 1904.

Wengst, K. *Bedrängte Gemeinde und verherrlichter Christus: Der historische Ort des Johannesevangeliums als Schlüssel zu seiner Interpretation*, Biblisch Theologische Studien 5, Neukirchen: Neukirchener Verlag, 1981.

Westcott, B. F. *The Gospel According to St John*, London: John Murray, 1898.

White, L. M. 'Crisis Management and Boundary Maintenance', in D. L. Balch, *Social History of the Matthean Community. Cross Disciplinary Approaches*, Minneapolis: Fortress Press, 1991, pp. 211–47.

Williamson, R. *Jews in the Hellenistic World, Philo*. Cambridge Commentaries on Writings on the Jewish and Christian World 200 BC–AD 200, vol. 1ii, Cambridge: Cambridge University Press, 1989.

Winter, P. *On the Trial of Jesus*, Berlin, Walter de Gruyter, 1961.

'A Letter from Pontius Pilate', *NovT* 7 (1964), 37–43.

Wiseman, T. P. (ed.) *Roman Political Life, 90 BC–AD 69*, Exeter Studies in History no. 7, University of Exeter, 1985.

Yadin, Y. 'Pesher Nahum (4Q Nahum) Reconsidered', *IEJ* 21 (1971), 1–12.

Zeitlin, S. *Megillat Taanit as a Source for Jewish Chronology and History in the Hellenistic and Roman Periods*, Philadelphia, 1922.

'Zealots and Sicarii' *JBL* 81(1962), 395–8.

'Did Agrippa write a letter to Gaius Caligula?' *JQR* 56 (1965–6), 22–31.

Ziolkowski, M. 'Pilate and Pilatism in Recent Russian Literature', in S. Duffin Graham (ed.), *New Dimensions in Soviet Literature*, New York: St Martin's Press, 1992, pp. 164–81.

INDEX OF TEXTS CITED

Other Jewish and Christian writings

INDEX OF MODERN AUTHORS

INDEX OF MAIN SUBJECTS

Gratus   8–9, 19, 20, 21, 68

handwashing   134
Herod I   6, 17, 53, 74, 106, 114
  buildings   7, 59
  coins   19, 21
  division of kingdom   1–3
  in Matthew   131, 136
Herodians   151
High Priesthood   18–19
Hyrcanus   113–14

Ignatius   120, 121
images, Jewish attitude to   42, 74, 79–83

Jerusalem   7–8, 39, 42
  Roman siege of   51
  garrison   13, 82
Jesus of Nazareth   76
  Testimonium Flavianum   65, 67, 71
Jewish leaders   110, 124, 126, 129, 134,
    146
  relations with governor   17–19, 89
Jewish revolt
  causes of   2, 15, 50–2, 63–4
  rebel leaders   50
Jewish trial of Jesus   99, 104–5, 131,
    141, 197
  lack of in John   168
John, gospel of   163–93
  author   163
  origin   163–5
  Roman trial   175–93
John the Baptist   98, 155, 188, 201–2
Joseph of Arimathea   95, 99, 103, 123,
    126, 139, 165
Josephus
  aims of *Ant.*   62–5
  aims of *JW*   49–52
  Flavian patronage   50, 51, 57, 63
Judaea
  aristocracy   17–8
  borders of province   5–6
  capital   7
  formation of province   1, 4–5
  population   6
  taxes   16–17
Judas Iscariot   98, 123, 124–5, 129, 130,
    188
Judas the Galilean   54, 61, 195
Judith, book of   29–30
Julia (Livia)   3, 20, 28

kingship   100–1, 169–71, 198

Lamia, L. Aelius   14, 46
Law, Jewish   122, 138
  in Philo   27–9, 31, 33, 34, 35, 37, 38, 44
  in Macc.   30
  in Josephus   50, 57, 63, 64–5, 70, 72,
    73, 74, 76, 77
  Pilate's attitude to   83, 84, 88
Longinus   5
Luke-Acts   138–62
  author   139
  origin   138–9
  relation to Roman Empire   140–3, 150
  Roman trial   152–62

Maccabees, books of   30–1
maiestas   43–4
Marcellus   8, 73, 92
Mark, gospel of   94–119
  origin of   94–5
  passion narrative   95–7
  Roman trial   104–19
Marullus   8
Matthew, gospel of   120–37
  origin of   120–2
  relation to Judaism   121–2
  Roman trial   129–34
Mount Gerizim   67, 89–90, 195

Nero xviii, 11, 63, 77
  persecution   95, 117–19
Nerva   122
Nicolas of Damascus   3

Papias   121
Passover   109, 113, 151, 180–2, 191,
    195, 196, 201
  amnesty (*privilegium paschale*)   109,
    130, 147, 156, 159, 180–2, 199
patronage   10–11
Paul   139, 141, 142, 145, 147–8, 154,
    158, 191
persecution
  Jewish   122
  Roman xviii, 147, 160, 179
  see also Nero
Petronius   5, 28, 34, 56, 58–9
Pharisees   54
  in Mark   98, 99, 108, 115
  in Matthew   122, 123
  in Luke-Acts   143, 151, 155
Philip   1–4, 5–6
Philo
  connections with Agrippa   24–5, 36,
    37